Better Homes and Gardens®

167 THINGS TO MAKE FOR CHILDREN

© Meredith Corporation, 1975. All Rights Reserved.
Printed in the United States of America. First Edition. First Printing.
Library of Congress Catalog Card Number: 74-25584
SBN: 696-00820-3

"Give a little love to a child, and you get a great deal back."
John Ruskin

BETTER HOMES AND GARDENS BOOKS

Editorial Director: Don Dooley
Managing Editor: Malcolm E. Robinson   Art Director: John Berg
Asst. Managing Editor: Lawrence D. Clayton   Asst. Art Director: Randall Yontz
Associate Editor: Marie Schulz
Assistant Editor: Jo Moore Stewart
Designers: Faith Berven, Harijs Priekulis, Candy Carleton

Contents

Introduction

It's always a treat to make something for a child, and when you
have 167 captivating projects—playthings, garments to wear,
and room decorating accessories—from which to choose, it's hard
to decide what to start first. What makes the undertaking
even more gratifying is that everything made by hand conveys a
personal message from its maker. Although we search for
perfection in machine-made articles, don't worry if your handcraft
efforts fail to achieve that same degree of flawlessness. Very
often, it's the little irregularities—an uneven stitch, a daub of paint
misplaced, or an uneven wood surface—that we cherish. All
of these are distinguishing characteristics that are the signature of the
hobbyist. These are the loving touches that will make the
gift more precious as the years go by.

As you browse through this book, you'll find that each item
has a photo, a brief description, a list of materials, and
instructions for making it. Many of these projects also have diagrams
and drawings that simplify construction. Often, these drawings
cannot be presented in their actual size, and this is where the *grid
system* enters the picture. This is the key that enables the "I-
can't-even-draw-a-straight-line" craftsman to come up with a design
drawn exactly to scale. Actually, there are two parts to the
grid system—the first is the combination of parallel horizontal and
vertical lines that form a graph, and the other is the line
drawing superimposed on top of the lines.
The first step is to look for the scale given with the grid that
accompanies the project you wish to make—one square
equals one inch, one square equals three inches, etc. Whichever
number is listed means that each square of the grid will
measure exactly those same dimensions after it has been enlarged.

When you enlarge your pattern, select paper large enough to accommodate the finished design (brown wrapping paper works well for large designs). Then, draw horizontal and vertical lines one inch apart (or whatever the scale indicates). Now that you have ruled ordinary paper into graph paper, transfer your drawing onto it.

This does take a little planning, but it won't take long to figure out just how the lines pass from square to square, and whether they move in a straight, curved, or diagonal line. As you work at it, you'll find that with practice it becomes easier to reenact the path of the line as it moves through the squares.

Use this same method, regardless of whether you wish to make a pattern smaller or larger. All you have to do is vary the size of the grids, according to the scale, and this will alter the size of the design.

There are several other helpful tips that will ensure the successful completion of the things you make. Whenever glue is required, be sure you use the right kind. If you need one that dries clear, use white glue. If you are attaching fabric, use fabric glue. If you are appliqueing designs on a window shade, use glue that will remain flexible after it dries.

If you are stuffing toys or pillows, use non-allergenic and mat-resistant polyester stuffing. (It comes in one- and three-pound bags.) If you are stuffing a quilt or comforter, use rolls of batting that you can unroll into large sheets. It, too, is non-allergenic.

Plastic foam comes in many shapes and sizes — balls, cones, cubes, and wreaths, plus blocks and sheets. You can re-shape or re-size them with a sharp knife. Pillow forms, either knife-edge or box-edge, are available in upholstery foam, which also comes in sheets.

The Children's Hour

Between the dark and the daylight,
When the light is beginning to lower,
Comes a pause in the day's occupation,
That is known as the Children's Hour.

Henry Wadsworth Longfellow

Things for Children
Infants through 2 years

During the first two years of a child's life, each day seems to reveal something new and wonderful in the growth process. Each time a smile, a tear, or a yawn appears, parents marvel at their tiny bundle of perfection. Even simple things such as watching the gains in weight and height make this a special time.

Although the needs of tiny infants are minimal—food, clothing, and shelter—before long the eyes begin to focus on colors and objects. It's fun to peek into their rooms in the early morning to see how their eyes will follow the gentle motions of a brightly colored mobile suspended above the bed. And their chubby little hands begin to grasp small toys. It's the time when a soft, stuffed doll or teddy bear cuddled in their arms gives a feeling of being protected. And playthings they can squeeze, pull from room to room (as soon as they can walk), or ride are favorites. Even eating is more fun if the dish and mug are their very own. And clothing should be suitable for the climate and allow freedom of movement, besides being pretty.

This is when you should start creating an environment that will awaken their senses to the beauty of the world around them.

Favorite playthings

This captivating collection of toys has been chosen both for play value and eye-appeal. All of the items are made from easy-to-find materials, are safe to play with, and will bring hours of pleasure to children you love. You'll find that making toys in your leisure hours is a rewarding activity that becomes more exciting with each new project.

Gingham Ducks

Children take to ducks like ducks take to water, and this family of ducks will have special appeal for babies and toddlers because of their bright and happy colors. Any one or all of them will bring squeals of delight from the happy recipient of this handmade gift.

Materials:
1 yd. checked material, solid-colored fabric, matching thread, and polyester filling.

Directions:
After cutting out the duck body pieces according to the patterns, sew the wings first (each wing is a half-circle). For each wing, snip around the edge of the inner wing piece about ⅛ inch inward and 1½ inches apart, turn under, and topstitch to the outer wing half-circle. Next, seam this half-circle and the other half of the wing with right sides together. Turn the wing right side out, pressing the straight edge ¼ inch under and stitching the wing from the underside of the wing to the duck body. Cut small, round pieces of contrasting fabric for the eyes and duck bill; stitch on the duck bill and the eyes.

Next, place the right sides of the duck together, then stitch, leaving from 4 to 6 inches open at the bottom sides to turn the duck right side out. Stuff, and sew up openings by hand.

Make the duck feet from the baby duckling wing pattern. Fold the circular shape in half and cut along the fold. With the right sides together, stitch ¼ inch around the edge, leaving the straight edge open, turn the feet right side out, and fill with the stuffing.

Then, fold the half-moon shape into a quarter-circle. With the back ends together, sew along the edge. Turn the piece right side out. (This will form a cone shape.) Sew it onto the body of the duck just under the wing area (seam side to the body).

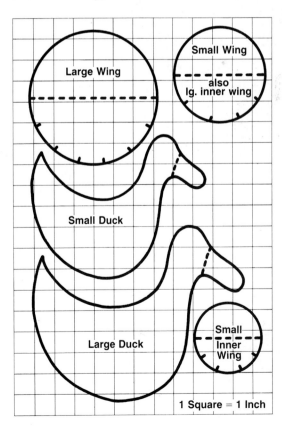

Large Wing

Small Wing
also
lg. inner wing

Small Duck

Large Duck

Small Inner Wing

1 Square = 1 Inch

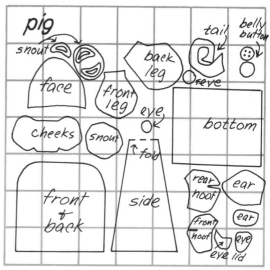

pig

snout back leg tail belly button

face front leg eye

cheeks snout eye bottom

fold

front & back side rear hoof ear

front hoof ear

eye lid eye

1 Square = 4 Inches

Felt Favorites

Felt toys to fondle on the way to the Land of Nod are favorites for the very young. Pudgy Pig, Cool Cat, and Kicky Cow offer new versions of soft sculpture for the nursery set. The squeezable, freestanding trio will adapt well to any environment and will brighten the daily bedtime ritual.

Materials:
Felt in your choice of a combination of bright and muted colors, spools of matching thread, polyester filling, and pipe cleaners.

Directions:
Enlarge the drawings to make the pattern pieces (one square equals 4 inches). Lay the pattern pieces on the felt and trace around each piece with the pencil. (Use the colors in the photos

or choose your own.) Cut them out. (No seam allowances are needed.)

Topstitch by machine all of the details, such as the eyes, nostrils, and spots, onto the animals' body pieces. Use matching thread.

Place the main pattern pieces that form the animals wrong side to wrong side, then machine-stitch with matching thread. Sew ¼ inch in from the cut edge of the pieces. Leave one seam with a large enough opening to insert the polyester stuffing. After the filling is in place, sew the opening closed.

With the smaller pieces, such as the cat's whiskers and the tail, lightly stuff them, then sew them onto the body of the animal. For any appendages that need stiffening, such as the cat's tail or the horns on the cow, give support by inserting a pipe cleaner bent to shape. Insert the pipe cleaner before stuffing.

To keep the like-new felt finish, add a stain-resistant coating to each character. Combine the selections of felt colors to create the mood of the animals of this zany zoo collection. In contrast to the hot pink of the Pudgy Pig character, the two cool shades of blue and a shade of green create Cool Cat. Muted colors give contentment to Kicky Cow.

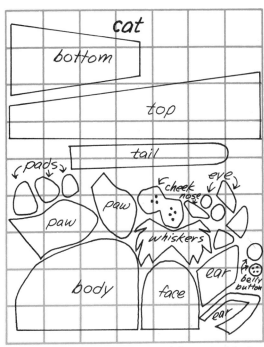

cat

bottom

top

tail

pads

paw

paw

cheek

nose

eye

whiskers

body

face

ear

belly button

ear

1 Square = 4 Inches

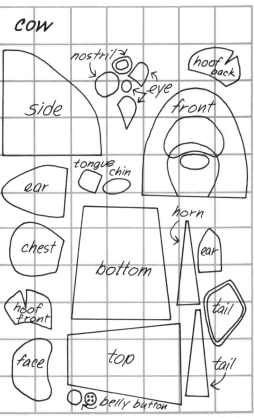

cow

side

nostril

eye

hoof back

front

ear

tongue

chin

chest

horn

bottom

ear

hoof front

tail

face

top

tail

belly button

1 Square = 4 Inches

11

Crocheted Alligator

Not all alligators are confined to zoos or swamps. In fact, you can crochet this lovable, luggable creation while you are watching your favorite television program. Children love soft, cuddly animals, and this one will be a welcome addition to their collection, regardless of the number they already have.

Materials:

Four-ply knitting worsted—5 ounces of olive green and 4 ounces of orange; size I and G crochet hooks; scraps of red, black, and white felt; one 4½ x 11-inch piece of shocking pink felt; polyester stuffing; and two 4-inch squares of cardboard.

Directions:

The animal is 39 inches long. Gauge: 3 puff sts=2 inches; 4 puff st rows=1¾ inches. 7 sc=2 inches; 4 sc rows=1 inch. (Be sure to check your gauge before starting the toy. Use the size crochet hook that will obtain the stitch gauge above.)

Underside: Starting at mouth end with orange and size I hook, ch 16 to measure 4½ inches. 1st row: SC in 2nd ch from hook, sc in each ch across—15 sc. Ch 1, turn. 2nd row: Sc in each sc across. Ch 1, turn. Repeat 2nd row until total length is 4¼ inches. Place a marker in each end of last row to indicate end of mouth. Ch 1, turn, and continue to repeat 2nd row until total length is 5 inches. Ch 1; turn.

Next row: Sc in each of first 2 sc, 2 sc in next sc—*inc made*; (sc in next 4 sc, inc in next sc) twice; sc in each of last 2 sc—3 sc increased. Ch 1; turn. Following row: Sc in each sc across—18 sc. Ch 1; turn.

Next row: Increasing 3 sc evenly spaced, sc in each sc across—21 sc. Ch 1, turn. Repeat 2nd row over these 21 sc until total length is 9 inches. Ch 1; turn. Following row: Sc in first sc, * draw up a loop in each of the next 2 sc, yarn over hook and draw through all 3 loops on hook—*dec made*; sc in each of next 2 sc.

Repeat from * across—5 sc decreased. Ch 1, turn. Next row: Sc in each sc across—16 sc. Ch 1; turn. Following row: Sc in each of first 2 sc, (dec over next 2 sc, sc in each of next 3 sc) twice; dec over next 2 sc, sc in each of last 2 sc—13 sc. Ch 1; turn.

Next row: Sc in each sc across. Ch 1; turn. Following row: Sc in first sc, (dec over 2 sc, sc in 2 sc) 3 times—10 sc. Ch 1; turn. Work even in sc (no more decs) until total length is 11½ inches. Mark both ends of last row to indicate end of neck. Ch 1; turn.

Now, work shaping for underside of body as follows: 1st row: 2 sc in first sc—*inc made at beg of row*; sc in each sc across—11 sc. Ch 1; turn. 2nd, 3rd, and 4th rows: Repeat last row 3 times—14 sc on 4th row. Ch 1; turn. 5th, 6th, and 7th rows: Sc in each sc across.

Ch 1; turn. 8th row: 2 sc in first sc, (sc in each of 2 sc, 2 sc in next sc) 4 times; sc in last sc—19 sc. Ch 1; turn. 9th row: Sc in each sc across. Ch 1; turn.

10th row: Increasing 2 sc evenly spaced, sc in each sc across—21 sc. Ch 1; turn. Work even in sc until length is 12 inches from end of neck markers. Ch 1; turn. Next row: Decreasing one st at both ends of row, sc in each sc across—19 sc. Ch 1; turn. Following 5 rows: Sc in each sc across.

Repeat last 6 rows 5 times more—9 sc on last row. Ch 1; turn. Work even in sc until length is 26½ inches from end-of-neck markers. Ch 1; turn.

Next row: Decreasing one st at both ends of row, sc in each sc across—7 sc. Ch 1; turn. Last row: Sc in each sc across. Break off and fasten.

Head: Starting at mouth end with green and size I hook, work as for *Underside* until total length is 11½ inches—10 sc. Mark both ends of last row to indicate end of neck. Ch 1; turn. Work shaping for body as follows: Next row: Inc in first sc, sc in each sc across—11 sc. Ch 1; turn. Repeat last row 4 times more—15 sc on last row. Ch 1; turn.

Following row: Increasing one sc at each end, sc in each sc across—17 sc. Ch 1; turn. Now, work in pattern as follows: 1st row: Sc in first sc, * (yarn over hook, draw up a 1-inch loop in same sc where last sc was made) twice; yarn over hook and draw through all 5 loops on hook—*puff st made*; skip next sc, sc in next sc. Repeat from * across—8 puff sts and 9 sc. Ch 3; turn. 2nd row: Sc in 2nd ch from hook, make puff st in same ch st where

last sc was made—*inc made*; sc in first sc, * puff st in same sc where last sc was made, sc in next sc.

Repeat from * across—9 puff sts. Ch 3; turn. 3rd row: Repeat last row—10 puff sts. Ch 1; turn. 4th row: Sc in first sc, * puff st in same sc where last sc was made, sc in next sc. Repeat from * across—10 puff sts. Ch 1; turn. Repeat last row for pattern. Work in pattern until length is 10½ inches from first row of pattern.

Ch 1; turn. Dec row: Draw up a loop in first sc, skip next puff st, draw up a loop in next sc, yarn over hook and draw through all 3 loops on hook—*dec made*; puff st in same sc where last loop was drawn through, sc in next sc and complete row in pattern—9 puff sts. Ch 1: turn.

Next row: Repeat Dec row, ending with sc in last st—8 puff sts. Ch 1; turn. Work in pattern over these sts until length is about 13 inches from first row of pattern. Ch 1; turn. Following 2 rows: Repeat Dec row twice—6 puff sts

(continued on next page)

Crochet Abbreviations

ch . . . . chain
sc . . . . single crochet
dc . . . . double crochet
sl st . . . . slip stitch
sp (s) . . . . space (s)
rnd . . . . round
inc . . . . increase
st (s) . . . . stitch (es)
comp. completely
sk . . . . skip
co . . . . continue

* Repeat whatever follows * as many times as specified. ( ) Do what is in parenthesis the number of times indicated.

remain. Ch 1; turn. Work in pattern until length is 17½ inches from first row of pattern. Next 2 rows: Repeat Dec row twice—4 puff sts. Ch 1; turn. Work in pattern until length is 26 inches from first row of pattern. Break off and fasten—this is tail end.

Back Leg (Make 2): Starting at top with green and size G hook, ch 4. Join with sl st to form ring. 1st rnd: Ch 1; 6 sc in ring. *Do not join rnds but carry a thread of a different color between last and first sc of every rnd to indicate beg of rnds.* 2nd rnd: 2 sc in each sc around— 12 sc. 3rd rnd: (Sc in next sc, 2 sc in next sc) 6 times—18 sc. 4th rnd: (Sc in each of next 2 sc, 2 sc in next sc) 6 times—24 sc. 5th rnd: Sc in each sc around.

Repeat 5th rnd until total length is 2½ inches. Next rnd: Decreasing 3 sc evenly spaced, sc in each sc around—21 sc. Repeat last rnd twice more—15 sc remain. Work one rnd, decreasing one st—14 sc.

Foot: 1st row: Sc in each of 7 sc. Ch 1; turn. Repeat last row 14 times more. Break off and fasten. Stuff leg firmly. Fold foot in half and sew last row to the free 7 sts on last rnd of leg. Stuff the foot and sew the side edges together.

Front Leg (Make 2): Work as for *Back Leg* until 3rd rnd has been completed—18 sc 4th rnd: Increasing 3 sc evenly spaced, sc in each sc around—21 sc. 5th rnd: Sc in each sc around. Repeat last rnd until total length is 2½ inches. Next rnd: Decreasing 3 sc evenly spaced, sc in each sc around—18. Repeat last rnd twice— 12 sc remain.

Foot: 1st row: Sc in each of 6 sc. Ch 1; turn. Repeat last row 13 times. Break off and fasten. Stuff the leg and finish the foot the same as for the *Back Leg.*

Leaving the mouth edges open to markers and having the right side of pattern out, pin outer edges of *Underside* to corresponding edges of top section, adjusting to fit.

Starting at the center of the tail end, sew side edges together to the mouth markers. Stuff the body as work progresses; sew the opposite side edges together. With green yarn, work back stitch across base of mouth from marker to marker. Tack or paste a cardboard square to the inside of the lower section of the mouth.

Having some stuffing between the crochet and the cardboard, tack the other cardboard square to the inside of the upper section of the mouth. Cut a 4½ x 8½-inch oblong of pink felt and, holding the mouth open, place the felt piece inside of the mouth covering the cardboards; stitch to the outer edges of the crochet. Sew the felt to the crochet across the base of the mouth between cardboards.

For the teeth, cut four ½ x 4-inch strips of white felt. Cut even points in one edge of each strip. Sew straight edge of a strip to each side edge of each section of mouth.

For the tongue, cut a 1 x 2-inch piece of red felt. Round off one narrow edge; sew the other narrow edge to the center of the lower piece of pink felt, ½ inch from center fold. Cut a 2 x 4-inch strip of pink felt; roll this piece of pink felt to form a tube and sew it to center fold inside of mouth, over tongue.

For the eyes, cut two ¾ x 1¼-inch black felt ovals, two white felt ovals slightly smaller than black ovals and two ½-inch diameter black felt circles. Paste or sew a white oval on top of each black oval; paste or sew a circle inside top half of each white oval. Paste or sew eyes to the top of the head, 2½ inches apart and 1½ inches from base of the mouth.

Claw (Make 4): Cut a ½-inch piece of red felt for each claw; taper the short edges enough so that one long edge measures 1½ inches. Trim the 2-inch edge of the claw into three ⅝-inch-deep points and sew the opposite edge to the fold of a foot.

With the foot of each leg pointing forward, pin a back leg to each side of the green section of the body, 16 inches from the end of the tail and 1 inch above the side seam, with the top of the leg extending 2 inches from the pin. Sew a front leg to each side of the green section of the body, 22½ inches from the end of the tail and ½ inch above the seam, with top of leg extending 1½ inches from the pin.

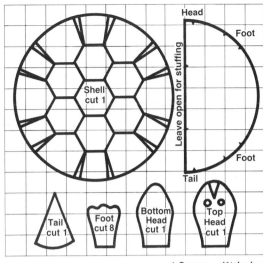

1 Square = 1½ Inches

Patchwork Turtle

You'll win the race for popularity with this toy turtle made from a batch of patched pieces. Its soft shell is a mosaic of brightly colored printed pieces of cotton, thoughtfully combined to provide a pleasing overall effect.

Materials:

½ yard of medium-weight solid-color green cotton or blend, scraps of patterned pink and green light- to medium-weight cottons or blends, ½ yard lightweight solid-color pink cotton or blend, polyester stuffing, and dark green embroidery floss.

Directions:

Enlarge all of the pattern pieces except the three back pieces on tracing paper, adding a ½-inch seam allowance and marking the darts and the position of the head, tail, and feet. Trace the patterns onto the fabric and then transfer the markings. Sew the dart in the top head of the turtle. Pin and sew the head, tail, and feet. Trim the seams and clip the curves. Turn. Sew the two bottom halves together, leaving an opening for the stuffing. Next, trace the three pattern pieces of the back and add a ¼-inch seam allowance, except around the outer row, which should have a ½-inch seam allowance. Arrange the colors of the fabric scraps in a balanced design. Trace and cut out the pieces.

Press under slightly more than ¼ inch around the edges, except the outer edge of the outer row of pieces. Baste the edges. Position the outer pieces between the dart notches (there should be about ⅜ inch between the pieces at the edge). Baste. Position and baste the hexagons in the center. Stitch down the pieces about ⅛ inch from the edge. Do not stitch the outer edges of the outer row. There should be a little background fabric showing between the pieces.

Make darts around the edge between the outside pieces (the darts should be about ¼ inch at the edge and should taper off 2½ inches from the edge). Lightly stuff the tail and feet to within ½ inch of the edge. Use a pencil or a crochet hook to push the stuffing into the narrow areas. Pin the edges of the tail and feet to the right side of the bottom, as indicated in the sketch.

Cut 3-inch bias strips from the pink fabric. Piece until the strip is 60 inches long. Sew the ends together to form a circle. Press in half lengthwise, with the wrong side inside. Sew a gathering stitch ½ inch from the raw edges. Gather to fit the top piece. Baste to the right side of the top piece. Pin the top piece to the bottom, with the right sides together. Sew around, leaving an opening for the head. Slip the head into the opening, with the right side out, and pin. Sew. Turn through the opening in the bottom. Stuff firmly, beginning with the head. Sew the opening closed. Embroider the eyes with a satin stitch.

Sock Toys

These super-soft, cuddly playmates, with their whimsical expressions, will appeal to all children — from the nursery set to teen-agers. Humpty Dumpty has a dual personality — an engaging grin when he surveys the scene from the top of the wall and a sober mouth and teardrops on the reverse side for the after-the-fall look. Soft toys made from Rockford socks were popular items many years ago. These updated versions of old favorites will bring a bit of nostalgia to the one who makes them.

Materials:

Sock dolls — one pair of size 13 Rockford socks (work socks) for each

Horse — one pair of size 13 Rockford socks

Octopus — ½ yard of white cotton knit fabric, four pairs of knee socks, yarn, buttons, and felt scraps

Humpty Dumpty — one yard of white cotton knit fabric, two pairs of argyle knee socks, felt scraps, yarn for hair, and buttons for eyes. Polyester stuffing for each character.

Directions:

Sock dolls: (see the separate cutting guide for each doll). After cutting out the pattern pieces, turn the body section of the doll inside out; stitch up the leg sections, leaving the bottom of the feet open. Take a small tuck in the red heel of the sock to define the center line of the mouth. Turn the sock doll right side out; insert the polyester stuffing into the

Boy Doll

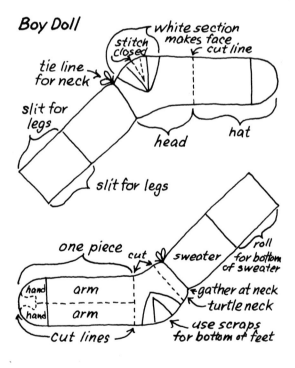

legs. Next, stitch round scraps of fabric to the bottom of the feet; slip-stitch the feet closed. Next, stuff the body up to the neckline; run a gathering stitch around the neckline, pull up stitches, and tie off. Stuff the head until plump; gather the closing at the back of head; stitch closed. (The hat will cover this area.)

Girl Doll

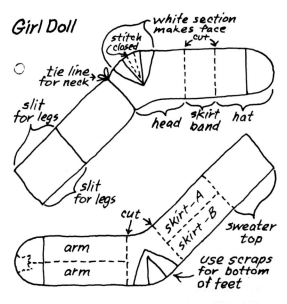

For the boy doll, slip the "sweater" section onto the body. (The boy's sweater is the same color as the doll body.) Roll down the top and stitch it to form the turtleneck. Roll up the white ribbing of the sock top, forming the bottom cuff of the sweater.

To finish the boy, fit the hat to the head, and turn the raw edges up into the brim; sew the hat in place. Sew on the buttons for the eyes; embroider the nose.

Make the girl's sweater from the white ribbed section. Cover the raw edge of the ribbing when the skirt is added. With the right sides together, stitch each arm piece, carefully delineating the hand outline. Clip the indentation between the thumb and hand; turn right side out and stuff. Turn the raw edges of each arm piece under; hand-stitch the arms to the body.

To finish the girl doll, join lengths A and B to make the skirt. Then, machine-hem the lower edge of the skirt; hand-stitch the skirt in place. Add the belt strip, the brown yarn bangs, the button eyes (fasten them securely), and the embroidered nose.

Horse: Cut the socks into sections, following the cutting diagram. Turn the body section inside out; take a tuck in the tail so the red section will not show when the body is turned right side out. Take a tuck between the body and the neck section so the neck stands at a 45-degree angle to the body (see sketch). Turn the body section right side out, and stuff until plump; leave both ends open.

Horse

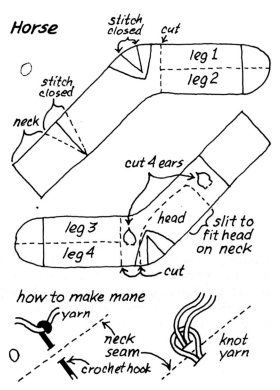

Snip the opening in the bottom of the head section to fit over the neck. Turn the head inside out; machine-stitch the head closed from the tip of the nose down the back of the head. Stuff; fit the head section over the neck. Turn raw edges under; stitch in place.

Cut out the four legs; stitch the legs on the wrong side, leaving open the ends that will

(continued on next page)

be attached to the body. Turn to the right side and stuff the legs. Fit the back legs to the back of the body sections; stitch in place. Add the front legs.

For the mane, cut lengths of red and orange yarn in 4-inch lengths; attach the mane two strands at a time along the back of the neck, across the crown of the head, and halfway down the nose. (Use a crochet hook to pull the yarn through the sock fabric and knot the yarn. See the diagram.)

For the tail, cut twelve 10-inch pieces of red and orange yarn; pull the yarn through the tail section with a crochet hook. Divide the yarn into three sections; braid the yarn. Tie off the tail with a scrap of yarn. Use a double thickness of sock fabric for each ear. Stitch the two sections together, then turn right side out; topstitch just inside the seam line to give the ears added stiffness. Turn the raw edges under; stitch the ears in place. Add black buttons for the eyes; fasten them securely.

Octopus: Cut the white cotton knit fabric 33 x 17 inches. With the right sides together, seam the short ends together. Run a gathering stitch around the top, turning the raw edges in; pull up the gathers and tie off. Stuff the head. Gather around the bottom edge of the head; tuck the raw edges inside; stitch the opening closed.

Cut the eyes from felt scraps; applique them to the front of the head (on the side away from the seam). Add the button nose. For the hair, wind 50 twists of yarn around an 8-inch cardboard strip. Tie off one end of yarn, then clip at the other end. Spread the ''hair'' over the crown evenly, stitch it in place, and trim it evenly with the scissors.

For the legs of the octopus, begin stuffing eight knee socks at the toe; tie off round bunches of the stuffed socks every two inches with the yarn. Leave the last 1½ inches of each leg limp so it will be easy to sew them to the head. Arrange the ends of the socks to fan out from the bottom of the head; stitch the eight legs in place. Add the bow tie made from the felt. The hat that the octopus wears is a child's beanie.

Humpty Dumpty: Following the cutting diagram, cut two large egg-shaped pieces from the white cotton knit fabric for the head, then cut out the facial features from felt.

With right sides of fabric together, stitch the two egg-shaped pieces together; leave a 5-inch opening at bottom of head. Turn right side out, and stuff head. Applique features with a slip stitch or with fabric glue. Put a smiling face on one side of Humpty Dumpty and a cracked face on the reverse side. Attach the yarn to the top of the head for the hair.

Turn the two socks inside out; stitch hand shape around toe. Clip between thumb and hand, and turn arms right side out; stuff arms

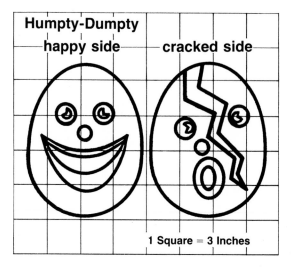

Humpty-Dumpty
happy side——— ——cracked side——

1 Square = 3 Inches

to desired length. Attach the arms to the head.

Cut the toes off the socks that are to be used for the legs about two inches from the heel. Stuff the legs, then fit the circles of the sock scrap fabric over the toe ends. Machine-stitch in place.

Insert the ends of the legs into the opening at the bottom of the egg head; leave ½ inch of the unstuffed sock at the top so the legs will be joined where they join the egg. Stitch the base opening closed.

sides together, stitch around the body, leaving the bottom open.

Pin the bottom section in place, easing where necessary. Leave the section open on the backside for stuffing. Next, stitch around the bottom. Then, clip the seams at the curves, turn the fabric to the right side, stuff the animal, and sew the back opening closed.

For the finishing touches, mark the embroidery pattern lightly with a pencil and work the design by using the full strand of embroidery floss with a chain stitch. Sew the features on by hand and add the collar and the bow.

Gingham often is a very lightweight fabric. If you choose this kind of material, make a complete body without ears of sturdy muslin, then cover this form with a second body of gingham with the ears.

Gingham Dog and Calico Cat

"The gingham dog and calico cat, side by side by the butter churn sat." Unlike their poetic counterparts, these updated versions of Eugene Field's fireplace-sitting toys don't eat each other. Instead, they serve as pillows or toys for your children to use.

Materials:
Gingham and calico print fabric; polyester stuffing; scraps of black, red, and yellow felt; and black embroidery floss.

Directions:
Enlarge the pattern pieces according to the drawing and cut the fabric. Next, with the right sides together, stitch the ear parts together, turn to the right side, and press. Then, with the right sides together, pin the ears as indicated on the patterns. Fold the dog ear in half at the top (lining to the inside) to sew. With the right

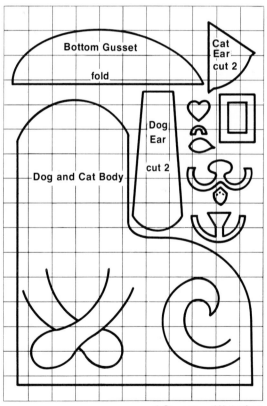

1 Square = 1½ Inches

19

Sleepy Babies

Soft cloth rag dolls made of simple clothing and yarn have been a popular children's item for many years. They seem to hold a particular fascination, especially with younger children. These sleepy-time huggables are completely washable; they're stuffed with foam rubber.

Materials:
Three bath-size Turkish towels, matching sewing thread, one 16-inch square 1-inch-thick foam rubber cushion pad, large scraps of sheets in a variety of prints, white lining, bias tape to match or blend with the fabrics, eyelet beading, ruffling, ribbon, embroidery floss, yarn for the hair, baby and regular rickrack, tracing paper, and lightweight cardboard.

Directions:
Enlarge the patterns by copying on paper ruled in 1-inch squares; complete all half-patterns indicated by long dash lines. The short dash lines on clothing patterns indicate seam and hem allowances.

Doll body: The foam pad contains enough stuffing for both dolls. Cut the two bodies and four arm pieces out of lightweight cardboard to make durable patterns. Place the patterns on the foam rubber padding; with a ball-point pen, mark the outlines on the padding. Cut the bodies and the arms out of the foam; trim away the sharp edges.

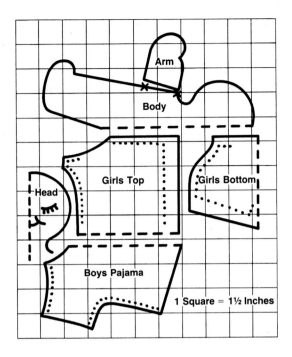

For each doll, fold a towel in half crosswise. Place one body and two arm patterns on one folded towel. Adding ½ inch on all the edges for the seams, cut the body and the arms through both thicknesses. Make a tracing of the face; pin on one terry cloth head as a guide. Using six strands of floss in the needle, embroider the features on the head through the tracing paper. Noses and cheeks are the satin stitch; mouths are the outline stitch; and the eyes are the straight stitch. After embroidering the facial features, tear away the tracing paper.

Place one foam body between two terry cloth bodies; turn in the seam allowance and overcast the cloth bodies together, making the terry cloth cover fit snugly. Overcast the two terry cloth arms together with the foam arm between; repeat for the second arm. Stitch the finished arm to each side of the body at the point indicated on the pattern by X's.

Hair: For the girl's hair, cut thirty 12-inch strands of yarn. Beginning at the center top of the head, stitch the center of each piece in parallel rows to halfway down the back. Bring the strands slightly across the face and stitch them flat in place at the temples. Pull the ends of hair together at the sides with an 8-inch-long ribbon for each; tie the ribbon bows. Trim the ends of the strands evenly. For the bangs, cut three 4-inch-long strands; stitch the centers of the strands at the center of the top of the head.

For the boy, cut eight 8-inch pieces of yarn. Place the strands of yarn in a line across the top of the head and stitch them down at the sides and above one side to give the effect of a side part, as shown. For the back of the head, cut fourteen 6-inch strands of yarn. Fold each strand in half and stitch the centers across the top back of the head. Tack the ends of hair at the bottom.

Clothes: For the girl, cut two tops and two pajama pants from the scraps of sheets or from permanent-press cotton, printed fabric. For the lining, cut two tops and two pants of plain white fabric. Place a lining and a fabric piece together, with the right sides facing, for the fronts and the backs of the tops and pants. Stitch together at the neckline the armholes, and around the legs. Turn right side out. Place the backs and the fronts together, with right sides facing; stitch the shoulders and the sides of the top and sides of the pants together, with 1-inch hems on the lower edge of the top and around the waist of the pants. Turn right side out. Stitch the eyelet beading around the neckline. Thread the ribbon through the eyelet; stitch the ribbon ends together at the seam. Stitch the ruffling on the top of the hem and the pant legs. Tie the bow after dressing.

For the boy, cut the front and the back pieces from the printed sheet fabric. Slash at the crotch up to the crossline. On the front, slash the centers of the neckline down to the crossline and around the top corners, as indicated by the short dash line on the pattern. With the right sides facing, sew the shoulders, sides, and crotch together; allow for ¼-inch seams. Bind the sleeves, legs, and neckline with bias tape. Make two large cross-stitches of black floss at the neck opening. After dressing the boy, pull the end of the floss to tighten the stitches.

Towel Teddy Bear

The teddy bear is a tradition of childhood. Now, a large jacquard weave bath towel will add a new dimension to your child's favorite companion. Personalizing this familiar plaything is easy, with the various towel patterns and colors available.

Materials:
One large bath towel (27x48 inches), one spool of thread, six-strand embroidery cotton or floss, polyester stuffing, and fabric glue.

Directions:
Arrange the pattern pieces on the towel so that the towel's pattern will be compatible with the features of the bear.

Body front and head front: Cut out the body front and the head front. Then, stitch along the seam line at the neck and leg edges. Clip to the stitching at the neck edge. With right sides together, pin body front to head side sections, having raw edges even. Stitch the neck edge, and clip the curves. Then, stitch the entire center front seam of the body up to the middle of the head. Clip curves. With the right sides together, stitch the head front to the head sections, breaking the stitching at the middle of the head. Clip the curves.

Ears, body back, and head back: Cut the ears of the bear from a solid color of the towel. With the right sides together, stitch the facing to the ear, leaving the flat edge open. Clip the curves. Then, turn the ears and press. Machine-stitch the raw edges together along the seam line. Clip to the stitching. On the outside, baste the ears to the head back (be sure the raw edges are even). Make a dart in the body back, then trim the dart and press open. Stitch along the seam line at the leg edge. With the right sides together, stitch the body to the head back. Clip the curves. Next, stitch the entire center back seam of the body and the head. Clip the curves.

Stitching the front to the back: With the right sides together, pin the front to the back, matching the seams (be sure the raw edges are even). Then, stitch, leaving the leg edges open. Clip the curves.

Soles: Cut the soles of the bear from a solid color of the towel. With the right sides together, pin sole to leg edge; stitch and clip curves.

Stuffing: Turn the bear right side out. Next, stuff the bear firmly, using less stuffing along the line in the legs. Slip-stitch the opening closed.

Facial features: Cut the eyes and nose from the solid colors of the towel. Attach them to the bear with fabric glue.

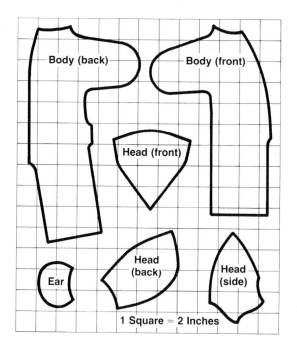

Body (back) Body (front)

Head (front)

Head (back) Head (side)

Ear

1 Square = 2 Inches

Pantry Animals

Children always are fascinated by the assortment of pots and pans that are stored behind the kitchen cabinet doors. If you want to divert them from strewing kitchen utensils all over the kitchen floor, create a menagerie of pantry animals that will satisfy this longing without upsetting the chef.

All you need is a collection of assorted pantry props, which you can find in discount stores and supermarkets. If and when your children's interest wanes in these humble pull toys, everything is reusable except for the pan.

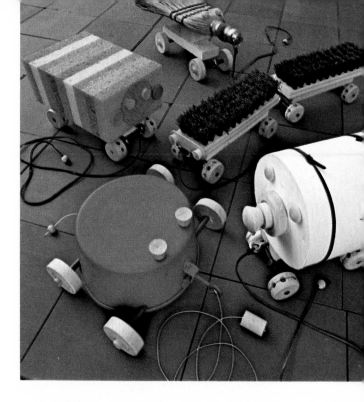

Materials:

Tissue pig—one roll of toilet tissue (white), four Tinkertoy wheels, five screw eyes, one leather thong, one 1x2x5-inch wooden block, two Tinkertoy dowel axles, two trim buttons, and a wooden drawer pull.

Brushes—two scrub brushes, eight Tinkertoy wheels, four Tinkertoy axles, two 1x2x6-inch wooden blocks, wooden trim buttons, one leather thong, and eleven screw eyes.

Sponges—one multicolor sponge approximately 5x7x3 inches, four Tinkertoy wheels, two Tinkertoy dowel axles, five screw eyes, leather, and wooden buttons.

Pan—one aluminum pan (4-cup size), four Tinkertoy wheels, two dowel axles, two drawer pull eyes, wooden beads, and fishing line.

Whisk broom—one whisk broom, one 1x2x6-inch wooden block, one 1-inch square wooden block, four Tinkertoy wheels, two axles, four screw eyes, wooden trim pieces, and a leather thong for a pull cord.

Directions:

Tissue pig: Glue the roll of white toilet tissue to the 1x2-inch wooden block. Then, tie the roll at either end with a leather thong. Next, attach the four screw eyes to the bottom of the block. Then, insert the axle through the screw eyes and attach the pull cord. Finally, glue on the buttons and wooden drawer pull for the face, and the tail trim pieces.

Brushes: Glue the wooden blocks to the top surface of both scrub brushes. Then, fasten eight screw eyes to the blocks (four on each

one), and insert the axles. Attach the Tinkertoy wheels. Connect the two brushes with two screw eyes and trim the toy with wooden buttons.

Sponges: Glue the multicolor sponge to the wooden block. Then, attach the screw eyes, axles, and wheels. Attach a cork disc to simulate a face, then glue the eyes and cheeks onto it. Attach the fifth screw eye and the cord on the front for pulling.

Pan: First, remove the plastic handle from the aluminum pan and insert a screw eye. Then, drill four ¼-inch holes in the edge of the pan to admit the axles and attach the wheels. Glue the drawer pulls onto the pan for eyes. Attach the fishing line pull cord.

Whisk broom: Glue the whisk broom to the square wood block. Then, attach the 1x2x6-inch block base. Next, attach the screw eyes and the Tinkertoy wheels. Glue the wooden eyes to the top of the whisk broom and attach the leather pull to the handle of the broom.

Wooden Pull Toys

Pulling around toys made from wood has been a favorite childhood pastime for generations. Any cherub will cherish these colorful wooden creations that they can lead around the home from the playpen to the parlor.

Materials:
Wood scraps, gesso, water-base paint (nontoxic acrylics or poster paints), 1-inch wooden beads, 1¾-inch screws, washers, clear enamel coating, yarn, and screw eyes.

Directions:
Following the patterns, cut out the shapes of the toy trio from wood scraps, using a coping saw or a saber saw. Next, sand the pieces and give them two coats of gesso. Then, paint them with water-base paints.

On the worm, draw the lines with hot pink, then alternate with blue and green for fill-in colors. For the fish, make purple lines, then fill in the other colors, using orange, yellow, hot pink, and green for the eye. On the lady bug, outline the body with blue, then paint the back hot pink with orange dots.

For the wheels, paint the 1-inch wooden beads green. Drill holes in each toy—six on the ladybug, four on the fish, and eight on the worm. Attach beads with 1¾-inch screws, and put a washer between the body and the head. Finish the toys with a coat of clear acrylic.

On the front of each toy, attach a screw eye; thread yarn through the screw eye, and tie a small wooden bead on the end.

1 Square = 2 Inches

Log Animals

These log animals, with their humorous expressions, soon will become your children's favorite pets. Because of the large size of the logs you use to create them and the wheels that add mobility, the animals will become a popular means of transportation for young toddlers, too. Besides having engaging personalities, these three characters are practically indestructible and will remain in tip-top condition for many years.

Materials:

Sections of logs (each a different diameter) cut to specified sizes, ¾-inch white pine board (platforms for small pig and hippo), epoxy cement, leather scraps for ears, 8 heavy casters (1½ inch diameter) for big pig and hippo, 4 casters (1 inch diameter) for small pig, rope scraps for tails, paint, trim, cork or dowels for teeth, and hosiery eggs for eyes.

Directions:

Big pig: Use a 16- to 18-inch-diameter log for the body. (Use a chain saw, which will make the required cuts easily.) Trim the bottom surface of the log with the saw to create a flat surface. Then, glue the heavy-duty rolling casters to each corner of the base, using epoxy cement. Use a 4-inch diameter log to serve as a snout. Glue the leather ears to the top of the head. Then, nail and glue a rope tail to the rear of the pig. Make the eyes of the pigs by cutting cork into discs and gluing them in place. Paint on the trim features.

The hippo and the little porker: Nail a ¾-inch white pine platform (cut to the largest diameter of the log so it won't tip) to one side. Make the hippo's body about 12 inches long and his head about seven inches long, with a slice of wood nailed between the two sections for a spacer. Chop out a triangular section for the mouth and paint the interior red. Use corks (or small pieces of wood dowel) for teeth and hosiery eggs for eyes. Then, attach leather scraps for the ears.

Make the little porker's body from a log about 12 inches long and about 8 inches in diameter. For the face, ears, and tail, follow the same instructions given for the big pig.

Build-It Barnyard

Your youngsters will have many hours of fun playing with this build-it-yourself barnyard, and you will take great pride in the fact that it is the result of your own handiwork.

The designs are so simple that you can conjure up a collection of these stylized domestic animals, plus your favorite children's storybook characters. The entire cast is created from plywood with the help of a jigsaw, and the set is collapsible, so it knocks down easily for storage in a toy chest. And, if you're making this barnyard creation for a child who lives in a distant place, it will be easy to pack for sending through the mail.

Materials:

⅛-inch-thick plywood, ¼-inch diameter dowels, a ¾x¾-inch strip of wood molding; red, blue, green, black, white, pink, brown, and beige acrylic paints, liquid gesso, carbon paper, and medium-weight sandpaper.

Directions:

To make the barnyard figures, trace and transfer the farm animals and the little girl to the plywood, enlarging the pattern pieces and using the carbon paper. Then, cut out the shapes of the figures on the ⅛-inch sheet of plywood with a jigsaw. After sanding all the edges of the figures smooth with medium-weight sandpaper, apply two coats of the liquid gesso. Let the first coat dry thoroughly before applying the second coat. Complete the barnyard figures by applying the acrylic paints. Use the photograph as a guide for choosing the different colors to use, and paint lighter areas first.

To construct the barnyard fence, cut out the posts from the ¾x¾-inch strip of wood molding. (You will need eight posts that stand about 6 inches high.) For the crosspieces of the fence, use 6-inch lengths of ¼-inch-diameter dowels.

1 Square = 1 Inch

Next, drill two ¼-inch holes in each post for the dowel fence to fit into. (Drill the holes 1½ inches from each end of the 6-inch posts.) Sand the ends of the dowel pieces so they will push easily and fit into the fence post holes.

To give the fence a stained wood finish, use acrylic raw umber that you first mix with a little polymer gloss medium. (Use this same mixture to finish tree trunks that are shown in the photograph.) Apply the same as paint.

Infants' and toddlers' wear

On the pages that follow, you will find many tasteful handcrafted fashions for infants and children. They will give your child's wardrobe that classic touch no matter what the season. The selection ranges from hand-knit and crocheted infant sweaters, sacques, bootees, and bonnets to a collection of intriguing bibs. A nostalgic knitted dress is featured as well.

Infants' Knits

Knitting and crocheting "little things" for new arrivals is still a favorite pastime. One reason for this popularity is the large number of captivating designs available today that make creating infantwear more fun than ever before. There is the added advantage of easy-care yarns that are machine-washable, dry quickly, need no blocking, are non-allergenic, and keep their original shape and good looks.

Materials:
Infants' sacque, cap, and bootees—Lollipop (Bucilla, 1 ounce balls). Sacque: 4 balls. Cap: 2 balls. Bootees: 1 ball. Size 2 and size 1 knitting needles, and size 3 crochet hook.
Crochet sacque—Winfant (Bear Brand, Fleisher's, or Botany, 1 ounce skeins). Color A—blue, 4 skeins; color B—white, 1 skein. Size E crochet hook, size 1 steel crochet hook for picot edges. Instructions are given for size 6 months and changes for size 1 in parentheses.
Quilted raglan cardigan and cap—Winfant (Bear Brand, Fleisher's, or Botany, 1 ounce skeins), 5 (6). Size 3 knitting needles and size 1 steel crochet hook. Instructions are given for size 6 months to 1 year and 2-3 are given in parentheses.

Gauge:
Infants' sacque, cap, and bootees—size 2 knitting needles—17 sts = 2 inches; 23 rows = 2 inches.
Crochet sacque—(sizes 6 mos.-1) size E crochet hook, 6 sts = 1 inch, 5 rows = 1 inch.
Quilted raglan cardigan and cap—(sizes 6 mos.-1 and 2-3) size 3 knitting needles and size 1 steel crochet hook, 13 sts = 2 inches; 27 rows = 2 inches.

Measurements for blocking:
Infants' sacque—chest: 19 inches.
Crochet sacque—width at chest: 21 (22) inches; width of back at lower edge: 10 (10½) inches; width of each front including the border: 5½ (5¾) inches; width of sleeves at underarm: 8¾ (8¾) inches.
Quilted raglan cardigan—width at chest, buttoned: 22 (24½) inches; width of back at underarm: 10¼ (11¼) inches; width of each front, including the border: 6¼ (6¾) inches; width of sleeves at underarm: 8¾ (9¼) inches.

Directions:
Infants' sacque, cap, and bootees: Pattern: Quaker Stitch-purl rib-row 1-right side-purl. K 1 row, p 1 row, k 1 row.
Knit rib—K 1 row, p 1 row, k 1 row, p 1 row. Repeat these 8 rows for pattern.

Sacque: *Left front*—with size 2 needles, cast on 47 sts. Work St. st (p 1 row, k 1 row) decreasing 1 st at beg. of k row every 8th row 5 times to shape underarm edge; 42 sts. Work even until 4 ins. from beg., end with a p row. Next row, bind off 4 sts, k to end. Slip these sts on extra needle. Do not break yarn.

Left sleeve—with size 1 needles, cast on 37 sts for cuff. Work Quaker Stitch until there are 3 purl and 2 knit ribs, end with a purl rib. *Inc. row*—right side—K 1, * inc. 1 st in next st, k 2; repeat from * to end. With size 2 needles, p 1 row, continue St. st, increasing 1 st each side every 6th row 5 times; 59 sts. Work even until 4 ins. above cuff, end with p row. Next row, bind off 4 sts, work to within 4 sts of end, bind off 4 sts. Slip sts on needle with front.

(continued on next page)

Back: With size 2 needles, cast on 86 sts. Working stockinette st, dec. 1 st each side every 8th row 5 times; 76 sts. Work even until same length as front, end with p row. Next row, bind off 4 sts, work to within 4 sts of the end, bind off 4 sts. Fasten off. Slip sts on the needle next to the sleeve. Make right sleeve and slip the sts on the needle next to the back. Make the right front to correspond to the left, shaping the underarm edge and binding off for the underarm at the end of k rows. Slip sts on the needle next to the sleeve.

Yoke: Slip to size 2 needle, 38 sts of right front, 51 sleeve sts, 68 back sts, 51 sleeve sts, 38 sts of left front; 246 sts.

Beg. at left front edge, with attached yarn, p 1 row. Continue St. st until 5½ ins. from lower edge of back, end with p row.

Short rows—row 1: K to within 10 sts of end. *Row 2:* Turn, slip 1, p to within 10 sts of end. *Row 3:* Turn, slip 1, k to within 14 sts of end. *Row 4:* Turn, slip 1, p to within 14 sts of end. Continue to work 4 sts less each row for 12 rows more. Break yarn, slip 38 sts on to the same needle with other sts.

Quaker Stitch Yoke: Join yarn at right front edge. *First Dec. Row:* right side—With size 1 needle, p 9, p 2 tog., * p 2, p 2 tog. *; repeat between *'s 6 times; + p 3, p 2 tog.; repeat from + 33 times; repeat between *'s 7 times, p 9; 197 sts. K 1 row, p 1 row, k 1 row, completing first purl rib. Work 4 rows of knit rib.

2nd Dec. Row: right side—P 5, * p 2 tog., p 6; repeat from * to end; 173 sts. Finish purl rib. Work 4 rows of knit rib. *3rd Dec. Row:* P 5, * p 2 tog., p 5; repeat from * to the end; 149 sts. Finish purl rib. Work 4 rows of knit rib. *4th Dec. Row:* p 5, * p 2 tog., p 4; repeat from * to end; 125 sts. Finish purl rib. Work 4 rows of knit rib. *5th Dec. Row:* P 4, * p 2 tog., p 3; repeat from *, end last repeat p 4; 101 sts. Finish purl rib. Work 4 rows of knit rib. *6th Dec. Row:* P 4, * p 2 tog., p 2; repeat from *, end last repeat p 3; 77 sts. Finish purl rib. Bind off tightly as to purl. Do not break yarn.

Finishing: Sew underarm and sleeve seams. Weave 8 underarm sts of sleeve to 8 underarm sts of front and back. Beg. at neck edge, work 17 sc on left front edge of yoke; 2 sc in every 3 rows to lower corner, 2 sc at corner, 1 sc in each st on lower edge, work right side to correspond.

Row 2: Ch 1, turn, 1 sc in first sc, * ch 4 for buttonloop, skip 2 sts, 1 sc in each of next 5 sts; repeat from * twice; continue sc to left corner of neck edge, working 2 sc at corners. Block—with wrong side up, pin out on pressing board to given measurements. Steam lightly with a moderately hot iron over a wet cloth, taking care not to let the weight of the iron rest upon any one spot. Allow to dry before removing from the board.

Bootees: With size 1 needles, cast on 36 sts. *Quaker St:* Row 1—wrong side—Knit. P 1 row, k 1 row, p 1 row for purl rib. P 1 row, k 1 row, p 1 row, k 1 row for knit rib. Repeat these 8 rows once. Repeat 4 rows of purl rib again. P 1 row.

Beading Row: * K 2 tog., yo, k 1; repeat from * to end. P 1 row.

Next Row: K 12, slip on holder for right side, do not break yarn; join another end of yarn and k next 12 sts for instep; slip remaining 12 sts on holder. Work back and forth in St. st—p 1 row, k 1 row—on 12 sts of instep for 2 ins., end with p row. Break yarn. Take up 12 sts of right side on free needle; pick up and k 16 sts on edge of instep; k 12 sts of instep; pick up and k 16 sts on the other side of the instep; take up and k remaining 12 sts; 68 sts. Repeat 8 rows of quaker st twice.

First Dec. Row: wrong side—K 2 tog., k 30, k 2 tog. twice, k 30, k 2 tog.; 64 sts. P 1 row.

2nd Dec. Row: K 2 tog., k 28, k 2 tog. twice, k 28, k 2 tog.; 60 sts. P 1 row.

3rd Dec. Row: P 2 tog., p 26, p 2 tog. twice, p 26, p 2 tog; 56 sts.

Next Row: K 28, break yarn, leaving 18-in. end. Weave sts on needles together.

Cord: Ch 12 ins. Fasten off.

Finishing: Sew seam at back. Block the same way as with the sacque. Run cord through beading. Make 2 small pompons and sew on ends of cord.

Cap: With size 1 needles, cast on 97 sts. Work quaker st as for sacque until there are 10 purl and 9 knit ribs, end with a purl rib.

Next Row: right side—bind off 34 sts, k until there are 29 sts, bind off 34 sts.

Back Part: Join yarn in last st worked. With size 2 needles, p 1 row, k 1 row and continue St. st on 29 sts for 3 ins., end with p row.

Dec. Row: K 12, k 2 tog., k 1 (seam st), slip, k and pass, k 12; 27 sts. Repeat decs. every 2nd row 5 times, decreasing 1 st each side of center seam st; 17 sts. Bind off.

Tie Cord: With size 1 needles, cast on 191 sts. Work St st for 5 rows. Bind off. Gather up the short ends and sew, having purl side for the right side.

Finishing: Sew sides of the back part of the cap to adjoining bound-off edges of the quaker st. With the right side of the cord to the right side of the cap, sew 17 sts at the center of the cast-on edge of the cord to the 17 bound-off sts of the back part of the cap; sew the neck edge of the quaker st part to the next 20 sts of cord at each side of the back. Sew the bound-off edge over the seam. Block the same way as with the sacque.

Crochet sacque: *Back*—With size E hook and A, ch 62 (65) for lower edge.

Row 1—right side—Work 1 hdc in 3rd st from hook and in each remaining st to end; 60 (63) hdc. Mark for right side.

Row 2—Ch 2, turn, 1 hdc in each hdc. Repeat row 2 for pat. Work even until 19 (23) rows from beg.—about 3¾ (4½) ins., end on right side.

Inc. row—wrong side—Ch 2, turn, 2 hdc in first hdc, 1 hdc in each hdc to within 1 hdc of end, 2 hdc in last hdc; 62 (65) hdc. Repeat inc. row 5 times; 72 (75) hdc. Work 1 row even.

Beg. Sleeves—*Back Sleeve Shaping*—*Row 1*—right side—Ch 7 (8), turn, work 1 sc in 3rd st from hook, 1 sc in next st of ch, 1 hdc in each of next 3 (4) sts of ch, 1 hdc in each st of row below; remove hook from loop, join a separate piece of A in top of turning ch of row below, just below last st worked, ch 6 (7), fasten off and break this yarn; work 1 hdc in each of next 3 (4) sts of ch, 1 sc in each of next 2 sts, 1 sl st in last st; 84 (89) sts; 6 (7) sts added each side. *Note*—Turning ch at beg. of row is counted as 1 st.

Repeat row 1 of sleeve shaping 5 times, end on wrong side at right sleeve edge; 144 (159) sts. Work 15 rows even, end on right side at left sleeve edge; 47 (51) rows from lower edge of back; about 9½ (10¼) ins.

Divide For Neck—Work 60 (66) hdc for Left Side. *Next row*—Ch 2, turn, work 60 (66) hdc.

First inc. row—Work to within 1 st of neck edge, 2 hdc in next hdc; 61 (67) hdc.

2nd inc. row—Ch 2, turn, 2 hdc in first hdc; 1 hdc in each hdc to end; 62 (68) hdc. Repeat first inc. row; 63 (69) hdc.

Next row—Ch 13 (14) for front neck edge, turn, work 1 hdc in 3rd ch from hook and in each of next 10 (11) sts on ch, 1 hdc in each hdc to end; 74 (81) hdc. Work 11 rows even, end at front edge; 32 rows even on sleeve edge.

Left Front Sleeve Shaping—*Row 1*—Work hdc to within 3 hdc of end, 1 sc in each of next 2 hdc, 1 sl st in last hdc. Fasten off.

Row 2—With loop on hook, turn, skip last 6 (7) sts of row below, work 1 sl st in next st,—the 7th (8th) st from sleeve edge; 1 sc in each of next 2 sts, 1 hdc in each hdc to end; 68 (74) sts.

Row 3—Work hdc to within 9 (10) sts of end of row below, 1 sc in each of next 2 sts, 1 sl st in next st; 62 (67) sts. Fasten off. Repeat rows 2 and 3 once; 50 (53) sts. *Row 6*—Repeat row 2, end at front edge; 44 (46) sts.

Row 7—Work to within 6 (7) sts of end of row below; 38 (39) sts.

Row 8—Ch 2, turn, work a decreasing hdc, as follows:—yo, draw up a loop in each of next 2 sts, yo, draw yarn through all 4 loops, work hdc to end; 37 (38) sts.

Row 9—Work hdc to within 2 sts of end, work a decreasing hdc; 36 (37) sts. Repeat rows 8 and 9 twice; 32 (33) sts. Work 19 (23) rows even, end at front edge. Fasten off.

Right Side—Leave 24 (27) hdc free for back neck edge. With loop on hook, work 1 hdc in 25th (28)th st from left side of neck and 1 hdc in each hdc to right sleeve edge; 60 (66) hdc. Work 1 row even.

First Neck inc. row—Ch 2, turn, work 2 hdc in first hdc, work hdc to end; 61 (67) hdc.

2nd inc. row—Work hdc to within 1 st of neck edge, 2 hdc in next hdc. Repeat first inc. row; 63 (69) hdc.

Next row—Work 63 (69) hdc; remove hook from loop; join a separate piece of yarn in top of

(continued on next page)

turning ch of row below and ch 11 (12) for front neck edge. Fasten off. Work 11 (12) hdc on ch; 74 (81) hdc. Work 11 rows even, end at sleeve edge—32 complete rows of hdc on sleeve edge.

Right Front Sleeve Shaping—Ch 1, turn, skip 1 hdc, 1 sc in each of next 2 hdc, 1 hdc in each hdc to end. *Note:* Turning ch at beg. of row is counted as 1 st. *Row 2*—Work same as row 3 of left front sleeve shaping; 68 (74) sts. Fasten off. *Row 3*—Work same as row 2 of left front sleeve shaping; 62 (67) sts. Repeat last 2 rows once; 50 (53) sts. *Row 6*—Repeat row 3 of left sleeve once, end at sleeve edge; 44 (46) sts. Fasten off. *Row 7*—Draw up a loop on hook, turn, skip 6 (7) sts of row below, work 1 hdc in next st, 1 hdc in each st to end; 38 (39) sts. *Row 8*—Same as row 9 of left sleeve. *Row 9*—Same as row 8 of left sleeve; 36 (37) sts. Repeat last 2 rows twice; 32 (33) hdc. Work even until same length as left front, end at underarm edge. Fasten off.

Finishing—Finish and block, see page 84.

Picot Edges—Sleeves—Row 1—Beg. at seam on sleeve edge, with size 1 hook and B, with loop on hook, from right side work 40 sc on sleeve edge—about 6 sc in every 5 rows; join with a sl st in first sc.

Row 2—Picot Row—Ch 1, turn, * work 1 sc in next sc, ch 3, 1 sc in same sc with first sc—a picot—1 sc in each of next 3 sc *; repeat between *'s around; join with a sl st to first sc; 10 picots. Fasten off.

Picot Edges—Sacque—Beg. at left underarm seam, work as for row 1 of sleeve, work 59 (61) sc on lower edge of back, 31 (32) sc on right front, 3 sc at corner, 45 (49) sc on right front edge. 3 sc at corner; 9 (10) sc on front neck edge; 1 sc in each of next 4 rows on side edge, draw up a loop in next row and in first st on back neck edge, yo and through all 3 loops on hook—a decreasing sc—* 1 sc in each of next 2 sts, draw up a loop in each of next 2 sts, yo and through all 3 loops on hook; repeat from * 4 (5) times, 1 sc in each of next 1 (2) sts; a decreasing sc in next st and next row on side edge, 1 sc in each of next 4 rows, 1 sc in each of 9 (10) sts on front neck edge. 3 sc at corner; continue sc on left front and lower edge to correspond to right front. Join with a sl st to first sc.

Row 2—Picot row—Ch 1, turn, work 1 sc in each of next 3 (2) sc, repeat between *'s of row 2 of sleeves, working a picot at each corner of left front, end with a picot at right corner of neck; ch 2 for buttonloop, skip next 2 sts, 1 sc in next sc. Continue picot row on right front and lower edge to correspond to left front. Join with a sl st to first sc. Fasten off. Steam lightly.

Quilted raglan cardigan: Pattern is a multiple of 4 sts plus 3. *Pattern*—P 1 row, k 1 row for 5 rows. *Row 6*—right side—K 3, * drop next st and ravel for 4 rows, insert right needle into dropped stitch and under the 4 raveled loops, k this st tog. with the 4 loops, k 3 *; repeat between *'s to end. P 1 row, k 1 row, for 5 rows.

Row 12—K 1, repeat between *'s of row 6, end last repeat k 1. Repeat these 12 rows for pat. Sleeves—Cast on 43 (47) sts. *Row 1*—wrong side—P 1, * k 1, p 1; repeat from * to end. *Row 2*—K 1, * p 1, k 1; repeat from * to end. Repeat these 2 rows for ribbing for 1¾ (2) ins., end with row 2. Work pat. for 27 (15) rows, end with pat. row 3.

Inc. Row—Inc. 1 st in first st, k to within 1 st of end, inc. 1 st in last st. With care to keep pat., repeat inc. row every 12th (24th) row 3 times, working inc. sts in pat. when enough sts have been added to have 1 st at edge next to a raveled st; 51 (55) sts. Work even until 6½ (8¼) ins. above cuff, end with 5 rows above a row worked as for pat. row 12.

Inc. 1 st each side of next row; repeat inc. each side every 2nd row twice; 57 (61) sts. P 1 row. Bind off 1 st at beg. of next row 2 rows, keeping pat.

Raglan Yoke—Mark for beg. of yoke. *Row 1—Dec. Row*—K 1, SKP, k to within 3 sts of end, k 2 tog., k 1. *Row 2*—P. *Row 3*—Same as row 1; 51 (55) sts. *Row 4*—P. *Row 5*—Work even, working as for pat. row 6. *Row 6*—P. Repeat these 6 rows 10 (11) times; sl remaining 11 sts to holder for neck ribbing. Break yarn.

Body—Cast on 139 (155) sts for lower edge. Work ribbing as for sleeves for 1 (1¼) ins., end with row 2. Work pat. until 5 (5¾) ins. above ribbing, end with pat. row 6. Mark for underarm.

Dividing Row—P 35 (39), sl to holder for left front, bind off 1 st for underarm, p until 67 (75) sts on needle for back; sl remaining 36 (40) sts to holder for right front and underarm. Work raglan yoke on 67 (75) sts of back for sleeves. Sl remaining 23 (27) sts to holder for neck ribbing. Break yarn.

*Left Front—Raglan Yoke—*Beg. at left front edge, sl 35 (39) sts to needle. Join yarn at underarm. *Row 1—Dec. Row—*K 1, SKP, k to end. *Row 2—*P. *Row 3—*Same as row 1. *Row 4—*P. *Row 5—*Work even, keeping pat. *Row 6—*P. Repeat these 6 rows until same length as back to neck, end at front edge. Sl remaining 13 (15) sts to holder for neck. Break yarn.

*Right Front—*Beg. at right front edge, sl 36 (40) sts to needle. Join yarn at underarm. Bind off 1 st for underarm, p to end of row; 35 (39) sts.

*Raglan Yoke—Row 1—Dec. Row—*K to within 3 sts of end, k 2 tog., k 1. Finish to correspond to left front, end with row 6. Break yarn. Sl remaining 13 (15) sts to holder. Sew raglan and sleeve seams.

*Neck Ribbing—*Beg. at left front edge, sl to needle 13 (15) sts of left front, 11 sleeve sts, 23 (27) back sts, 11 sleeve sts and 13 (15) sts of right front; 71 (79) sts.

*Joining and Inc. Row—*Join yarn at right front edge; k 5 (7), * inc. 1 st in next st, k 3, inc. 1 st in next st *; k 2, k 2 tog., k 9, k 2 tog., k 6, inc. 1 st in next st, k 7 (11), inc. 1 st in next st, k 6, k 2 tog., k 9, k 2 tog., k 2; repeat between *'s once, k 5 (7); 73 (81) sts. Work ribbing as for sleeves for 6 rows. Bind off in ribbing.

*Note—*Border with buttonholes on right front is for a girl's sweater. For a boy, work 3rd row of border on left front as for buttonhole row of right front and omit buttonholes on right front.

*Right Front Border—*Join yarn on right front edge in first row of ribbing at lower edge.

Work 5 (6) sc on front edge of ribbing, 67 (76) sc to neck ribbing, about 1 sc in every 2nd row—4 sc on neck ribbing; 76 (86) sc.

*Row 2—*Ch 2, turn, work 1 hdc in each sc.

*Row 3—Buttonhole Row—*Ch 1, turn, work 1 sc in each of first 2 hdc, * ch 2 for buttonhole, skip 2 hdc, 1 sc in each of next 12 (14) hdc; repeat from * 5 times, end last repeat 2 sc.

*Row 4—*Repeat row 2. Fasten off.

*Row 5—*From right side, join yarn in first row of sc on lower edge of border, work 1 sc in each row on end, 3 sc at corner, 1 sc in each hdc to neck, 3 sc at corner, 4 sc on top of border. Fasten off.

*Left Front Border—*Join yarn on left front edge in last row of ribbing at neck edge. Work border to correspond to border on right front, omitting buttonholes. Finish and block, see page

Cap: *Back—*With size 3 needles, cast on 77 (81) sts for neck edge. *Row 1—wrong side—*P 3, * k 1, p 1; repeat from *, end last repeat p 3. *Row 2—Dec. Row—*K 1, SKP, work ribbing to within 3 sts of end, k 2 tog., k 1. *Row 3—*P 2, work ribbing to within 2 sts of end, p 2. Repeat rows 2 and 3 times, repeat row 2 once again; 67 (71) sts.

*Pattern and Shaping—Row 1—*P. *Row 2—Dec. Row—*K 1, SKP, k to within 3 sts of end, k 2 tog., k 1. *Row 3—*P. *Row 4—*Same as row 2; 63 (67) sts. *Row 5—*P. *Row 6—right side—*K 3, * drop next st and ravel for 4 rows, insert right needle in 5th row below and under the 4 raveled loops, k this st tog. with the 4 loops, k 3; repeat from * to end. Repeat these 6 rows 9 (10) times, repeat rows 1, 2, 3, 4 and 5 again; 23 sts.

*Next Row—*Sl 1, k 2 tog., pass sl st over the k 2 tog., work as for pat. row 6 to within 3 sts of end, k 3 tog.; 19 sts. Sl these 19 sts to holder. Break yarn.

*Front—*Cast on 89 (93) sts. Work same as for back; 31 sts.

*Dec. Row—*P 2 tog. twice, * p 2 tog., p 1; repeat from * 6 times, p 2 tog. 3 times; 19 sts. Break yarn leaving 20 in. end for weaving. Weave these 19 sts to 19 sts of back.

*Finishing—*Sew edges of back to edges of front.

*Chin Strap—*Ch 36 (40). Work 1 sc in 2nd st from hook and in each remaining ch, working under 1 loop only; ch 5 for buttonhole; work 1 sc in each st of other side of foundation ch.

*Row 2—*Ch 2, turn, work 1 hdc in each of 35 (39) sc working under both loops, 1 hdc in each of next 2 sts of ch; 3 hdc in center st of ch, 1 hdc in each of next 2 sts of ch; 1 hdc in each of next 35 (39) sc. Fasten off. Sew straight edge of chin strap to edge of ribbing at right corner for girl, left corner for boy. Sew button on other side at center of ribbing on seam.

Hooded Knit Outfit

Little Red Riding Hood never had it this good! Protect your baby's ears in style with this soft hand-knit outfit. The fashionable double-breasted cardigan, hood, and mittens will keep your child warm on chilly days and the set is perfectly suited for either a boy or girl.

Instructions are given for size 1-2, and changes for size 3-4 are given in parentheses.

Materials:
Win-knit (Bear Brand, Fleisher's, or Botany, 4 ounce packs) or Softex (Bucilla, 4 ounce balls). 3 (3). Size 7 needles, size 4 needles for ribbing, size 4 double pointed needles for mittens, size F crochet hook.

Gauge:
Size 7 needles—pattern stitch—5 sts = 1 inch, 7 rows = 1 inch; size 4 needles—mittens—6 sts = 1 inch, 8 rnds = 1 inch.

Measurements for blocking:
Width at chest with 3 (3½) inch overlap: 24½ (26½) inches; width of back at underarm: 12 (13) inches; width of each front, including borders: 7¾ (8½) inches; width of sleeve at underarm: 9½ (10) inches.

Directions:
Cardigan: *Sleeves*—With size 4 needles, cast on 30 (34) sts. Work k 1, p 1 ribbing for 3 ins. increasing 1 st at end of last row; 31 (35) sts.

With size 7 needles, begin pat. *Row 1*—wrong side—P. *Row 2*—K 1, * p 1, k 3; repeat from *, end last repeat k 1. *Row 3*—P. *Row 4*—K 3, * p 1, k 3; repeat from * to end. Repeat these 4 rows for pat. Work pat. for 7 rows.

Inc. row—right side—Inc. 1 st in first st, work pat. to within 1 st of end, inc. 1 st in last st. With care to keep pat., repeat inc. row every 8th row 1 (4) times, every 4th row 6 (3) times, working increased sts in pat.; 47 (51) sts. Work even until 6¾ (8½) ins. above ribbing, end with pat. row 3. Inc. 1 st each side of next row; 49 (53) sts.

Work 2 rows even. Bind off 2 sts at beg. of next 2 rows; 45 (49) sts. Mark for beg. of Raglan Yoke. *Raglan shaping*—Row 1—P. Row 2—Dec. Row—SKP, work pat. to within 2 sts of end, k 2 tog. Repeat rows 1 and 2, 17 (19) times; 9 sts. Break yarn. Sl sts to holder for neck ribbing.

Body—With size 4 needles, cast on 143 (155) sts. *Row 1*—wrong side—P 1, * k 1, p 1; repeat from * to end. *Row 2*—K 1, * p 1, k 1; repeat from * to end. Repeat these 2 rows for ribbing for 1 in. end with row 2. *Next row*—With size 7 needles, work 18 (20) sts in ribbing for the left front border, place a marker on the needle, p to within 18 (20) sts of end, place a marker on the needle, work ribbing to end for right border.

Next row—Work 18 (20) sts in ribbing, sl marker, work as for pat. row 2 to 2nd marker, sl marker, work ribbing to end. Sl markers every row. Continue to work ribbing on borders and pat. between markers until 6¼ (7¾) ins. above ribbing, end with pat. row 3 (1) at right front edge.

Divide for underarm—Work 40 (44) sts and sl to holder for right front, bind off 3 sts for underarm; work until 57 (61) sts for back; sl remaining 43 (47) sts to holder for left front and underarm. Mark for beg. of raglan yoke.

Back—Work raglan shaping same as for sleeve; 21 sts.

Right front—Beg. at front edge, sl 40 (44) sts to size 7 needle. Join yarn at underarm.

Row 1—Work even. *Row 2*—Work to within 2 sts of end, k 2 tog. Repeat rows 1 and 2, 17 (19) times; 22 (24) sts. Break yarn. Sl sts to holder.

Left front—Beg. at front edge, sl 43 (47) sts to size 7 needle. Join yarn at underarm and bind off 3 sts as before, work to end of row; 40 (44) sts. *Raglan shaping*—*Row 1*—Work even. *Row 2*—*Dec. row*—SKP, work to end. Repeat rows 1 and 2, 17 (19) times; 22 (24) sts. *Do not break yarn.* Sl sts to holder. Sew sleeve seams. Sew sleeves to raglan yoke edges of back and fronts, matching pat.

Neck ribbing—Beg. at right front edge, sl to size 4 needles 22 (24) sts of front, 9 sleeve sts, 21 back sts, 9 sleeve sts, 22 (24) left front sts; 83 (87) sts. *Dec. row*—wrong side—Work 18 (20) sts in ribbing, p 3, p 2 tog., p 7, p 2 tog., p 19, p 2 tog., p 7, p 2 tog., p 3, work ribbing to end; 79 (83) sts.

For separate cardigan only—Work ribbing on all sts for 1 in. Bind off in ribbing.

For hood (attached only)—Work ribbing on all sts for 1½ ins., end at right front edge.

Inc. row—Bind off 10 (12) sts in ribbing, work until 8 sts in ribbing, * inc. 1 st in next st, p 1; repeat from * 19 times, work 11, bind off remaining 10 (12) sts; 79 sts. Break yarn. Join yarn in last st on needle. With size 7 needles, work 8 sts, place marker on needle, p to within 8 sts of end, place marker on needle, work 8.

Next row—Work 8, sl marker, work as for pat. row 2 to marker, sl marker, work 8. Sl markers every row. Continue ribbing and pat. until 8 (8½) ins. from inc. row, end with pat. row

4. Break yarn, leaving a 40 in. end of yarn for weaving together.

Sl 39 sts to piece of string, pass 2nd st on needle over the first st; sl remaining 39 sts to string. Fold hood at center with front edges meeting. Thread end of yarn in tapestry needle. From right side, weave edges of ribbing tog., weaving the k sts only and skipping the p sts; weave remaining sts tog.

With another piece of yarn, weave the k sts on wrong side of ribbing which were skipped when weaving right side. Join yarn on right front edge at lower edge. Work 1 sc in every 2nd row on front edge, 2 sc at corner of neck.

For girl only—Ch 2 for buttonloop, skip next 2 bound-off sts, 1 sc in each of next 8 (10) sts, 1 sc in every 2nd row on edge of hood, continue sc on left front to correspond, omitting buttonloop. Fasten off.

For boy only—Work 1 sc in each of 10 (12) bound-off sts on right neck edge, 1 sc in every 2nd row on edge of hood, 1 sc in each of the next 8 (10) bound-off sts, ch 2 for buttonloop, skip next 2 sts, 2 sc at corner, 1 sc in every 2nd row on the front edge. Fasten off. Block, see page 84.

Frogs—Ch 20 (22), working under 1 loop only work 1 sc in 7th st from hook and in each of remaining 13 (15) sts of ch, ch 6, join with a sl st to first st at beg. of foundation ch.

Row 2—Ch 1, turn, work 1 sc in each of 6 ch sts, working under 1 loop only; 1 sc in each of 14 (16) sc of first row, working under both loops; 1 sc in each of 6 ch sts; 1 sc in each of 14 (16) sc on the other side of the foundation ch, working under both loops. Join with a sl st to ch 1 at the beg. of the 2nd row. Fasten off. Make 4.

Sew a small button on front opposite buttonloop at neck edge. Sew 4 buttons evenly spaced on the front which overlaps other front, sewing to the 20th (22nd) st from front edge, placing the top button on the row below the neck ribbing, the lower button on the row above the ribbing at the lower edge.

Sew 4 buttons on other front, placed as for first front, but sewing them to the 21st (23rd) st from front edge. Button sweater at neck edge. Button frogs over buttons. Pin and sew frogs to ribbing, sewing through the 14 (16) center sts of frog.

(continued on next page)

Mittens: *Cuff*—With double pointed needles, cast on 30 (34) sts divided on 3 needles. Join with care not to twist sts on needles. Work k 1, p 1 ribbing for 2 (2½) ins.

Hand—K around for St. st for 1¼ (1½) ins. from cuff. With a piece of contrasting yarn, k 5 (6) sts for thumb; sl these sts back to left needle; then k around on 30 (34) sts as before until 3½ (4) ins. from cuff, or ½ in. less than desired length.

First Hand Dec. Round—K 2, * k 2 tog., k 2; repeat from * to end; 23 (26) sts. K 1 round. *2nd Hand Dec. Round*—K 1, * k 2 tog., k 1; repeat from *, end last repeat k 2; 16 (18) sts. K 1 round. *3rd Hand Dec. Round*—K 2 tog. 8 (9) times; 8 (9) sts. Break yarn leaving a 6 in. end. Draw the end twice through all of the sts. Fasten off.

Thumb—Remove contrasting yarn. Pick up 5 (6) sts below opening on one needle and 6 (7) sts above on another needle. *Note:* The half st at each side of 4 (5) center sts above opening is counted as a st. Sl these 11 (13) sts to 3 needles. K around for 1¼ (1½) ins., or ¼ inch less than desired length.

First Thumb Dec. Round—K 1, * k 2 tog., k 1; repeat from *, end k 2 tog., k 2 (k 2 tog, 1); 8 (9) sts. K 1 round. *2nd Thumb Dec. Round*—K 2 tog. 4 times, end k 0 (1) st; 4 (5) sts. Finish same as top of mitten. Steam, see page 84.

Cap Sleeves For Cuties

Your toddler will display her winning ways in this knitted cap sleeve dress. Designed with comfort in mind, it fits perfectly over little chubby arms and offers just enough flare to display those darling sturdy legs. Directions are given for 6-month size, with changes for 1, 2, and 3 years in parentheses.

Materials:
Knit-Cro-Sheen (J. & P. Coats, 250 yd. balls of white), 3 (4, 5, 6) or Knit-Cro-Sheen (175 yd. balls of colors), 5 (6, 7, 8). Size 3 needles, 1 yd. ½-inch-wide ribbon.

Blocking measurements and gauge:

Chest: 20 (21, 22, 23). Width across back at underarm: 10 (10½, 11, 11½). Width across each front section at lower edge of bodice: 8¼ (8¾, 9¼, 9¾). Length from neck to lower edge: 12 (14½, 16½, 17½). Width across back or front at lower edge: 16½ (17, 18, 19).

Gauge: 15 stitches = 2 inches; 10 rows = 1 inch.

Directions:

Back: Starting at lower edge of skirt, cast on 125 (128, 134, 143) sts. K 5 rows for garter st border. P next row. Work in pattern as follows: *Row 1 (right side):* K 2, * yo, K 2 tog., k 1. Repeat from * across. *Rows 2 through 5:* Repeat Row 1. *Row 6:* K 1, p across to within last st, k 1. *Row 7:* K across. *Row 8:* Repeat Row 6. Repeat last 8 rows (Rows 1 through 8) for pattern. Work in pattern until total length is 7 (8½, 9½, 10½) inches, end with Row 8 of pattern.

Next row (Dec. row): K 3 (5, 8, 6), * (k 2 tog.) 5 times; k 2. Repeat from * across to within last 2 (3, 6, 5) sts, k 2 (3, 6, 5) — 75 (78, 84, 88) sts.

Bodice: Rows 1, 2 and 3: k across. *Row 4 (Eyelet row):* K 3 (2, 2, 4), * k 2 tog, yo, k 4. Repeat from * across, end last repeat with k 4 (2, 2, 4). *Row 5:* K across. Starting with a k row, work in stockinette st (k 1 row, p 1 row) for 10 (14, 20, 20) rows.

Sleeve Shaping: Row 1: Cast on 4 sts, k across, cast on 4 sts at end of row — 83 (86, 92, 96) sts. *Row 2:* Sl 1, k 4 — sleeve border; p across to within last 5 sts, K 5 — sleeve border. *Row 3:* Sl 1, k 4, k 2 tog. — dec made at sleeve edge; k across to within last 7 sts, k 2 tog., k 5. Repeat last 2 rows (Rows 2-3) alternately 3 more times — 75 (78, 84, 88) sts.

Continuing to work first and last 5 sts as before for sleeve borders, work in stockinette st until length is 4½ (5½, 6½, 7½) inches from first row of bodice, end with a p row.

Shoulder shaping: Continuing in stockinette st, bind off 9 sts at beg. of next 4 rows; then 7 (8, 9, 10) sts at beg. of following 2 rows. Bind off remaining 25 (26, 30, 32) sts.

Front: Work same as for Back until eyelet row has been completed. *To divide for left and right sections: Next row:* k across to within last 13 (13, 14, 15) sts, place these 13 (13, 14, 15) sts on a stitch holder. Turn.

Right front section: Work over 62 (65, 70, 73) sts on needle only. *Row 1 (right side):* sl 1, k 4 for border, sl 1, k 1, psso — dec made inside border; k across. *Row 2:* P across to within last 7 sts, p 2 tog. — another dec made; k 5 for border. Repeat Rows 1-2 alternately 4 (6, 9, 9) more times — 52 (51, 50, 53) sts, end at front edge.

Sleeve Shaping: Row 1: Sl 1, k 4, sl 1, k 1, psso, k across, cast on 4 sts at end of row — 55 (54, 53, 56) sts. *Row 2:* Sl 1, k 4 — sleeve border; p across to within last 7 sts, p 2 tog., k 5. *Row 3:* Sl 1, k 4, sl 1, k 1, psso, k across to within last 7 sts, k 2 tog., k 5. Repeat last 2 rows (Rows 2-3) alternately 3 more times — 43 (42, 41, 44) sts. Keeping sleeve edge straight and working 5 sts of sleeve border as before, continue to dec one st inside front border every row as before 6 (4, 2, 2) times; then dec one st inside front border every 2nd (3rd, 4th, 4th) row 7 (7, 7, 9) times — 30 (31, 32, 33) sts. Working front and sleeve borders as before, work even in stockinette st until length of armhole is same as on back, end at armhole edge.

Shoulder Shaping: Row 1: Continuing front border as before from armhole edge, bind off 9 sts; complete row. *Row 2:* Work even. *Rows 3-4:* Repeat Rows 1-2. *Row 5:* Bind off 7 (8, 9, 10) sts; complete row — 5 sts. Continue to work border sts as before until length from last bound-off sts is 1¾ (1¾, 2, 2¼) inches for half of back of neck. Bind off.

Left Front Section: Cast on 49 (52, 56, 58) sts, with wrong side of dress facing, with same needle, k sts on stitch holder — 62 (65, 70, 73) sts. *Row 1 (right side):* K across to within last 7 sts, k 2 tog., k 5. *Row 2:* Sl 1, k 4, p 2 tog, p across. Repeat Rows 1-2 alternately 4 (6, 9, 9) more times, end at side edge — 52 (51, 50, 53) sts.

Sleeve Shaping: Row 1: Cast on 4 sts on needle with sts. Sl 1, k across to within last 7 sts, k 2 tog., k 5 — 55 (56, 53, 56) sts. *Row 2:* Sl 1, k 4, p 2 tog., p across to within last 5 sts, k 5. Complete to correspond with right front section, reversing shaping.

Block to measurements. Sew cast-on edge of left front section loosely to wrong side of first row of right front section. Sew side and shoulder seams. Sew ends of back of neck borders together, sew to back of neck. Starting at beg. of right front section, draw ribbon through eyelets in bodice, tie ends into a bow.

Sugar 'n Spice

You'll add variety to your little girl's wardrobe when you make this feminine, soft pink knit overblouse that may also serve as a dress.

It features picot edgings, a round Peter-Pan collar, and a kangaroo pocket. Instructions are given for size 6 months to 1 year, and changes for size 2-3 are given in parentheses.

Materials:
Winfant (Bear Brand, Fleisher's, or Botany, 1 ounce skeins). Color A−4 (4), color B−1 (1). Silverflake (Bucilla, 1 ounce skeins). Color A−5 (5), color B−1 (1). Size 3 14-inch knitting needles, and size 1 steel crochet hook.

Gauge:
Size 3 needles−8 sts = 1 inch, 21 rows = 2 inches.

Measurements for blocking:
Width at chest, buttoned: 27 (29) inches; width of sleeve at underarm: 8¾ (9¾) inches; width at lower edge: 32½ (34½) inches.

Directions:
One Half of Collar−With size 3 needles and A, cast on 31 (33) sts for neck edge, P 1 row.

Inc. row−K 2 (1), * inc. 1 st in next st, k 1, repeat from *, end last repeat k 2 (1); 45 (49) sts. Work St. st−p 1 row, k 1 row−until 11 rows from beg., end with p row. Join A on end of collar at beg. of cast-on row. From right side with free needle, pick up and k 9 sts on end, about 3 sts in every 4 rows; inc. 1 st in first st on left needle, k to within 1 st of end, inc. 1 st in last st, pick up and k 9 sts on other end; 65 (69) sts. Break A.

Picot Hem−With B, p 1 row.

Openwork row−* K 2 tog., yo; repeat from * to within 1 st of end, k 1. P 1 row, k 1 row, p 1 row. Repeat openwork row once. With size 2 needles, p 1 row, k 1 row. Bind off as to p. Make other half of collar in same way.

Pocket−With size 3 needles and A, cast on 31 (35) sts for top edge. Work St. st for 21 rows, end with a p row−about 2¼ ins. Join A on end of pocket at beg. of cast-on row. From right side, pick up and k 16 sts on end, inc. 1 st in first st on left needle, k to within 1 st of end, inc. 1 st in last st, pick up and k 16 sts on other end; 65 (69) sts. Break A. With B, work picot hem as on collar.

Overblouse−With size 3 needles and A, cast on 89 (95) sts for neck and P 1 row. *Inc. row*−K 3 (4), * inc. 1 st in next st, k 1; repeat from *, end last repeat k 3 (4); 131 (139) sts.

Raglan Yoke−Left Side−Short rows−Row 1−P 43 (46), leave remaining sts on needle. *Row 2*−Turn, sl 1 st, k 1, * yo−an inc.−k 1, place marker on needle, k 1, yo−an inc. *; k 12 (14) for left sleeve; repeat between *'s once, k 25 (26) sts for back. Sl markers every row. *Row 3*−P 47 (50), p 2 sts from left needle. *Row 4*−Turn, sl 1, * k to within 1 st of marker, yo, k 2, yo; repeat from * once, k to end. *Row 5*−P all sts of last row and p 2 sts from the sts remaining on needle. Repeat rows 4 and 5 twice, repeat row 4 once. *Row 11*−P all sts of last row, p the sts remaining on needle.

Right Side−Short rows−Row 1−K 25 (26) back sts, * yo, k 1, place marker on needle, k 1, yo; * k 12 (14) sts for right sleeve, repeat between *'s once, k 2, leave remaining sts on needle. *Row 2*−Turn, sl 1, p to end. *Row 3*−* K to within 1 st of marker, yo, k 2, yo; repeat from * once, k 3, k 2 sts from the sts remaining on needle. *Row 4*−Turn, sl 1, p to end. *Row 5*—* K to within 1 st of marker, yo, k 2, yo; repeat from * once, k remaining sts of last row, k 2 sts from sts remaining on needle. *Row 6*—Turn, sl 1, p to end. Repeat rows 5 and 6 twice, completing short rows; 171 (179) sts.

Yoke Inc. row—* K to within 1 st of marker, yo, k 2, yo; repeat from * 3 times, k to end; 179 (187) sts. *Next row*—P. Repeat yoke inc. row every 2nd row 19 (21) times, end with an inc. row; 331 (355) sts.

Divide for Body and Sleeves—P, sl to holder 51 (54) sts for left side of back, 64 (70) sts for left sleeve, 101 (107) sts for front; p and leave on needle 64 (70) sts for right sleeve; sl remaining 51 (54) sts to holder for right side of back. Mark for beg. of sleeve.

Right Sleeve—Cast on 3 (4) sts for underarm. Turn and k these 3 (4) sts, k the 64 (70) sts, cast on 3 (4) sts for underarm; 70 (78) sts. P 1 row. *Dec. row*—SKP, k to within 2 sts of end, k 2 tog. Repeat dec. row every 2nd row twice; every 4th row 5 (7) times; 54 (58) sts. Work even until sleeve measures 3 (5) ins. from marker or desired length to cuff, end with p row.

Cuff dec. row—K 4 (6), * k 2 tog., k 2; repeat from *, end last repeat k 4 (6); 42 (46) sts. With size 2 needles, work k 1, p 1 ribbing for ¾ in. Bind off in ribbing.

Left Sleeve—Beg. at back edge of left sleeve, sl 64 (70) left sleeve sts to needle. Join A at front edge, work to correspond to right sleeve. Sew sleeve seams. Beg. at right back edge, sl 51 (54) sts of back to needle. Join A at underarm edge and p these sts. Mark for beg. of body.

Body—*Next row*—Turn, k 51 (54) back sts, pick up and k 6 (8) sts on underarm sts of right sleeve; beg. at left back edge and sl to free needle 51 (54) sts of back, 101 (107) sts of front; k the 101 (107) front sts, pick up and k 6 (8) sts on underarm sts of left sleeve, k 51 (54) back sts; 215 (231) sts. P 1 row, k 1 row until 9 (13) rows from marker for beg. of body, end with k row.

Next row—P 18 (21), * place marker on needle, p 36 (38); repeat from *, end last repeat p 17 (20). Sl markers every row. *Inc. row*—* K to within 1 st of marker, inc. 1 st by knitting a st in the side of next st in row below, k next st, sl marker, k 1 st for seam st, inc. 1 st as before; repeat from * 5 times, k to end; 227 (243) sts. Repeat inc. row every 10 (14)th row 3 times; 263 (279) sts. Work even until 6 (7½) ins. from beg. of body or desired length to hem, end with k row. Break A. With B, work picot hem as on collar.

Finishing—Turn back picot hems, folding along line of 2nd openwork row and hem. Block, see page 84.

Crochet Border—Join A on left back edge at lower edge of picot hem. From right side, work 3 sc in picot hem, 77 (91) sc to neck—about 2 sc in every 3 rows; 80 (94) sc. *Row 2*—*Buttonhole row*—Ch 1, turn, 1 sc in next st, * ch 2, skip 2 sts for buttonhole, 1 sc in each of next 12 sts; repeat from *, end last repeat 1 sc in each of last 7 sts. *Row 3*—Ch 1, turn, 1 sc in each st of row below. Fasten off.

Join A on right back edge at neck. Work, to correspond to left border, omitting buttonholes. Join A on lower edge of left border in first row of sc. From right side, work 2 sc on end of border, 2 sc at corner, 1 sc in each sc to top of border, 2 sc at corner, 2 sc on top of border, * draw up a loop in each of next 2 cast-on sts, yo and draw yarn through all 3 loops—a decreasing sc—1 sc in each of next 3 sts, repeat from * around neck; work 2 sc on end of border; 75 (80) sc on neck; 2 sc at corner, finish right border to correspond to left border. Fasten off.

Pocket Border—With A, draw up a loop on hook, from right side, work 1 sc in first cast-on st, * work a dec. as before in next 2 sts. 1 sc in each of next 2 sts; repeat from * to end; 23 (26) sc.

Row 2—Ch 1, turn, 1 sc in each st. Fasten off. Sew the ends of the hem on the pocket to the ends of the crochet edge. Sew on the collar and the pockets as illustrated, making sure that you have them positioned correctly.

Infants' Sweater Sets

◀ Hand-knit and crocheted sacques, caps, and bootees have always been the perfect choice for "showing off" a new baby, as well as keeping him warm. The designs shown here range from tailored knits for boys to outfits with a feminine flair. Instructions are given for size 6 months and changes for size 1 are given in parentheses.

Materials:

Raglan sleeve sacque, cap, and bootees — Winfant (Bear Brand, Fleisher's, or Botany, 1 ounce skeins). Color A — 4 (4), color B — 1 (1). Size 3 14-inch knitting needles, size E crochet hook.
Sacque and cap — Winfant (Bear Brand, Fleisher's, or Botany, 1 ounce skeins). Color A — 3, color B — 1. Silverflake (Bucilla, 1 ounce skeins). Color A — 4, color B — 1. Size 3 and 1 knitting needles, and size 3 crochet hook.
Three-piece baby set — Winfant (Bear Brand, Fleisher's, or Botany, 1 ounce skeins). 5 (6). Size 3 knitting needles and size 1 crochet hook.

Gauge:

Raglan sleeve sacque, cap, and bootees — St. st 8 sts = 1 inch, 21 rows = 2 inches.
Sacque and cap — size 3 needles 8 sts = 1 inch, 21 rows = 2 inches.
Three piece baby set — size E hook — slipper stitch — 7 sts = 1 inch, size G hook — lace pattern — 1 pat. (1 shell and 1 sc) = 1 inch; 6 rows = 2 inches.

Measurements for blocking:

Width at chest: 21 (22½) inches; width of back at underarm: 10 (10¾) inches; width of sleeve at underarm: 7½ (8) inches.

Directions:

Raglan sleeve sacque, bootees, and cap:
Sacque: *Quaker Rib Yoke* — With A, cast on 76 (80) sts for neck. *First Purl Rib* — P 1 row, k 1 row, p 1 row. *Next row* — wrong side — K 16 (17) sts for right front, * put marker on needle, k 8 sleeve sts, put marker on needle *; k 28 (30) for back; repeat between *'s once, k 16 (17)

for left front. Sl markers every row. Carry color not in use along edge. *Yoke Pattern* — Knit Rib — *Row 1* — right side — With B, K. *Row 2* — With B, P. *2nd purl rib* — *Row 3* — With A, K. *Row 4* — Inc. Row — wrong side — * With A, k to within 1 st of marker, yo, k 1, sl marker, k 1, yo; repeat from * 3 times, k to end; 84 (88) sts. *Row 5* — With A, P. *Row 6* — With A, repeat inc. row; 92 (96) sts. Repeat these 6 rows of yoke pat. 9 (10) times; 236 (256) sts — 11 (12) purl ribs and 10 (11) knit ribs from beg. Break B. This completes Quaker Rib Yoke. Remainder of raglan yoke is worked with A, in St. st — k 1 row, p 1 row. *Next Row* — right side — Work inc. row as before; 244 (264) sts. P 1 row. Repeat last 2 rows 5 times; 284 (304) sts. *Dividing Row* — right side — Dropping markers, k and sl to holder, 42 (45) sts. for left front; 60 (64) sts for left sleeve; 80 (86) sts for back; k and leave on needle 60 (64) sts for right sleeve; sl remaining 42 (45) sts to holder for right front.

Right Sleeve — Mark for beg. P 1 row. *Dec. Row* — SKP, k to within 2 sts of end, k 2 tog. Repeat dec. row every 4th row twice, every 6th row 4 (5) times; 46 (48) sts. Work even until 4 (4¾) ins. from beg. of sleeve, end with a p row — 41 (49) rows. *Cuff Dec. Row* — right side — K 3, * k 2 tog., k 1; repeat from * 13 times, end last repeat k 2 (4); 32 (34) sts. *Quaker Rib Cuff* — K 1 row, p 1 row, k 1 row for first purl rib. With B, k 1 row, p 1 row for knit rib. With A, k 2 rows, p 1 row, k 1 row for 2nd purl rib. Repeat knit and 2nd purl ribs 2 (3) times, having 4 (5) purl and 3 (4) knit ribs in all. Break B. Bind off with A, as to p.

Left Sleeve — Beg. at front edge, sl 60 (64) sts from holder to needle. Join A at back edge. Work same as right sleeve. Sew sleeve seams, weaving edges of Quaker Ribs tog. Beg. at right front edge, sl 42 (45) sts from holder to needle. Join A at underarm edge and k 1 row. Mark for beg. of body. *Body* — *Next Row* — P right front sts. Beg. at left front edge, sl 42 (45) sts to free needle, sl 80 (86) back sts to same needle, and p these sts with needle holding right front sts; 164 (176) sts. Work St. st until 4¾ (5¼) ins. from marker for beg. of body, end with a k row at right front edge — 50 (56) rows.

Lower Border — K 1 row, p 1 row, k 1 row, p 1 row for Quaker Rib. Bind off as to k.

Left Front Border — Beg. at neck edge, with A, pick up and k 1 st in first purl rib — in

(continued on next page)

4th row from cast-on row; pick up and k 3 sts in each of next 10 (11) purl ribs; 43 (46) sts on St. st to beg. of border on lower edge—about 2 sts in every 3 rows; 74 (80) sts. K 1 row, p 1 row, k 1 row, p 1 row for Quaker Rib, end at lower edge.

Next Row—K 43 (46) sts, bind off remaining 31 (34) sts as to k. Join A in last st on needle and k 1 row, p. 1 row on the 43 (46) sts for St. st hem facing. Bind off as to k.

Right Front Border—Beg. at lower edge, with A, pick up and k 43 (46) sts on the St. st part of front edge, and 31 (34) sts on yoke to correspond to left border; 74 (80) sts. K 1 row, p 1 row, k 1 row, p 1 row for Quaker Rib, end at neck. *Next Row*—Bind off 31 (34) sts as to k, k to end. K 1 row, p 1 row on remaining 43 (46) sts. Bind off as to k.

Finishing—Hem bound-off edge of 31 (34) sts of front yoke border to "pick up" row on yoke and tack first row of St. st hem facing to "pick up" row on St. st part. Hem bound-off row of hem facing to wrong side of front. Weave ends of Quaker Ribs of front borders to ends of Quaker Ribs on neck and lower edges.

Sew 3 buttons on each front yoke, sewing to "pick up" row at inner edge of front borders; placing top button at center of first k rib and lower button at center of last k rib of yoke, with other button centered halfway between.

Make 3 button loops on left front for boys or right front for girls as follows: Join yarn at base of button and work a button loop long enough to fasten over button on opposite front so that front edges meet.

Bootees: With A, cast on 48 (56) sts for center of sole. *First Row*—wrong side—With A, p 25 (29), put marker on needle, p 23 (27).

First Purl Rib—*Inc. Row*—right side—With A, inc. 1 st in first st, k to within 1 st of marker, inc. 1 st in next st, sl marker, k 1, inc. 1 st in next st, k to within 2 sts of end, inc. 1 st in next st, k 1; 52 (60) sts. Sl markers every row. With A, k 1 row, p 1 row. Carry color not in use along edge.

First Knit Rib—With B, repeat inc. row; 56 (64) sts. With B, p 1 row. *2nd Purl Rib*—With A, repeat inc. row; 60 (68) sts. With A, k 1 row, dropping markers. With A, p 1 row, k 1

row. *2nd Knit Rib*—With B, k 1 row, p 1 row. *3rd Purl Rib*—With A, k 2 rows, p 1 row, k 1 row. *3rd Knit Rib*—With B, k 1 row.

Next Row—P 23 (27), put marker on needle, p 14, put marker on needle, p 23 (27). *4th Purl Rib*—*Dec. Row*—With A, k to marker, k 2 tog., k to within 2 sts of 2nd marker. SKP, k to end; 58 (66) sts. With A, k 1 row, p 1 row, k 1 row. Break A. *4th Knit Rib*—With B, repeat dec. row; 56 (64) sts.

Next Row—With B, p 12 (14) and sl to holder for right side, p 32 (36), p and sl to holder remaining 12 (14) sts for left side. Break B. *5th Purl Rib*—Join A, repeat 4th Purl Rib; 30 (34) sts. *5th Knit Rib*—With B, repeat dec. row; 28 (32) sts. With B. p 1 row. *6th Purl Rib*—With A, repeat dec. row; 26 (30) sts. With A, k 1 row, p 1 row, dropping markers.

Next Row—With A, k 11 (13), k 2 tog., k 2 tog., k 11 (13); 24 (28) sts. Break A.

Next Row—With B, k 12 (14), leave remaining 12 (14) sts on needle. Break B, leaving a 16 in. end for weaving. Thread B in tapestry needle and weave the 12 (14) sts on needles tog. for center of instep.

Ankle Border—Beg. at left side of instep, sl 12 (14) sts from holder to needle. Join A at back edge. *Row 1*—right side K 12 (14), pick up and k 3 sts in each of the 4 Purl Ribs on instep; beg. at right back edge, sl 12 (14) sts from holder to free needle and k these sts; 36 (40) sts, K 1 row. *Dec. Row*—P 10 (12), p 2 tog., p 2 tog., p 8, p 2 tog., p 2 tog., p 10 (12); 32 (36) sts. K 1 row. Bind off as to p.

Ankle Strap—With A, cast on 32 (34) sts. K 2 rows. *3rd Row*—K 2, yo for buttonhole, k 2 tog., k to end. K 1 row. Bind off. Make 2nd strap to correspond to first strap, working 3rd row as follows: K to within 4 sts of end, k 2 tog., yo, k 2.

Finishing—With A, weave back edges, weaving Purl Ribs only. Weave cast-on edge tog. With B, weave back edge of Knit Ribs from wrong side. Sew 12 sts at center of cast-on edge of strap to 12 bound-off sts at center back of ankle border. Sew strap on other bootee with buttonhole at opposite side. Work buttonholes in blanket st. Block, see page 84. Sew a button on end of straps opposite buttonholes.

Cap: With B, cast on 64 (72) sts for center back. *First Purl Rib*—With A, k 2 rows, p 1 row. *Next Row*—wrong side—With A, k 32 (36) sts, put marker on needle, k 32 (36). Sl marker every row. Carry color not in use along edge.

*Back Shaping—Knit Rib—Row 1—*right side —With B, k. *Row 2—*With B, p. *2nd Purl Rib— Row 3—*With A, k. *Row 4—Inc. Row—*wrong side—* With A, k to within 1 st of marker, yo, k 1, sl marker, k 1, yo; k to end; 66 (74) sts. *Row 5—*With A, p. *Row 6—*With A, repeat inc. row; 68 (76) sts. Repeat these 6 rows 5 times; 88 (96) sts.

*Quaker Rib. Pat.—*With B, k 1 row, p 1 row for knit rib. With A, k 2 rows, p 1 row, k 1 row for purl rib. Repeat knit and purl ribs 10 (12) times, having 18 (20) purl ribs in all from beg.—about 6 (6½) ins. and ending with a Purl Rib. With A, bind off as to p.

*Finishing—*Fold cap at center. With B, sew cast-on sts tog. for seam at center back.

*Neck Border—*Beg. at left corner of front edge, from right side, with A, pick up and K 2 sts in each purl rib on neck edge of cap; 72 (80) sts. K 1 row, p 1 row; k 1 row, p 1 row, k 1 row. Bind off as to k. Hem bound-off edge to "pick-up" row. *Tie String—*With two strands of A and size E hook, ch 6, 1 sl st in first st of ch; ch 23 (24) ins. 1 sl st in 6th st from hook. Fasten off. Run tie string through hem of neck border.

Infant's sacque and cap:

Sacque: *Body—*With size 1 needles and A, cast on 284 sts for lower edge of back and fronts. P 1 row, k 1 row for 6 rows for facing. K next row from wrong side inserting needle in back loop of each st for turning ridge.

*Pattern—Row 1—*right side—With size 3 needles, k. *Row 2—*K 10 for left front border, p to within 10 sts of end, k 10 for right front border. Repeat rows 1 and 2 twice. Drop A. Carry A loosely along edge of work. With B, k 2 rows. Break B. Repeat these 8 rows for pat. Work even in pat. until about 7¾ ins., or desired length above turning ridge, end on wrong side at right front edge with 2nd row of B ridge. Mark for underarm.

*Dividing row—*Continuing pat., k 64, place these sts on holder for right front, bind off next 16 sts for underarm, work until 124 sts on needle, place these sts on 2nd holder for

back, bind off next 16 sts for underarm, finish row; 64 sts for left front.

*Left Front—*Continuing pat., work 4 rows even, end on right side at front edge. *Dec. Row—*K 10, p 2 tog. 22 times, p 10; 42 sts. With size 1 needles and B, k 2 rows. *Next Row—* right side—With B, p to within 10 sts of end, k 10. *Next Row—*K. Break B. With size 3 needles and A, keeping 10 sts in garter st for front border, work St. st—k 1 row, p 1 row—on remaining sts for 16 rows, end with p row.

*Neck—*K to within 15 sts of end; place remaining 15 sts on holder for neckband. Dec. 1 st at beg. of next row. Repeat dec. at neck edge every row 6 times, end on wrong side; 20 sts. Work 2 rows even. Bind off.

*Right Front—*From right side, take up 64 sts of right front from holder to size 3 needle, with A from wrong side, p to within 10 sts of end, k 10.

*Buttonhole Rows—*K 4, bind off next 2 sts for buttonhole, k to end. On next row, cast on 2 sts over bound-off sts to complete buttonhole. K 1 row.

*Dec. Row—*P 10, p 2 tog. 22 times, k 10; 42 sts. With size 1 needles and B, k 2 rows. *Next Row—*With B, k 10, p to end. *Next Row—* K. Break B. With size 3 needles and A, keeping 10 sts of front border in garter st, work St. st—k 1 row, p 1 row—on remaining sts for 6 rows, end with p row. Work buttonhole on next 2 rows. Continue to work 8 more rows, end on wrong side at front edge. Break A, join again where necessary.

*Neck—*With B, work first 15 sts, place on holder for neckband, drop B; join A and finish row. Dec. 1 st at end of next row. Repeat dec. at neck edge every row 6 times, end on wrong side; 20 sts. Work 2 rows even. Bind off.

*Back—*From right side, sl 124 sts of back to size 3 needle. With A, beg. on wrong side work 4 rows even, end with k row. *Dec. Row—*P 12, p 2 tog. 50 times, p 12; 74 sts. Drop A. With size 1 needles and B, k 2 rows. With B, p 1 row, k 1 row. Break B. With size 3 needles and A, continue St. st—k 1 row, p 1 row—for 35 rows, about 3½ ins., above dividing row, end with p row. *Shoulders—*Bind off 20 sts at beg. of next 2 rows for shoulders. Sl 34 sts of back to holder for neckband. Sew shoulder seams with a weaving st.

*Sleeves—*With size 1 needles and B cast on 45 sts. *Ribbing—*Row 1—P 1, * k 1, p 1;

(continued on next page)

repeat from * to end. Break B. *Row 2* — With A, k 1, * p 1, k 1; repeat from * to end. With A only, repeat last 2 rows for ribbing until 2 ins. from beg. With size 3 needles, work St. st — k 1 row, p 1 row — for 6 rows. Inc. 1 st each side of next row. Repeat inc. each side every 8th row 7 times; 61 sts. Work 1 row even. Mark for end of sleeve. K 1 row, p 1 row for 10 rows. Bind off.

Neckband — From wrong side, sl the 15 sts of back to size 1 needle; from right side, sl 15 sts of right front to free size 1 needle. With attached strand of B, pick up and k 9 sts on right neck edge, k across 34 sts of back, pick up and k 9 sts on left neck edge, k across 15 sts of left front; 82 sts. K 1 row; break B. With A, k 2 rows. Continuing garter st, work a buttonhole on next 2 rows. K 2 rows; break A. With B, k 1 row. Bind off as to k.

Finishing — Sew sleeve seams to marker for end of sleeve. Sew in sleeves, sewing ends of rows left free at top of sleeve to sts bound-off for underarm. Finish buttonholes in blanket st. Block, see page

Bows — With size 3 hook and B, ch 46. Inserting hook in single thread at back of ch, work 1 sc in 2nd st from hook and each remaining st of ch; 45 sc. Fasten off. Tie into bow. Make 2. Sew 1 bow to each front on last B ridge, having bow about 3 ins. from each front edge.

Cap: With size 1 needles and A, cast on 96 sts for front edge. P 1 row, k 1 row for 12 rows for facing. K next row from wrong side inserting needle in back loop of each st for turning ridge. With size 3 needles, k 1 row, p 1 row for 12 rows, end with p row. With B, k 2 rows. Work pat. as for body of sacque until 7 B stripes are completed. Break B. With A, k 1 row, p 1 row.

Ribbing — *Row 1* — Work k 1, p 1 ribbing to within 2 sts of end, k 2 tog.; 95 sts. *Row 2* — wrong side — P 1, * k 1, p 1; repeat from * to end. *Row 3* — K 1, * p 1, k 1; repeat from * to end. Repeat rows 2 and 3 twice; repeat row 2 once more.

Dec. Row — With size 1 needles, * k 1, p 3 tog.; repeat from * to within 3 sts of end, k 1, p 1, k 1; 49 sts. *Next Row* — P 1, * k 1, p 1; repeat from * to end. Work ribbing for six more rows. *2nd Dec. Row* — K 1, k 2 tog. 24 times; 25 sts. *3rd Dec. Row* — P 2 tog. 12 times; p 1; 13 sts. Break yarn, leaving a 12-inch end.

Finishing — Thread end of yarn in tapestry needle and run through sts on needle, slipping them off; draw up tightly and fasten. Sew back seam neatly for about 3 ins. Turn back facing on turning ridge and sew to wrong side.

From right side, beg. at left front edge, working through double thickness of facing and cap, work 1 row sc on lower edge of cap. Make 2 bows as for sacque. Sew bows to first B ridge, having each bow about 2½ ins. from each side edge.

Three-piece crocheted baby set:
Sacque: *Note:* Always work through both loops of first and last sts and through *back* loop only of all other sts for *slipper stich.*

Yoke — With size E hook, ch 66 for neck edge. *Row 1* — Work 1 sc in 2nd st from hook and in each remaining st to end of ch; 65 sc. Mark for right side. *Row 2* — *slipper st.* — Ch 1, turn, work 1 sc working through both loops, working in *back* loop only, work 1 sc in each sc to within 1 sc of end, work 1 sc in last sc working through both loops. *Row 3* — *Inc. Row* — Work sc as before, working 2 sc in back loop of every 3rd st 21 times, finish row; 86 sts. Work 3 rows even. *Row 7* — Inc. 1 sc as before in every 4th st 21 times, finish row; 107 sts. Work 3 rows even. *Row 11* — Inc. 1 sc in every 5th sc 21 times, finish row; 128 sts. Work 3 rows even. *Row 15* — Inc. 1 sc in every 13th sc 9 times, finish row; 137 sts. Work 2 rows even, end on right side. This completes yoke.

Lace Pattern — *Row 1* — With size G hook, ch 1, turn, 1 sc in first sc, * skip 1 sc, a shell of 1 dc — ch 2 — 1 dc — ch 2 — 1 dc — all in next st inserting hook through both loops, skip 1 sc, 1 sc through both loops of next sc; repeat from * to end. *Row 2* — right side — Ch 5, turn, 1 dc in first sc, * 1 sc in center dc of next shell, a shell of 1 dc — ch 2 — 1 dc — ch 2 — 1 dc — all in next sc; repeat from *, end last repeat with ½ shell of 1 dc — ch 2 — 1 dc in last sc.

Row 3 — Ch 1, turn, 1 sc in top of first dc, * 1 full shell in next sc, 1 sc in center dc of next shell; repeat from *, end last repeat with 1 sc in 3rd st of ch 5; 34 full shells, plus 1 sc. Repeat last 2 rows for lace pat. Work even until 6 rows from Yoke, end on *right* side. Fasten off.

Right Sleeve — *Row 1* — Turn, with loop on hook, working from *wrong* side, skip ½ shell and 5 full shells for right front, 1 sc in center dc of next shell, * 1 shell in next sc, 1 sc in center dc of next shell; repeat from * 5 times; 6 shells for sleeve.

Row 2—Ch 5, turn, 1 dc in first sc, work to end of row 1. Continue lace pat. until 13 rows on sleeve below underarm, end on wrong side.

Cuff—With size E hook, ch 1, turn, work 1 sc in each sc and in each dc; 25 sc. Work 6 rows more of Slipper St, end on right side. Fasten off leaving a 14 in. end. With this end, sew sleeve seam.

Left Sleeve—With loop on size G hook, working from wrong side, skip ½ shell and 9 full shells from sleeve for back; 1 sc in center dc of next shell. Finish as for right sleeve.

Body—With loop on size G hook, from wrong side, work 1 sc in top of first dc on right front edge, continue pat. until 6 full shells, 1 sc in underarm seam of sleeve, continue pat. across back until 10 full shells, 1 sc in underarm seam of sleeve, continue pat. across back until 10 full shells, 1 sc in underarm seam of sleeve, continue pat. across left front; 22 pats. plus 1 sc. Work even in pat. until 15 rows from underarm, end on wrong side. Fasten off.

Front and Neck Edging—With loop on size E hook, from right side, work 1 sc in end sc of last row on right front edge; * ch 3, 1 dc in same sc, skip 1 row, 1 sc in next sc on edge; repeat from * to beg. of Yoke; continue edging on Slipper St. Yoke, skipping 3 rows instead of 1 row, end 1 sc in corner st of foundation ch, work around neck edge, skipping *3 sts*. work left front edge to correspond to right front edge. Fasten off. Steam lightly, see page 84. Sew 3 buttons on left front edge; use edging for button loops.

Bonnet: *Back*—With size G hook, ch 8 for back of neck. *Row 1*—Mark for right side—1 sc in 2nd st of ch, * a shell of 1 dc—ch 2— 1 dc—ch 2—1 dc—all in next st, 1 sc in next st; repeat from * to end; 3 shells plus 1 sc. Work lace pat. until 14 rows from beg., end on wrong side. Fasten off.

Front—Row 1—Turn, from right side, with loop on hook, work 1 sc in end sc of first row on right side edge of bonnet, skip 1 row, 1 full shell in end of next row, skip 1 row, 1 sc in next sc, continue shell pat., end 1 sc in

top of last dc of last row; work 3 shells across last row of back; 1 sc in 3rd st of ch 5; continue on left side of back to correspond, end 1 sc in end sc of first row; 11 pats. Work shell pat. back and forth until 13 rows from beg. *Do Not Fasten Off.*

Neckband—With size E hook, from right side, work 18 sc on neck edge of front, 8 sc on back and 18 sc on other side; 44 sc. Work Slipper St for 6 more rows, end on right side. Fasten off. Finish and block, see page 84. Make Ties or trim with ribbon if desired.

Ties—With Size E hook, ch 77. Work 75 sc on ch working in 1 loop only, 3 sc in last ch; continue sc on other side of ch. Fasten off leaving an end. Make 2 loops on end of Tie and sew to side edge of Neckband, see illustration. Make 2 Ties.

Bootees: *Instep*—With size E hook, ch 10 for front edge of instep. Work Slipper St for 11 rows; 9 sc. Mark last row for right side. Ch 24, join with sl st in first sc of last row. Fasten off. *Foot*—With loop on hook, from right side, work 1 sc in 13th st from beg. of ch, 1 sc in each of next 11 sts, work 1 sc in end st of each of 11 rows on side edge of instep, 7 sc on foundation ch, 11 sc on other side and 12 sc on ch, mark for center back; 53 sc. Work Slipper St back and forth for 10 rows more.

First Dec. Row—wrong side—Work 25 sc, insert hook in *back* of each of next 3 sc, yo, work off as 1 sc. Mark this st for center front, finish row; 51 sts. *2nd Dec. Row*—Work to within 1 st of marker, dec. as before, finish row. Repeat 2nd dec. row once; 47 sts. Fasten off leaving an end. Sew back seam. Fold last row in half from right side, sew seam neatly for sole, sewing *back* loop of st only.

Top of Bootee—With loop on size G hook, from right side, work 1 sc in first st of ch, from back seam on top of foot, skip 2 sts, 1 shell as on sacque in next st, skip 2 sts, 1 sc in next st, skip 2 sts, 1 shell in next st, skip 2 sts, 1 sc in 2nd st of last row of instep, 1 shell in center of sc of instep, skip 2 sc, 1 sc in next st, skip 2 sts of ch, 1 shell in next st, finish row; 5 shells plus 1 sc. Work even in Lace Pat. until 7 rows in all. Fasten off. Sew back seam. Steam lightly. Make tie-cord or trim with ribbon if desired.

Tie-Cord—With size E hook, ch 97. Work 96 sc on ch. Fasten off. Draw through top of foot. Make a knot in each end of cord.

Bold Bibs for Babies

◄ No matter how hard you try to prevent them, spills inevitably occur whenever young children are around food. Although these quaint bibs won't solve the spillage problem, they may catch some edibles that otherwise would go astray.

When the bibs become soiled, simply wash them by hand and they'll be just like new. They are made with fashionable flairs, including bow ties, in fabrics that are both pretty and practical. The bold colors and patterns of these bibs will add high style to the highchair set.

Materials:
Snoopy Bib and Friends Bib — Washcloths (select those that allow you to cut neck opening without destroying motif); ⅓ yard 54-inch wide, flexible clear plastic that can be sewn (enough for four bibs); 2⅓ yards bias tape; polyester stuffing; and decorative items such as eye buttons, bells, beads and acrylic yarn.
Shirt Bib and Bow Tie Bib — Cotton/polyester fabric (12x12½-inch piece for each bib, ¼ yard for collar and pocket for shirt bib, ¼ yard for bow tie and pocket for bow tie bib); ⅓ yard 54-inch-wide clear plastic (enough for four bibs); 39 inches bias tape for each bib; and two snaps.

Directions:
Snoopy Bib: First, cut the rounded neck opening in the washcloth and round the upper two corners. Then, cut a piece of the clear plastic material slightly larger than bib. (Making plastic larger than bib allows for it drawing up slightly during the quilting process.)

Next, cut polyester filling and place it underneath Snoopy; pin the two layers together carefully. Machine-stitch outline of Snoopy; cut away excess filling. Repeat this same process for bird and for knapsack. Outline the pole with stitching, too. Sew eye button on bird. Sew bell on knapsack.

With white thread, machine-stitch washcloth to piece of plastic; leave a ¼-inch edge all the way around the bib. (This will hold the two layers together while you are sewing on bias tape.) Sew contrasting color bias tape around outer edges of bib, omitting neck opening.

Cut 39 inches of bias tape for ties and neck opening. Fold under end of bias tape and seam 15 inches of binding closed. Continue sewing binding around neck opening. Sew remaining 15 inches of binding closed and fold it in at the end.

Friends Bib: Follow the Snoopy Bib instructions, except for directions that refer to polyester filling and to eye button and bell. Instead, after cutting the clear plastic, fill in girl's hair with strands of acrylic yarn, using satin stitch. Repeat this same procedure for girl's hair bow and for boy's hair and hat.

Then, add beads and bells, being sure to sew with a double thread. Knot thread securely so child who is wearing bib cannot remove them. Continue with binding and bias as you did for Snoopy.

Shirt Bib: Start by cutting cloth and plastic bib sections. With bib fabric doubled, cut collar and pocket pieces. With right sides together, seam collar sides and top and sides of pocket. Trim seams, clip corners, and turn pieces right side out. Press. Sew sides of pocket to bib. Baste collar to neckline. Next, pin plastic bib section to right side of cloth bib. Seam them together, leaving a 4½-inch opening at bottom of bib for turning right side out. Do not press, as heat would melt plastic. Cut 39 inches of bias tape for ties and neck opening binding. Fold under end of bias tape and seam 15 inches of the binding closed. Continue sewing binding around neck opening. Sew remaining 15 inches of bias binding closed and fold it in at the end. Hand-sew opening at bottom of bib closed.

Bow Tie Bib: Cut cloth and plastic bib sections. With fabric doubled, cut out pocket and sash for bow tie. With right sides together, sew seams of sash, leaving one end open. Seam top and sides of pocket. Trim seams, clip corners, and turn right side out. Press. Sew sides of pocket to bib.

Next, pin piece of plastic material to right side of cloth bib. Seam together, leaving a 4½-inch opening at bottom of bib. Trim seam. Turn right side out. *Do not press,* as heat would melt plastic. Then cut 39 inches of bias tape for ties and machine-stitch neck opening and proceed as for shirt bib. Hand-stitch end of sash closed, and press. Then, tie sash into a bow tie knot. When you have the bow tied the way you want it, sew through knot by hand. Sew two snaps on backside of knot, and sew the other half of the snaps onto bib at center of neckline.

Baby Carrier and Tote

This matching baby carrier and tote bag set is an ideal gift for a new infant. This particular set offers a bright, fashionable approach to some very practical items.

The cuddly carrier is designed to look like a flower, with the zipper incorporated to be the stem. The sleeping and carrying bag has a companion tote sack to hold baby's indispensables.

Materials:

3 yards terry cloth, ⅛ yard fabric for leaf applique, ½ yard polka dot fabric for flower petal applique, ⅓ yard fabric for flower center applique, and a 20-inch zipper.

Directions:

Carrier: Enlarge the pattern pieces for the basic carrier bag and cut both the pieces from terry cloth. Pin the two pieces of terry cloth with the right sides together, and stitch along the top outline from one side of the zipper closing to the other side. Clip the seams to ease the turning. Turn and press lightly.

Stitch the zipper to the outer layer of the terry cloth. Turn under the seam allowance and hand-stitch the inner layer of the terry cloth to the zipper tape, clipping at the top edge to eliminate the bulk.

Lay the bag out flat, making sure that the zipper is centered. Mark for pleats at the bottom edge. Stitch down. Then, turn the bag inside out and stitch all of the layers together across the bottom edge.

Enlarge the patterns for the applique pieces and cut from the appropriate fabric. Top-stitch the center of the flower to the large petal piece.

Stitch this entire piece to the top of the bag, right sides together, and turn to right side.

To make the front edge petals, pin the petal piece and the terry cloth piece with the right sides together, and stitch at the top and the outer side edges. Turn and press well. Fit over the terry cloth bag top front edge at the place that corresponds with the petals of the applique below. Hand-stitch the applique in place.

Place the leaf appliques on either side of the zipper and hand-stitch.

Tote: (finished size 12x16 inches: Cut two pieces of terry cloth 13x18½ inches. Cut one boxing piece 5x50 inches (may be pieced, but be sure to include seam allowances).

Enlarge the patterns for the applique pieces and cut from the appropriate fabric. Place the leaves on the tote and stitch them in place. Stitch the center piece to the flower shape. Then, stitch the flower to the tote, overlapping the leaf applique slightly.

Stitch the boxing strip to the front and the back of the tote, using a scant ½-inch seam allowance. Trim the seams to ¼ inch and turn the tote right side out.

Fold on the stitch line and stitch again on the right side ¼ inch from the fold as you would for a French seam. (This will keep the seams from raveling inside and give the tote a finished look.) Turn the 2-inch hem at the top edge and hand-stitch down.

To make the handles, cut two 3x18-inch pieces of terry cloth. With the right sides together, stitch along the 18-inch side to form the tube. Turn right side out. Turn the ends back into the tube about ½ inch, and baste in place to hold. Top-stitch along the seamed edge of the tube for a finishing effect. Place the tote handles 2½ inches from the outside edge and 2 inches down from the top. Machine-stitch at the bottom of the handle. Stitch across the handle where the handle joins the top of the tote (stitch twice for extra strength).

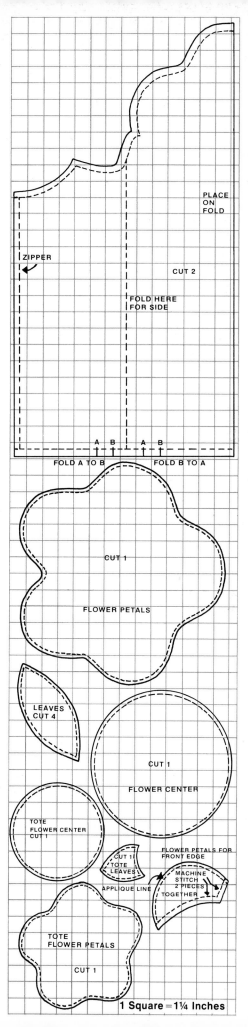

PLACE ON FOLD

CUT 2

FOLD HERE FOR SIDE

ZIPPER

A B A B
FOLD A TO B FOLD B TO A

FLOWER PETALS

CUT 1

LEAVES CUT 4

CUT 1

FLOWER CENTER

TOTE FLOWER CENTER CUT 1

CUT 1 TOTE LEAVES

FLOWER PETALS FOR FRONT EDGE

MACHINE STITCH 2 PIECES TOGETHER

APPLIQUE LINE

TOTE FLOWER PETALS

CUT 1

1 Square = 1¼ Inches

Lively ideas for the nursery

Creating a cheerful, functional nursery requires much thoughtful planning, but it can be lots of fun, too, as you can see by looking at the exciting handcrafted touches in this chapter. Whether your tastes in decorating lean toward modern or reflect an old-fashioned air, you'll find just what you are looking for to spruce up your child's private world.

Baby's Rainbow Retreat

◄ No longer are nurseries restricted to colors that are soft, pastel, and restful. Now, you can decorate with wild, bright, happy ones. The painted crayon-box floor and wavy striped window shade shown at left, for example, contrast with the stark white walls and furniture and set the stage for today's infant. These decorating projects are easy to do and are bound to be big with little ones. And with this basic, bold background of colors, you can springboard into endless combinations of decorating ideas as your baby grows.

Materials:
A rainbow assortment of enamel paint (½ pint of enamel covers 25 square feet; 1 quart of enamel covers 110 square feet); scuff-resistant, high-gloss varnish; one 1-inch-diameter dowel cut to size; and brightly striped, sturdy cotton fabric (either sailcloth or duck) to use with a window shade laminating kit, or a plain white room-darkening window shade and a rainbow assortment of textile paints.

Directions:
For the window shade: Once you have decided on the cotton fabric, let that choice dictate the color scheme of your floor. Laminate the fabric to a room-darkening window shade (use either a press-on or iron-on laminating kit). With the plain white window shade, paint your own design with textile paints in a rainbow color choice.

For the floor: Use masking tape to protect the adjacent floor boards and paint each floor board with a different color of enamel. Be sure to give each board two coats, and let each dry thoroughly before you paint the one next to it.

Give the stark white nursery walls a dominant accent color by painting the majority of the floor boards one particular color. After painting the floor boards, give the entire floor at least two coats of clear, high-gloss varnish. This will keep the colors brilliant and make the floor scuff-resistant.

For the clothes bar: Cut the 1-inch dowel to size. Then, pick one of your favorite colors from the striped floor boards and paint the bar with the enamel paint. Use several coats to prevent hanger scratches.

Other nursery essentials: Use side-by-side drawer units that provide plenty of good storage space for baby clothes. You can buy these in finished or unfinished versions. Or if there's a handyman in the family who enjoys simple carpentry projects, these are not difficult to make.

Build in a cantilevered shelf that can serve as a changing table for the baby and as a readily accessible area for nursery essentials. Paint the shelf with an accent color.

Crib Carrousel

Long before your baby is old enough to take his first ride on the merry-go-round at the amusement park, he'll spend many hours enjoying this fanciful carrousel with its collection of 16 brightly painted miniature animals suspended from rickrack streamers.

Just hang this handcrafted mobile above or near his crib where he can focus his eyes on it. It not only will provide entertainment for baby, it also will brighten his nursery decor.

Materials:

Sixteen wooden animal cutouts (either ready-made ones purchased in a toy department or handcrafted ones cut out with a jigsaw from ¼-inch-thick plywood, one large wooden embroidery hoop, enamel (non-toxic) in bright orange plus other colors for the animals, 16 small brass screw eyes, baby rickrack (orange), a brass curtain ring, and heavy-duty thread.

Directions:

Drill 16 holes, spaced an equal distance apart, around the perimeter of the wooden embroidery hoop. Paint the hoop with bright orange enamel. Paint the animals in various colors so that you'll include tan and black horses, black dogs, tan sheep, orange cows, gray elephants, and pink pigs. Or, you can choose other animals just as long as you have a total of 16 so the mobile will be correctly balanced. Next, insert small brass screw eyes in the tops of each one of the painted wooden animals.

Cut the orange baby rickrack in lengths of 15, 17, and 19 inches. Knot one end of each length of rickrack in the screw eye on the top of each animal. Apply a small dab of white glue to each knot so it won't come untied.

Thread the other end of each piece of rickrack through one of the holes in the embroidery hoop. Loop the rickrack into a knot and continue it above the hoop for a canopy effect at the top. Loop and knot all of the cutouts, letting the animals fall at different levels. Keep the rickrack at approximately the same lengths above the loops (about six inches). Form the canopy by bringing all of the extensions of the rickrack to the center. Trim the rickrack ends so they are all equal lengths.

Loop all of the ends through a brass curtain ring. Tie the gathered loop together at the ring with a heavy thread.

Suspend the mobile by the curtain ring over the crib, or hang it in front of a window where a gentle breeze will keep it in motion.

Child's Play Tent

Most babies outgrow their infant swings by the time they are 12 to 18 months old. When this happens, parents usually store the swing for possible future use by another child, sell it to someone else, or give it away.

There is another use for the swing, though. The A-frame of an infant swing is ideal as a frame for a toddler's play tent. Simply disconnect the swing from the frame and cover the frame with fabric. When the fabric becomes soiled, slip it off of the frame and launder it.

Materials:
4½ yards of 45-inch patterned fabric, one package of twill tape, 1½ yards of lining fabric, and one spool of heavy-duty thread.

Directions:
Drape the fabric over the frame from what was the swing's front to the back. (This will form the sides of the tent.) Cut the fabric the width of the frame plus a ¾-inch seam allowance on each side. (The frame probably will taper slightly narrower toward the top, so be sure to cut the fabric while it is draped over the frame.) Allow for a 2-inch hem on the bottom at each end.

To cut the back of the tent, lay the fabric on the floor or on a large cutting surface, then lay the swing frame on top of the fabric. Cut the piece to shape, allowing a ¾-inch seam allowance on both sides, plus a 2-inch hem allowance at the bottom.

To cut the front of the tent, fold the back fabric piece in half lengthwise and use it for a pattern to cut two front halves. Be sure to add a ¾-inch allowance for the center seam. Do not add the 2-inch hem allowance. Instead, add a ¾-inch seam allowance at the bottom.

Cut the right and left front pieces of the tent fabric and the two pieces of contrasting lining fabric. (If the swing frame has a crank for winding the swing, place it at the back of the tent and cut a slit in the tent's back piece so the crank will slip through.) If the fabric tends to ravel, overcast cut edges of slit before joining the back piece to the sides.

To construct the tent, sew the back piece to the side pieces, right sides together, with a ¾-inch seam allowance. Sew the two outer panels together at the top (from the top to below the swing frame cross brace). Sew the two lining panels together the same way. Then, place the lining panel and the outer flaps together, right side to right side, and sew down the front edges and across the bottom edges. Next, turn right side out and press the front section. Next, join the lined front piece to the side pieces and sew them together.

Use a 2-inch hem allowance for the hem at the sides and the back. Add twill tape ties to the corners at the bottom. Tie these around the swing frame legs to secure the cover to the frame. Finally, add a length of twill tape to the outside front corners and the center of the front flaps in order to either tie the front flaps closed or to tie them back open.

Children's Corner

The addition of these items to a bare corner of a child's room will transform it into a very special place. Under a coat tree with toy containers suspended from every arm, place a large, colorful toy chest. Then, make teatime with dolly completely cozy with a custom-designed mini-tablecloth and matching chair cushions that complement the painted youth-size table and chair set.

Materials:

For the table and chairs—paint (one pint should be enough to cover a child's table and chair set), clear varnish, two yards washable fabric (for a 26x20-inch child's table and two small chairs with 11½x11½-inch seats), eyelet ruffling, lace edging, daisy chain, and ½-inch-thick foam rubber padding.

For the toy box—a large corrugated carton, masking tape, adhesive-back paper, paint, fold-over braid, band trim with ABC motif, jumbo yarn, and felt.

For toy containers—empty food cans, felt, yarn.

Directions:

Table and chairs: Apply two coats of paint to unpainted table and chairs. Then finish the set with two coats of clear varnish.

Cut fabric for the tablecloth, allowing an 8-inch drop on all sides. Narrowly hem, then stitch the eyelet ruffling under the hem and the lace edging over the hem. In the center of each daisy cut from the daisy chain, tack a tiny stitch to give it dimension.

For the chair cushions, cut the fabric 1 inch smaller than the chair seat. Cut a ½-inch-thick piece of foam rubber ½ inch smaller than the fabric. Stitch the eyelet ruffling to the top edge of the cushion, adding fullness at the corner; add the daisies. Seam the top and bottom, leaving five inches open. Insert the padding and hand-stitch the opening.

Toy box: The best choice is to use a large corrugated carton whose top is still hinged on one side. Use masking tape at the hinged area for support. Cover the box with adhesive-back paper to hide the printing on the box.

Paint the box the desired color. Glue fold-over braid around the lid edge and around the top and bottom edges of the box. Glue the band trim with ABC motif around the top and bottom. Measure the sides of the box and then punch holes in the sides for centered handles. Braid bulky yarn and insert the ends. Knot them to prevent them from slipping out. As a finishing touch, cut the letters from felt and glue them to the front of the box.

Toy containers: To make containers for small toys and trinkets, clean out the coffee cans and the small and large juice cans. Then, glue felt to the inside and the outside of the cans. Next, glue colorful trims to each of the cans, as shown in the photograph. Make a hole at each side of the top of each container. Use yarn with knotted ends for the handles.

Clown Door Caddy

Welcome to the greatest door decor on earth! This slip-over-the-door caddy features a happy clown on one side; the backside has stash-away pockets and a mirror.

Materials:

2¼ yards ticking, 1½ yards yellow fabric, ½ yard each of green and pink fabric, 9 yards fold-over braid, 2¼ yards ball fringe, ¾ yard brush fringe, ¾ yard ruffling, ⅜ yard ¾-inch elastic, 1 yard jumbo rickrack, 9x9-inch mirror, 2⅜ yards black bias tape, and 1 yard yellow bias tape.

Directions:

To duplicate this fanciful caddy, cut two pieces of ticking 22x81 inches (door height plus 4 inches). For the front, cut a yellow triangle 53x20 inches wide at the base. Cut white face circle (9¾ inches in diameter). Mark facial features as shown. Stitch fold-over braid for mouth, cheek circles, black double-fold bias tape for eyes, and 4½ inch braid fringe rolled up for the nose. Stitch two rows of jumbo rickrack 7 inches from top of triangle. Then, stitch green ball fringe, 31 inches high. Stitch face 1½ inches above. Cut one green and one pink circle (5 inches in diameter). Cut them in half. Use green ones for hands and pink ones for shoes. Stitch triangle 10¾ inches from bottom of ticking. Hair is two rows of brush fringe, hat top is 4 inches brush fringe rolled and tacked, and collar is two rows of ruffling. Cut balloons (8½ inches in diameter). Use double-fold bias tape for the "HI" and the strings.

For the pockets on back side of door, cut pink fabric 14x26 inches and green fabric 12x26 inches. Make a 2-inch box pleat at center and 1-inch pleats at each side ½ inch from edge. Bind top and bottom edge in contrasting colors. Pin pink pocket 8½ inches from bottom and green pocket 6 inches above pink pocket. Stitch sides, bottom, and through the center.

Cut 12x12-inch yellow fabric and interfacing. Bind together. Stitch 8½-inch-diameter circle in center and cut out; stitch jumbo rickrack around hole. Stitch to caddy above green pocket to hold mirror. Seam top of caddy, hem bottom, and bind sides. Stitch four 3-inch pieces of elastic at hem of caddy in order to keep clown caddy snug when you slip it over door.

Infant Seat Pads

The very young spend a considerable amount of time lying around, so why not have them do it in high style? These adorable and colorful infant seat pads are so comfortable that the child may decide that there really isn't all that much to cry about after all.

Materials:
½ yard of two or more assorted print fabrics and one 16x28-inch piece of lining fabric (cotton-polyester), 2½ yards eyelet ruffling or wide bias tape, one 16x28-inch piece polyester stuffing, acrylic yarn, and thread.

Directions:
Eyelet Trim Infant Seat Pad: Cut 28 4½-inch-square patches. (If you are using several patches of one fabric, tear strips 4½ inches wide. Then, cut at 4½-inch intervals to make the squares.)

Next, lay out your design in a pleasing arrangement. Join each row of seven patches. Press the seams down. Now, join the four rows of patches. Press the seams in one direction.

Cut the backing fabric to the size of the patchwork. Round the upper corners of the pad.

Then, pin eyelet ruffling to right side of the patchwork. Leave a ⅝-inch seam allowance. Baste. Join the front and back, right sides together. Stitch on the eyelet-basted seam, leaving an 8-inch opening at the bottom for turning right side out and filling. Trim the seams and turn. Press.

Cut the polyester padding the same size as the finished pad. Carefully lay the padding flat inside the pad. Sew the opening closed.

Sew through the three layers at each of the squares' corners with acrylic yarn. Clip the yarn and tie a knot.

Bias-Edged Infant Seat Pad: Follow the instructions for the Eyelet Trim Pad, except omit directions that refer to the positioning of the eyelet trim, and use the following: With wrong sides together, pin bias tape around the edge of the patchwork, leaving an 8-inch opening at the bottom for filling. Stitch.

Fanciful Clothes Hangers

Sized just right for small children's clothes, these decorative padded hangers will be a welcome addition to any nursery room closet. And they're so inexpensive to make that you'll probably want to fashion a whole collection of novel clothes hangers—each one depicting a different storybook character.

Materials:
Ordinary wire clothes hangers, felt scraps in different colors, 3 yards of thick orange yarn for the girl's hair, twelve 2- or 2½-inch lengths of yellow yarn for the boy's hair, two 2½-inch-diameter velour-type powder puffs, polyester stuffing, and 18 inches of ribbon to tie around the girl's braids.

Directions:
Cut the wire hanger at the center of the cross bar. Re-bend the hanger to a 12-inch width, overlap the ends, and tape them together.

For the arms, cut two pieces of felt 1½x11½ inches. Stitch the two pieces together with a narrow seam along one long edge, leaving ¼ inch free at the center. Turn the piece right-side out and slip it over the hanger hook. Pad the felt lightly with polyester stuffing. Pin the bottom edges together and stitch close to the edge, using a zipper foot.

From the beige felt, cut the hands about two inches long and wide enough to fit snugly on the ends of the hanger arms. Stuff the hands lightly, slip them over the hanger ends, and tack them to the wire. Glue the ends of the sleeves over the tops of the wrists.

For the face, open the seam of the powder puff a little way at both the top and the bottom. Slip the powder puff over the hanger hook, and add a little more stuffing through the top of the puff. Sew the bottom of the puff to the hanger and the top of the puff closed. After doing this, attach the collars— a round one for the girl and for the boy a pointed shirt collar topped with a bow tie.

To make the girl's wig, cut six 15-inch-long strands of orange yarn, and machine-stitch them together at the center. For the bangs, cut six 3-inch loops from orange yarn. Machine-stitch these together at the center of the loops. Position the center stitching of the strands at the back top center of the powder puff head. Stitch the yarn to the puff. Then, bring six strands to the front of the head on each side, whipstitch the yarn to the puff, and braid the ends of the yarn. Next, tie the ribbon (9 inches each) bows to the braided yarn. Then, wrap the machine-stitched bangs around the hanger wire and sew them to the powder puff head.

For the boy's hair, stitch the pieces of yellow yarn together, pushing one piece of the yarn under the presser foot at its center. Apply the hair as you did the girl's bangs.

To finish the hangers, glue on the felt eyes and the mouths.

Country Creations

Add a rural restfulness to the nursery scene with this wall hanging and companion pillows. These familiar farm animals will delight your youngsters and the barnyard atmosphere of the wall hanging will help to lighten your chores when it comes to decorating for juveniles.

Materials:

36-inch-square wall hanging—⅔ yard green fabric (grass); ½ yard blue fabric (sky); one 9x18-inch piece of yellow fabric; scraps of red and blue, red and white print, brown, beige, peach, yellow, and white for the balance of the barn, silo, chickens, and cows; gold felt for the ears; one package polyester filling or batting; and 1 yard lining fabric.

You'll also need rings for hanging, three yards jumbo rickrack (yellow for the roof), 3 yards of wide bias tape (red for the siding), 1 yard of red/white/blue woven braid, 4½ yards of hem facing (red), ⅓ yard brush fringe (green for grass), bits of brush fringe (brown for the cow), red ball fringe (chicks), and small amounts of lace trims, braid, middy braid, and fold-over braid for the flowers, barn door, chicken legs, and cow legs.

Pillows—two 12x12-inch knife-edge pillow forms, ½ yard yellow fabric, ½ yard blue fabric, two 10-inch zippers in colors to match, and an assortment of fabric scraps.

Directions:

For the wall hanging: Seam the blue and green fabric together, and press the seam flat. Cut the barn pieces and the animals as illustrated on the drawings. Determine the location for the fabric scene and baste or pin the barn pieces on the background fabric. Use the trim to outline the shapes of the window, the barn front, and the silo. Baste all of the pieces in place.

For the barn siding, use rows of 1-inch-wide bias tape. Stitch the bias tape at the top edge

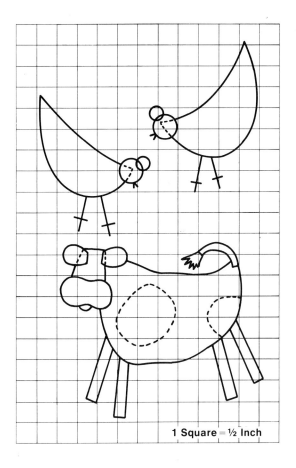

1 Square = ½ Inch

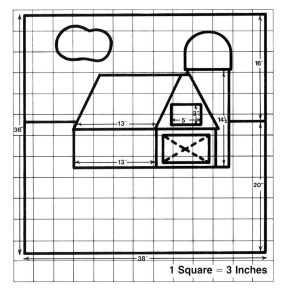

1 Square = 3 Inches

only; overlap tape slightly to give a clapboard effect. Give the roof a shingled effect by stitching overlapping layers of jumbo rickrack, starting at the bottom. Place the layer of batting under the background fabric and the lining fabric under the batting. Baste through all three layers to avoid shifting. Stitch barn in place through all of the layers.

Where no decorative trim is shown, use the satin stitch to applique the motif in place. Repeat the same process for the animals. For the chickens, stitch two layers of ruffled lace on the upper and lower edge of the bodies before placing them on the background. Stitch the chickens and the cow in place, adding bits of trim such as the ball fringe, the felt ears, and the brush fringe for details as shown. Cut and

stitch the cloud in place, and tack the tiny embroidered flowers on the green fabric and stitch them in place. Press the hem facing in half and bind around the entire edge of the wall hanging. Add rings at top under the binding.

For the pillows: For each pillow top, cut the fabric 14x14 inches square. For each back, cut two pieces 14x7½ inches. Turn under ½ on the long edge of each piece and press. Seam two inches at each end, and stitch a 10-inch zipper in the opening. Arrange the animal designs on front sections. Stitch them in place.

If you wish to give the pillows a more luxurious, puffy look, place a layer of quilt batting and lining fabric under the pillow top, then baste in place. Stitch the pillow front to the back with the right sides together. Clip the corners and turn the pillow right side out. Place the knife-edge pillow form inside and zip it closed. When it needs laundering, simply unzip the cover and remove it.

Crib or Carriage Covers

Mothers have been making handmade shawls to wrap their babies in as long as fathers have been hunting rabbit skins. Whether in the crib, the bassinet, or the carriage, your baby will have beautiful protective covering with these three easy crochet and knit blanket designs.

Materials:

Thermal crib blanket — Winfant (Bear Brand, Fleisher's, or Botany, 1-ounce skeins), 9; 5 yards nylon blanket binding; and a size F crochet hook.
Wrapping shawl or carriage cover — Win-Tot, Winsom, Win-Knit (Bear Brand, Fleisher's, or Botany, 4-ounce packs) or Softex (Bucilla, 4 ounce balls), 2. Size 10½ knitting needles.
Ripple carriage or crib cover — Material requirements are for crib size and in parenthesis for carriage size. Win-Knit (Bear Brand, Fleisher's, or Botany, 4-ounce packs) or Softex (Bucilla, 4 ounce balls), 1(2) color A, 2(4) color B, and 1(2) color C, and a size G crochet hook.

Gauge:

For the thermal crib blanket — 4 spaces = 2 inches; 21 rows = 4 inches.
For the wrapping shawl or carriage cover — for the size 8 needle — 7 sts = 1 inch, 13 rows = 2 inches; for the size 10½ needles — 21 sts = 4 inches, 4 rows = 1 inch.
For the ripple carriage or crib cover — 9 sts = 2 inches; diagonal pattern — 13 sts = 2 inches, 13 row = 4 inches.

Measurements for blocking:

For the ripple carriage or crib cover — width: carriage cover — 26 inches and crib cover — (36½) inches; length: carriage cover — 31 inches and crib cover — (45½) inches.

Directions:

Thermal Crib Blanket (36x45 inches): *Pattern* — multiple of 4 plus 2. Chain 218. *Row 1* — 1 sc in second ch from hook, * ch 3, skip 2 ch, 1 sc in next ch, repeat from * to end; 72 spaces. *Row 2* — Ch 1, turn, 1 sc in first sc, * ch 3, 1 sc in space under next ch 3; repeat from *, end 1 sc in last sc. Repeat last row for pat. until about 45 ins. from beg. Fasten off. *Finishing* — steam lightly. Bind with blanket binding as illustrated.

Wrapping shawl or carriage cover (34½ x 27½ inches): Bound-off edge is pictured. Cast-on edge begins and ends with half a pat. Cast on 192 (144) sts.
Pattern — K 2 rows. *Row 3 — Openwork Row* — wrong side — K 2 tog. 4 times, * k 1, yo, k 1, yo, k 1, yo, k 1, yo, k 1, yo, k 1, yo, k 1, yo, k 2 tog. 8 times; repeat from * 6 (4) times, k 1, yo, k 1, yo, k 1, yo, k 1, yo, k 1, yo, k 1, yo, k 1, yo, k 2 tog. 4 times; 192 (144) sts. *Row 4* — K. Repeat these 4 rows for pat. until 34½ ins. from beg. or desired length. Steam lightly.

Ripple carriage or crib cover: With A, ch 170 (238). *First stripe* — *Row 1* — With A, 1 sc in 2nd ch from hook, 1 sc in each of next 6 ch, * 3 sc in next ch, 1 sc in each of 7 ch, skip 2 ch, 1 sc in each of next 7 ch; repeat from *, end last repeat 1 sc in each of 6 ch, skip 1 ch, 1 sc in last ch. *Row 2* — Turn, skip first st, * 1 sc in back loop of each of 7 sts, 3 sc in back loop of next st, 1 sc in back loop of each of next 7 sts, skip 2 sts; repeat from *, end last repeat 1 sc in back loop of each of 6 sts, skip 1 st, 1 sc in back loop of last st.

Repeat row 2 twice, having 4 rows in first stripe. Break A. When changing colors always draw new color through last loop on hook. *2nd stripe* — with B, repeat row 2 of first stripe 4 times. Break B. *3rd stripe* — with C, repeat 2nd stripe. Break C. *4th stripe* — with B, repeat 2nd stripe. Break B. *5th stripe* — with A, repeat 2nd stripe. Break A. Repeat 2nd, 3rd, 4th and 5th stripes 5 (8) times. Fasten off.
Finishing — Run ends into stripes of same color. Block with wrong side up; pin out on pressing board to given measurements. Steam lightly with a moderately hot iron over a wet cloth, taking care not to let the weight of the iron rest upon any one spot. Allow to dry before removing from the board.

The Wind

I saw you toss the kites on high
And blow the birds about the sky;
And all around I heard you pass,
Like ladies' skirts about the grass—
 O wind, a-blowing all day long,
 O wind, that sings so loud a song!

Robert Louis Stevenson

Things for Children
3 through 6 years

This is the age of discovery. Children in this age group wonder about the people around them and why they react the way they do, about mechanical devices and what hidden parts make them perform, and about the glories of nature that surround them.

And, their imagination knows no bounds. During this time, the world of "let's pretend" occupies many hours and transports them on magic carpets to faraway places where they can play the role of knights in shining armor or astronauts in a spaceship. It is also during this period that tea parties attended by little girls dressed in their mothers' discarded finery take on all the formality of a prestigious social event. Whatever part they choose to play, they do it naturally—being self-conscious has not entered their childish minds yet.

Children in this age group are very sensitive about their innermost feelings—joy, sorrow, anger, and guilt—and they depend on their parents for reassurance. Even at this tender age, life-long habits can be formed—consideration for others, unselfishness, good table manners, politeness, and grooming. These are all traits that parents can instill during these formative years.

Toys for little people

Most children in the three- to six-year age group are bursting with energy. Their eagerness and curiosity are at a high pitch and, as a result, they are extremely receptive to creative play ideas. On the following pages, there is a variety of playthings that will fascinate your children and provide new channels for them to expend their energies as well.

Stepladder Playhouse

◄ With this super step-up playhouse, there is no room for the old walking-under-a-ladder superstition. And regardless of whether it is stationed indoors or outdoors, it leaves plenty of room for your child and his playmates to develop their imagination. In the world of "let's pretend," this unpretentious playhouse can change instantly to become a Swiss chalet at a ski resort, a cabana at the beach, or a medieval castle high on a hill.

The playhouse has its practical side, too. First, your children can use it year-round. During the summer, it's a shady spot for favorite hideaways, games, and other activities. And as winter approaches, you can bring it into the family room, a winterized porch, or the children's playroom to use as a cozy retreat. And second, walking up and down the ladder steps is great exercise for the children and will help to develop and coordinate their arm and leg muscles.

Materials:
Two 6-foot ladders, 4½ yards of 48-inch-wide lightweight canvas material (7 ounces per square yard), wood braces, brightly colored enamel paints, staples, nylon rope, and a board the length of the two ladder tops.

Directions:
First, remove the leg braces and the paint platforms from the ladders. Then, paint the ladder steps—each one a different vivid color of enamel. Next, paint the rest of the ladder in one solid bright color that will complement the color of the canvas.

Nail on the new stationary wood braces to replace the leg braces that were removed. Join the tops of the ladders together with a board cut the same width as the ladder tops and the same length as the two ladder tops combined. Nail or screw this board securely across the top of the two ladders so they will stay in the A-frame position side by side. Paint the braces and board to match the ladders.

Now that you have this sturdy frame for the playhouse, select a bright happy color of lightweight canvas material. Cut the canvas to fit the inside of the frames of the ladders, then staple it to the inside of the frames. Just above the second step, drill a hole on either side of the ladder through the outside edge. For a professional effect, take the canvas to a tent and awning company before you staple it to the ladders and have metal grommets inserted for the two tieback holes. Pull a nylon rope through each hole in the ladder and the holes in the canvas underneath to serve as tiebacks for the canvas.

Be sure to select extra-sturdy ladders for playful climbing use. Sand down rough edges before you start painting. Check for any repairs or repainting needs before taking the playhouse in or out of doors with the changing seasons.

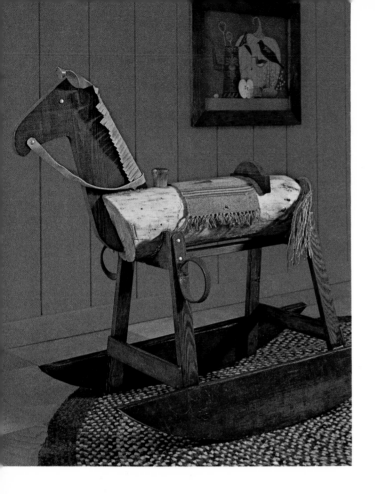

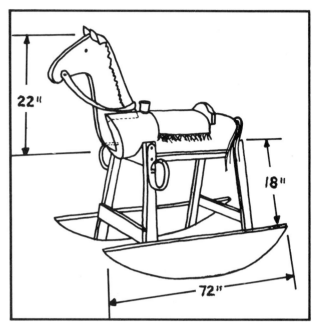

Antique Rocking Horse

If you're looking for a toy project that is steeped in nostalgia, this new version of an old-fashioned rocking horse is bound to be your choice. Long before mass-produced toys were readily available, handmade rocking horses were carved painstakingly by hand. Now, handcrafted toys are popular once again, and you can delight your child with this handsome replica of an old-time favorite.

Since the rocking horse may tip if trotted or galloped, use guidance when your young cavalry corporal takes off on a mission.

Materials:
24-inch-long log (6 to 8 inches in diameter); 4 1x2-inch legs; 1-inch-thick 22-inch-long board for horse's head; 1x6-inch board for rockers; 1x2-inch lumber for saddle back; leather strips, pieces, and belting; walnut stain; thin rope or heavy cord; small Indian place mat; an end of an old baseball bat or short dowel; stiff wire brush; and thumbtacks.

Directions:
To make the rocking horse, follow the measurements that are given in the drawing at the right.

Start by cutting out the 18-inch-long legs and the saddle back from 1x2-inch scrap lumber. Cut the 72-inch-long rockers and the head from one-inch-thick boards. Cut the horse's body from a 24-inch-long piece of log that measures 6 to 8 inches in diameter. Remove the bark from the log body, then sand the log, if necessary.

Trim the head with ears that you cut from a piece of leather. Then, add thumbtack eyes or glue on small circles cut from a piece of felt. Glue and tack on leather strips to simulate the horse's mane and reins.

Join all of the parts together by cutting slits for drilling holes in the horse's body. Secure all of the limbs and rockers in place with glue and nails. Use the leather belting to form the loop stirrups. Attach them to the forelegs, making sure that they are secure enough to hold the weight of a child. Use the end cut from a baseball bat or dowel for the saddle horn.

Stain the horse, except for the log body, with walnut stain. Make the tail from thin rope or heavy cord; nail to the end of log. Place a small Indian place mat on the back for a saddle blanket. Scrape body of horse with a wire brush to produce a rustic or antique effect.

Stair-Step/Rocker

Provide versatile fun for your child's playtime with this reversible stair-step toy. Even though it has a rocker on one side and a step platform on the other, it is an easy woodworking project that you can complete easily in an evening.

Materials:
¾-inch plywood, epoxy paint, and primer.

Directions:
Cut the shapes of the rocker sides and the steps out of ¾-inch plywood. (Adapt the dimensions of the project to the age and size of your child. And for safety's sake, keep the unit wide enough so it won't tip easily.) Make the step risers and the treads at least eight inches deep.

Lay out and mark the step design on the sidepieces before gluing and nailing the unit together. Sand the versatile stair-step toy and then seal it with a coat of primer. Then, finish the project by painting it with epoxy to give it a long-lasting finish.

Sandpile Seating

In spite of the fact that your youngsters build beautiful castles of sand, the sandpile is often an eyesore in your yard. But yours won't be if you incorporate this pleasing design for your "sandpile set." The closely spaced wooden blocks prevent the sand from spreading to other areas of your yard.

These same blocks make convenient seats for the children, so don't be surprised if more of the sand stays in the sandpile rather than invading your house. Place this sturdy creation where you can keep an eye on sandpile activities from inside the house.

Materials:
Railroad ties or 4x6s (scraps or inferior pieces).

Directions:
Cut the railroad ties or 4x6s into a variety of lengths for three sides of the 4½x2½-foot sandbox. Stand the vertical pieces on end, setting them in the ground about half their length. Lay some pieces horizontally for seating around the three sides, and install a single 2½-foot length at one end for seating. Be sure to sand the rough edges to avoid splinters. If you plan to leave the wood outdoors in inclement weather, treat the pieces to a coat of waterproofing.

Noah's Ark and Animals

The Ark proved to be the salvation of Noah as well as the two-of-a-kind animals during the Flood. This plywood ark and wooden versions of Noah and the animals may rescue you when you need to entertain your children some rainy day.

Materials:

Noah's Ark — 1 4x8-foot sheet ½-inch plywood, ¾-inch finishing nails, wood glue, sandpaper, watercolors, and one 2x26-inch strip of leather.
Noah, the animals, and the rainbow — ½-inch plywood (remains of the ark plywood), ½-inch dowel approximately 6 feet long, watercolor paints, a sponge, a No. 3 small paintbrush, and felt-tip pens or acrylic paints.

Directions:

Noah's ark: Cut all the parts of the ark from the ½-inch plywood, following the ark sketch. Glue and nail the ark sides (B) and the ark ends (C) together. Glue the house shell to floor (D) and nail. Add roof (E) on one side only.

Build the base of the ark, using A, F, G, and H. Glue and nail these pieces in place. Paint the base red, and the waves blue. Antique all the pieces by rubbing a thin wash coat of watercolor over the paint. Be sure the paint is completely dry, first.

Paint the top of the ark, windows, door, and the inside. Give the ark a coat of fast-drying varnish. Attach the second side of the roof with the leather strip. Glue this piece tightly in place to secure the roof.

Noah, the animals, and the rainbow: Enlarge the pattern and cut two of each animal from ½-inch plywood, following the sketch. Peg the birds and the beasts together with two or three 1½-inch-long dowels to make them steady before you paint them.

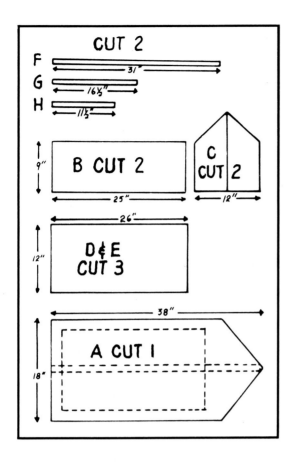

CUT 2

F |——— 31" ———|
G |—— 16½" ——|
H |— 11½" —|

9" B CUT 2
|——— 25" ———|

C
CUT 2
|— 12" —|

|——— 26" ———|
12" D & E
CUT 3

|———— 38" ————|
18" A CUT 1

Cut one each of Noah, the rainbow, and the bush at the foot of the rainbow from ½-inch-thick plywood.

Wipe a wash of watercolor over the wood, then add the detailing with a felt-tip pen or acrylic paints. Add large painted letters of the alphabet to each animal. Prop up Noah and the rainbow with out-of-sight small size blocks.

1. kangaroo 2. turtle 3. giraffe 4. camel 5. birds 6. alligator 7. Noah 8. bush 9. hair 10. elephant 11. chicken

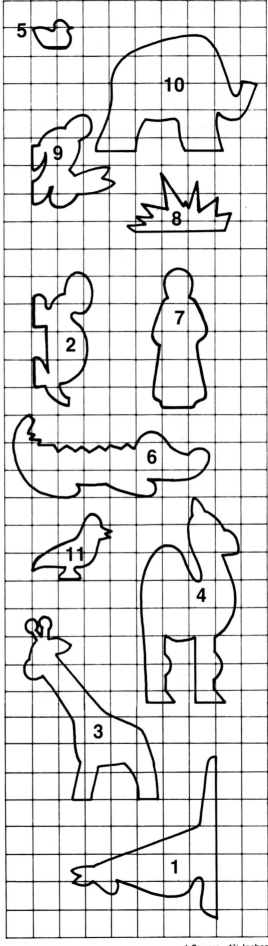

1 Square = 1¾ Inches

Whittled Wooden Toys

The art of whittling has seen more popular days, but wooden toys such as this tumbling clown and the pull horse are still popular. The tumbling clown has an old-world charm with its jester appearance. The pull horse is based on an original Mexican design, traditionally adorned with a variety of decorations.

Materials:

Tumbling clown — pine, balsa wood, dowels, medium-weight cardboard, poster paints, varnish, metal washers, and a knife.

Wheeled horse — soft pine or balsa wood, a sharp knife, a razor blade or whittler's knife, tempera paint, string, a bead, and a dowel.

Directions:

Tumbling clown: Make an 8-inch-long inclined ramp out of pine for the tumbling clown to teeter down. Cut the pine base and the balsa wood rails as shown in the sketch. Cut the dowels for the support rods. Drill holes in the base and the rails. Then, glue dowels in place. Glue a dowel under one end of ramp so it will slant slightly.

Cut the clown from medium-weight cardboard. Glue a ½-inch dowel through the hands. Paint the clown with poster paint and then finish with a coat of clear varnish. For balance, glue metal washers to the sides of the head and feet. Paint the washers to match the clown.

Wheeled horse: Make the platform for the horse from a 4x6-inch piece of scrap lumber that is rounded at the front. Make a small hole in the front of the platform and insert a string with a bead at the end for pulling.

Make two axles from a dowel. Round them at the ends to accept the wheels. Nail or glue the two axles in place.

Cut or carve the wheels from soft pine or balsa. Make the wheels about 1 inch in diameter and mount them on the axles. Hold them in place with smaller wheels.

Carve the horse from soft pine or balsa wood. Use a sharp knife for the basic cuts, then use a razor blade or a whittler's knife for the details and the finishing. Complete the model with a coat of tempera paint. For an old-fashioned look, use a flat finish rather than a high-gloss varnish or lacquer.

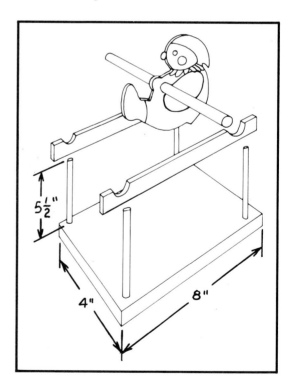

$5\frac{1}{2}$"

4"

8"

Wooden Pull Train

You're bound to be on the right track when you make this sturdy wooden pull train for the young child in your family. This toy circus train will follow your child obediently down the sidewalk, over the sandpile, and even through a mud puddle because it is designed for that kind of normal wear and tear. And since this train runs on "pull power," more cars can always be added for the next big trip.

Materials:

16 small rubber wheels (these can be from junked toys), one 28-inch-long 2x4, one small juice can, wire, black tape, cardboard mailing tube or a small dowel, one 48-inch-long ½x3-inch board, wood screws, hook and eye screws, long braided cord, paint, animal cutouts or decals, and clear varnish.

Directions:

For each one of the cars, cut a 7-inch rectangle from the length of 2x4. Use a small juice can or a similar small can for the boiler mounted on the engine. Hollow out the engine block so the can fits into the front of it. Wire the can in place and conceal the wires with bands of black tape.

Add a smokestack made from a cardboard mailing tube or insert a dowel through the boiler. Make the roof of the engine and the caboose and the base of each car out of an 8-inch piece of ½x3-inch board. This allows for a small edge or overhang. Paint the cars in patriotic red, white and blue (nontoxic paint).

Attach the rubber wheels to the base with wood screws and tighten them until they are secure but still turn easily. Join the cars with the hook and eye screws (attach a hook screw at the rear of the caboose). Attach a long braided cord for the pulling power.

Make the animals for this circus train by painting or drawing them on the side of the cars. Or, you can use cutouts from a child's book or magazines, or animal decals which you can buy in paint departments. Finish the project with a protective coating of clear varnish for longer wear.

Storybook Toys

Familiar storybooks featuring Pinocchio, Jack and the Beanstalk, the Three Little Pigs, and the Adventures of Arab are early childhood favorites. So, when you present these mini-size, carefree characters to your children, they are bound to loom large in the children's eyes.

In addition to their play value, these wooden creations are ideal for birthday party decorations and as aids when you are teaching your children these popular bedtime stories.

Materials:
Playful Pinocchio — wooden beads, balsa wood, wood filler, bright colored enamels, cardboard, and wire or heavy cord.

Jack and the Beanstalk — wooden figure used to hold birthday cake candles, wooden dowels, wood filler, balsa wood, paint, insulating wire, and green enamel paint or artificial greens.

Carrousel from The Adventures of Arab — fine wire spool made of wood, wooden dowel, balsa wood, paint (enamel), and horses from a toy farm set.

Three Little Pigs — wooden beads, matchsticks, buttons, glue, and pastel pink paint.

Directions:
Playful Pinocchio: To reproduce this beloved storybook character, start by threading children's wooden beads onto a length of fine wire until the little fellow stands 4 inches tall. Shorten some of the beads in order to get the proper proportions for the storybook figure.

Once you have sized the beads correctly, carve a hat, nose, and shoes out of balsa wood, then glue them in place onto the body. Fill the cracks between the shoes and the legs, the legs and the knees, the wrists and the hands, and the hat and the head with wood filler.

After you glue together the two cylindrical beads that form his shorts, use the filler to shape Pinocchio's shorts. Leave most of the joints of the figure mobile so he'll be an easy-to-manipulate, puppet-like lad.

When you have the figure constructed, paint him with bright enamels, make tiny books out of balsa wood for him to hold in his hand, and add a jaunty red feather to wear in his hat. Make the red feather out of cardboard. Use wire or heavy cord for the book carrying strap.

Jack and the Beanstalk: Start the project by using the tiny wooden birthday figure, and shape the wooden dowel legs and arms in the same way as the Pinocchio figure, then glue them to the basic figure. Fill in any open area at the joints with the wood filler.

Carve Jack's hat from balsa wood and glue it in position on his head. Attach the wooden hands, then paint the entire figure.

Make the beanstalk holding Jack by twisting insulating wire to resemble the vine. Squeeze the tips to get the vine-look, then paint the vine with green enamel. As an alternative for the insulating wire stalk, use a couple of stems of artificial greens.

Carrousel from The Adventures of Arab: Drill a small hole in the center of a fine wire spool made of wood. Insert a wood dowel in the hole and secure it with glue. Shape a canopy of balsa, and drill a hole in the center. Then, cut a dowel to the height you want and glue it in place.

Paint the carrousel with enamel in the desired designs. Use horses from a child's farm set or carve some from balsa wood. Paint the horses in your choice of colors. When the paint is dry, glue them in position for a merry ride.

Three Little Pigs: Use large wooden beads for the bodies of the pigs, smaller ones for the legs, matchsticks for the ears, and small buttons for the noses.

Glue all the parts of the pig together. After the glue is dry, coat the figures with pink nontoxic paint. Finally, add the facial features.

Primary Puzzles

Basic, large-sized puzzles are good beginning games for the three-to-six age group because they teach coordination. And since these uniquely designed playthings are constructed of a variety of durable materials, they will stand up well to many hours of play.

Materials:

Pony puzzle — 29 9-inch square indoor-outdoor carpet squares: 8 gold (A), 10 blue (B), and 11 red (C); chalk; mat knife; and sharp scissors.

Piglet puzzle — ¾-inch plywood, acrylic paints, burnt umber, fiberboard, and flat varnish.

Owl puzzle — ¾-inch plywood, ¼-inch plywood (for backing piece), ¾-inch picture molding (6 feet), acrylic paint, and polymer medium finish.

Cookie cutter puzzle — Five cookie cutters in a variety of shapes, artist knife, heavy cardboard, gesso, fluorescent paint, and clear enamel.

Directions:

Pony puzzle: Following the sketch of the pony pattern, draw the pieces on the backside of carpet squares with chalk. Cut top part of carpet with a mat knife; use sharp scissors for cutting rubber section (rubber backing shreds if it is cut with a knife). For a younger child, make a paper tracing of outline on a large sheet of brown wrapping paper to help him in putting the puzzle together. Once the puzzle is put together, number pieces on the backside, and key the numbers on the large-sized tracing you made from wrapping paper.

Piglet puzzle: Cut a 16½x11½-inch piece of plywood. Sand the board lightly and draw piglet shape onto board, following sketch. Cut out puzzle pieces with a saber saw, using a metal-cutting blade for a closer fit. Begin cutting at a junction of lines. Hold the blade almost flat to the surface to begin, then gradually turn it in to start. (The neck is a good place to start cutting). First, cut the large shapes such as the body. Then, cut smaller ones, as they are less apt to break. Sand the pieces until they are smooth and will easily release from puzzle form.

Using acrylics, paint the sections pink, blue, and red according to sketch. While paint is drying on the puzzle pieces, rub burnt umber on the frame with your finger.

Cut the fiberboard backing same size as top piece, and glue onto frame. Nail the fiberboard

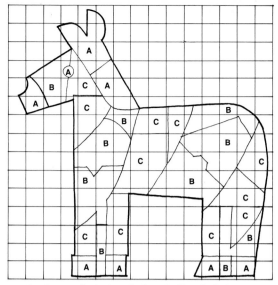

One Square = One Inch   A = Gold, B = Blue, C = Red

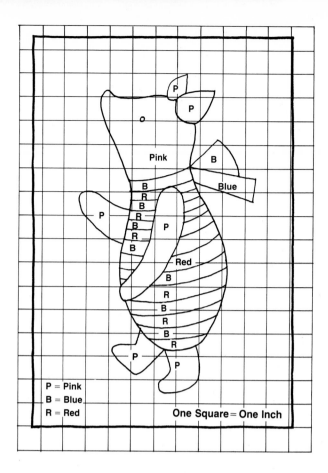

P = Pink
B = Blue
R = Red

One Square = One Inch

to frame at corners. Finally, arrange the puzzle pieces in place, then smoothly coat the entire puzzle with flat varnish.

Owl puzzle: Cut a 14x17½-inch backing placque from ¾-inch plywood. Following the sketch, draw motifs and cut out with a saber saw. Begin cutting at the top and work downward. Clamp the board when you get close to the bottom to hold it together.

Sand all of the pieces, then paint motifs with various colors of acrylics, following the sketch. Decoration of owls should vary: use individual motifs—dots, lines, etc.

Cut picture molding to frame and hold puzzle pieces in place. You will need two 15½-inch strips and two 17½-inch strips. Nail the pieces onto the plywood backing. Coat the puzzle pieces and the frame with polymer medium finish for longer wear.

Cookie cutter puzzle: Select five cookie cutters and trace each shape onto heavy cardboard. For ease in cutting, select simple shapes. Cut out designs with an artist's knife. Leave ¹/₁₆-inch margin around each one so that cookie cutters will release easily. Sand edges of cardboard and coat entire surface with gesso.

Cut a piece of cardboard same size as first piece and glue this backing to cutout piece. In recessed areas, paint figures that depict cutters used. (See snowman and chicken in photography). Use fluorescent paints and be sure to touch up recessed edges. Finish the puzzle with a coat of clear enamel.

1 Square = 1 Inch

Fortress of Fun

Your young knight will spend hours in "round-table" play sessions with this sturdy wooden castle. This little fortress also will serve as a storage place for his tiny men in shining armor.

Materials:

18-inch-square piece of plywood, red and black construction paper, round wooden beads, glue, 3/16-inch hardboard, scrap wood, blocks, primer, acrylics, artist's brush, popsicle sticks, balsa wood, and wood braces.

Directions:

Use plywood for: base (A). Cut out the following pieces from hardboard (see sketch): two side walls (B) 5x17 inches, two front walls (C) 5x18 inches, one back tower (F) 12x9 inches, one front tower (G) 6x8 inches, two sides (H) 2x8 inches, one roof (I) 5½x2 inches, 2 walkways (N) 1x14½ inches, 4 back and front pieces (P) 1x5 inches, 2 stair sides (R) 3¾x4⅝ inches, and one gate (T) 4½x4½ inches.

From the scrap lumber: 8 posts (D) 1x1x5 inches, 2 gate posts (E) 1x1x4 inches, 2 towers (J) 1x1x4 inches (pointed at one end), 2 towers (K) 1x1x4 inches, 4 braces (L) ½x½x7 inches, 1 brace (O) ½x½x14 inches, 4 braces (Q)

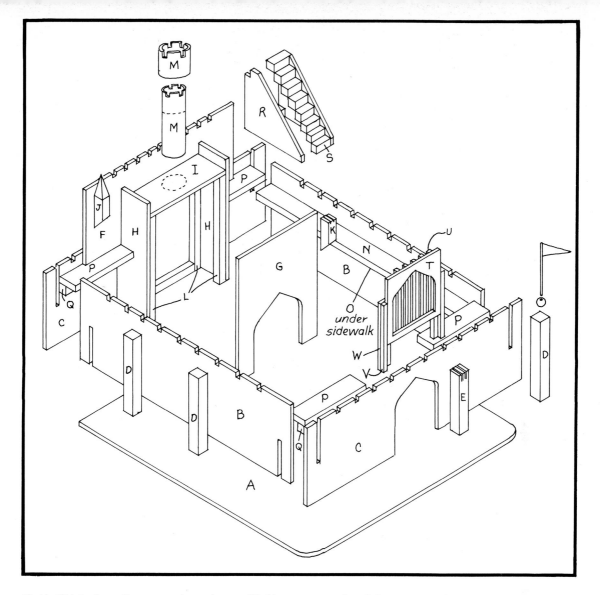

½x½x3½ inches, 8 steps and one brace (S) ½x ½x1¼ inches, 2 gate slots (V) ¼x¼x5 inches, and 2 gate slots (W) ¼x½x5 inches. Cut from balsa wood 5 bars (U). Then, use a wood dowel 2 inches in diameter and 4 inches long for round tower (M).

To assemble castle, mark braces and walkways on sidewalls. Nail and glue walkways in place. Be sure that all the sidepieces fit under the front and rear walkways. Following the sketch, build the gate. Glue gate slot to inside of front wall so gate will slide up and down.

Assemble walls, then glue them to base with rear and sidewalls 1 inch from outer base edges, as shown in photograph. Glue corner posts at outside of slot corners. Glue on front gate posts. On tower section, cut out wood towers. Then, glue and nail them in place. Glue and nail braces to tower sides, matching edges.

Glue and nail sides to tower back and tower front. Nail tower roof in place at brace tops. Glue round tower to roof (see sketch). Put assembled tower in place against back wall. Mark base at inside tower back. Remove tower and glue a piece of scrap wood along line, forming slot to hold tower in place.

Build staircase. Mark pattern for stairs on sides. Glue blocks to sides and glue in brace.

Use a coat of primer on all of the parts. Then, paint with fast-drying acrylics, following photograph for color suggestions. Permanently landscape the castle with motifs painted on the walls with an artist's brush. Add wooden beads to tower tops to hold paper flags. Use red and black construction paper for flags, and use popsicle sticks for flagstaffs.

Doll and Carriage Set

... ...shioned ... when ... one will ... matching ... ed here ...

... ng and ... g plus edging on pillowcases, small amount of yarn for tying comforter, and felt-tip pens for drawing facial features.

Directions:

Doll: Remove the beige hem and lace from the edge of one of the pillowcases; open all the fabric and press it flat. Following the drawing, cut the pattern pieces for the doll from the beige border fabric.

Pin the two arm pieces face to face and stitch along the edges, leaving the bottom edge open. Do this with both arms and legs. Turn the arms and legs right side out, and stuff them. Do the same with the head pieces.

Pin the body pieces together and seam along the edges, leaving them unsewn between the dots indicated on the pattern. Turn right side out.

Pin the legs in place at the bottom holes of the body, turning the raw edges under, and sew in place. Do the same with the arms at the holes on the sides of the body. Stuff the body.

Pin the head in place, making sure that the raw edges are turned under; sew in place. Using felt-tip pens, draw on the facial features.

For the dress, cut out the four bodice pieces and a 38x10-inch strip of the printed fabric for the skirt. Seam two bodice pieces together in the same manner. Press the seams flat. Now, pin the two bodice sections together, right sides together, and stitch along the outside edges. Turn the bodice right side out. Pin the raw edges under around the neck, clipping at the corners, and slip-stitch in place.

Using a basting thread, stitch along the length of the rectangular piece of fabric. Pull the thread so that the fabric gathers to fit around the waistline of the bodice. Pin in place and stitch. Pin the back skirt seam closed and sew it up. Edge the skirt with eyelet ruffling.

For the bonnet, use a compass or dinner plate to draw a 9-inch circle on printed fabric. Draw another line 2 inches outside the edge (13 inches in diameter) and cut around larger circle.

Using a basting thread, sew along the inner circle. Gather the stitches by pulling one end of the thread until it fits the doll's head. Stitch eyelet edging around edge of bonnet, and sew the bonnet in place on the doll's head.

Comforter: Cut two 20x22-inch pieces from the other pillowcase. With right sides together, seam around three sides, stitching eyelet edging in the seam. Turn right side out, insert a layer of quilt batting, and hand-stitch the open side closed. Make tufts of yarn at evenly spaced points about 5 inches apart to hold batting in place. Tie yarn in a double knot.

Pillow: Cut two 12x15-inch pieces of fabric. Proceed in the same manner as you did with the comforter, except stuff the pillow with polyester filling instead of the quilt batting.

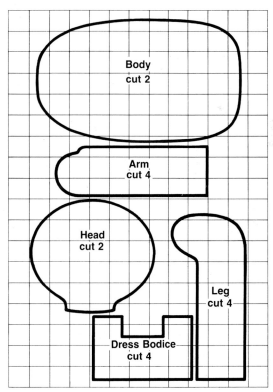

Body cut 2

Arm cut 4

Head cut 2

Leg cut 4

Dress Bodice cut 4

1 Square = 1 Inch

Surprise Travel Kits

Whether you travel by plane, train, car, or camper, the trip will be more relaxing for you and more fun for your children if they have something with which to occupy themselves. And that's precisely where these lunch buckets-turned-decorated travel kits come in so handy. They hold a multitude of surprises—from crayons to crackers! They also are indispensable when you visit someone who doesn't have a supply of children's toys.

Materials:
Tape-covered travel kit—workman's lunch bucket, (minus the thermos), ¾-inch-wide plastic-coated tape, ⅛-inch-wide white pinstripe tape, and a mat or X-acto knife.
Patchwork travel kit—workman's lunch bucket, scraps of fabric, clear-drying fabric glue, cotton balls, rickrack, cardboard, and felt scraps.

Directions:
Tape-covered travel kit: First decide on your four colors of tape. Then with the open lunch bucket facing you, start taping on the front bottom left side. Attach the tape down the side and cut it at the bottom with the mat knife. Proceed with alternate colors, cutting around the latches when necessary.

Next with the back facing you, do the same thing to the back bottom. Keeping the color sequence in order, now cover the top of the box, cutting around the hinges and the handle holder with the knife.

At both ends of the box, start in the center and work in rows toward the edges. Cut the tapes in the curve, using the knife. When the top and bottom of both ends are finished, cover the underside of the kit. Starting at one edge, cover all the uneven tape ends and work toward the other side. Alternate colors as you have been doing. The covered underside will prevent the furniture from being marred.

Finally, overlay with white pinstripe tape all the seams where tapes meet each other.

Patchwork travel kit: First, divide the front bottom of the lunch bucket into thirds. Cut a cardboard pattern piece according to the ⅓ measurements of the bucket.

Fit that piece of cardboard in the left bottom front corner, and cut away the section for the latch. Now, use that piece of cardboard, reversed, for the pattern piece for the right front bottom.

Cut another piece of cardboard the same size as the first one for the top front. Fit this piece over the upper latch on the left side, and cut an opening to fit. This piece, reversed, is also the right top front. Without the hole, it is the center top front, too.

Cut a third piece of cardboard to be used as a pattern for the top of the box. This piece is the same size as the previous two, but it must have an opening cut for the hinge that holds the handle on. Cut through the cardboard to make the opening. This reverses for the right top, and another one without the hole is for the center top. Use any pattern piece for the back top (No holes in this section).

Since the back bottom section is usually slightly smaller than the front bottom section, measure it into thirds again to make a pattern. Then, cut the pattern pieces for the ends.

Choose the fabrics and lay them out in front of you before you cut them to ensure that the same pieces of fabric are not going to be next to each other anywhere on the bucket.

Then, starting at the bottom left front, cut a piece of fabric. Place ½ of a cotton ball, slightly spread out, in the center of the back of the fabric. Apply glue around the edges of the fabric and attach it to the bucket. Glue each piece to the bucket as you cut them out to keep them in order. Proceed across the bottom. Next attach the left front top pieces. Then do the bottom back and the center back pieces, leaving the top until these are done. Then, do the top of the box.

Next, attach the fabric to the ends. (The end pieces will require slightly more cotton padding because they are larger.)

When all the pieces are applied and allowed to dry, cover the seams with rickrack. Use either plain or patterned rickrack, but be sure that the latter doesn't conflict with the patterns in the fabric. Cut the rickrack to fit over all the seams and around the edges. Glue the vertical pieces first and then the long horizontal pieces to cover the ends of the shorter pieces. Cover the underside of bucket with felt.

Organize Craft Supplies

● Store all your craft supplies in one particular area that is readily accessible.

● Collect shoe boxes or purchase the see-through plastic ones (uniform sizes will allow them to stack easier). If you use regular shoe boxes, cover them with adhesive-backed paper in colorful patterns.

● Sort out the items you use most, and arrange them by categories—bias tape, rickrack, lace, and trims in one container; buttons, beads, and sequins in another; felt scraps; small amounts of fabric; decorative press-on tapes; adhesives; and so on.

● Label the end of each container so that you can find just what you need easily.

Styles for action

*Sewing, knitting, and crocheting for the three- to six-year-old set
can be a real budget saver, as well as an opportunity to
provide clothing that is attractive, comfortable, and that fits well.
On the pages that follow, you'll find a variety of little
garments with that one-of-a-kind look that you will enjoy making
and that young children will love to wear.*

Granny-Square Pinafore

◀ Your little charmer will be all set to go and visit her Grandma or attend a birthday party as soon as she dons this colorful, crocheted pinafore. Fashioned from a bib and skirt composed of granny-squares and the two pieces joined together with an elasticized waistband, this garment is comfort and fashion at its best. Its vibrant colors will flatter any little girl.

Although the crocheted pinafore is shown here worn over a long-sleeved white pullover sweater, it will combine with a blouse or turtleneck top and matching tights equally as well (choose a color that matches one of the pinafore colors).

Materials:
A variety of colors of washable knitting worsted; a size F crochet hook (for toddler size 2), a size G crochet hook (for toddler size 4), or a size H crochet hook (for toddler size 5); elastic for waistband; and 2 buttons.

Gauge:
With an F crochet hook: 1st square = 1 inch, 2nd square = 2 inches, 3rd square = 2½ inches, 4th square = 3¼ inches; with a G hook: 1st square = 1¼ inches, 2nd square = 2¼ inches, 3rd square = 3 inches, 4th square = 3¾ inches; with an H hook: 1st square = 1½ inches, 2nd square = 2½ inches, 3rd square = 3½ inches, 4th square = 4¼ inches.

Measurements:
Directions are given for a toddler size 2. Changes for sizes 4 and 5 appear in parentheses. To make a size 4, use a G hook; for size 5, an H hook. There are four different sizes of squares in all—one in the bib and three in the skirt.

To enlarge the squares further, add extra rows by repeating third row of second and third strips of skirt.

Directions:
Bib: With F (G-H) hook, ch 4, join with a sl st to form a ring. Ch 3 to count as 1 dc, 2 dc in ring, ch 2, * 3 dc in ring, ch 2, repeat from * twice, join in top of ch 3. Fasten off.

Make 16 squares. On wrong side sew squares tog., 4 across and 4 down. On right side, work 1 row sc around 3 sides of bib.

Skirt, Second Square: Work as Row 1 of bib square. *Row 2:* Join another color in a ch 2 corner, ch 3 to count as 1 dc, 1 dc in same sp, * dc in next 3 dc, 2 dc, ch 2 and 2 dc in next corner sp, repeat from * around, ending 2 dc in first corner, ch 2, join in top of ch 3. Fasten off. Make 10 squares and join them in a circle.

Third Square: Ch 4, join with a sl st to form a ring. Ch 4 to count as 1 dc and ch 1, (1 dc and ch 1) 7 times in ring. Join in 3rd st of ch 4. Fasten off.

Row 2: Join another color in any ch 1 sp, ch 3, 2 dc in same sp, ch 1, * 3 dc in next sp, ch 1, repeat from * around. Join in top of ch 3. Fasten off.

Row 3: Join another color in any ch 1 sp, ch 3, 2 dc in same sp for start of a corner, ch 1, * 3 dc in next sp, ch 1, 3 dc, ch 2 and 3 dc in next sp for a corner, ch 1, repeat from * around, ending 3 dc in first corner, ch 2, join in top of ch 3. Fasten off. Make 10 squares and join in a circle.

Fourth Square: Work first 3 rows of 3rd square.

(continued on next page)

Fasten off. *Row 4:* Join another color in any corner, ch 1 (2-3), sc (hdc, dc) in same sp, work 1 sc (hdc, dc) in each st and ch 1 around, working 2 sts, ch 2 and 2 sts in each corner. Fasten off. Make 10 squares and join in a circle.

Sew circles together to form skirt, easing in larger squares to previous squares. Skirt measures approximately 8 (9½-11) inches long.

Waistband: Working over round elastic, work 1 row of sc around the waist edge. Knot the elastic to the desired waist size. Sew the lower edge of the bib to the waistband.

Straps: Use assorted colors for straps, working 3 or 4 rows of each color. When changing colors, draw new color through the last 2 lps of last dc. Ch 8, dc in 3rd ch from hook, dc in next 4 ch, ch 3, turn. Dc in each dc. Ch 3, turn. Repeat the last row until the strap reaches from the back waistband to the top of the bib. Sew the straps to each side of the center back, sew buttons to free ends. Use the ch 2 corners of bib for buttonholes.

Blocking Instructions

To give knit and crochet garments a truly finished appearance, block them, following the steps given below:

● With the wrong side up, pin the garment to the board with rustproof pins, stretching it to the desired measurements.

● Steam lightly with a moderately hot iron over a wet cloth, taking care not to let the weight of the iron rest in any one spot. Also, do not iron back and forth.

● Steam press the seams.

● Leave the garment pinned to the board until it is dry, then remove the pins. **Note:** Because 100% acrylic yarns will stretch permanently if they are steam-blocked, you must treat them differently. First, pin them to a padded surface according to the blocking measurements. Then, lay a damp cloth over the garment and allow it to dry.

Crocheted Dress

This tastefully simple crocheted dress is easy to make and will add a fashionable touch to a young lady's wardrobe. Instructions are given for size 4, with changes for 6 in parentheses.

Materials:
Knit-Cro-Sheen (J. & P. Coats, 250 yd. balls of white), 5 (6) or Knit-Cro-Sheen (175 yd. balls of colors), 8 (9). Size 3 steel crochet hook, and 4 ¼-inch-diameter buttons.

Blocking measurements and gauge:
Body chest size: 23 (24) inches; *crochet measurements:* 24½ (25½); width across back or front at underarm: 12¼ (12¾); width across back or front at lower edge: 16 (17); length from shoulder to lower edge: 18 (21); length of side seam: 13½ (16).
Gauge: 7 sts = 1 inch; 6 rows = 1¼ inches.

Directions:
Back: Starting at lower edge, ch 113 (119) to measure 17 (18) inches. Row 1 (right side): Dc in 4th ch from hook, dc in each of next 42 (45) ch, * ch 1, *thread over hook, draw up a loop in next*

ch, pull up this loop to measure ⅜ inch, (thread over hook, draw up ⅜ inch loop in same ch as last loop) 4 times. Thread over hook and draw through all 11 loops on hook, ch 1 tightly— puff st made. Skip next 2 ch, sc in next ch, ch 3, skip next 2 ch, sc in next ch, skip next 2 ch, make a puff st in next ch same as before, ch 1, dc in each of next 3 ch. Repeat from * once more; dc in each of remaining 41 (44) ch. Ch 1, turn.

Row 2: Sc in each of first 44 (47) dc, * ch 4, skip next puff st, sc in next ch-3 loop, ch 4, skip next puff st, sc in each of next 3 dc. Repeat from * once more; sc in each remaining dc, sc in top of turning chain. Ch 3, turn. Always count turning ch 3 as 1 dc.

Row 3: Skip first sc, dc in each of next 43 (46) sts, * ch 1, make puff st in same sc as last dc made, sc in next ch-4 loop, ch 3, sc in next ch-4 loop, puff st in next sc, ch 1, dc in same sc as last puff st, dc in each of next 2 sc. Repeat from * once more; dc in each remaining sc. Ch 1, turn. Last 2 rows (Rows 2-3) form pattern. *Rows 4 through 7:* Repeat Rows 2-3 alternately twice. Ch 1, turn.

Row 8 (Dec row): Sc in each of first 6 dc, *draw up a loop in each of next 2 dc, thread over and draw through all 3 loops on hook—dec made;* sc in each dc to within 5 dc before next puff st, dec over next 2 dc, sc in next 3 dc, * ch 4, skip next puff st, sc in next ch-3 loop, ch 4, skip next puff st, sc in each of next 3 dc. Repeat from * once more; dec over next 2 dc, sc in each dc to within last 7 dc and turning chain, dec over next 2 sts, sc in next 5 dc, sc in top of ch 3—4 decs made. Ch 3, turn.

Row 9: Skip first sc, dc in each sc to within next ch-4 loop, * ch 1, puff st in same sc as last dc made, sc in next ch-4 loop, ch 3, sc in next ch-4 loop, puff st in next sc, ch 1, dc in same sc as last puff st, dc in each of next 2 sc. Repeat from * once more; dc in each remaining sc. Ch 1, turn.

Row 10: Sc in each dc to within next puff st, * ch 4, skip next puff st, sc in next ch-3 loop, ch 4, skip next puff st, sc in each of next 3 dc. Repeat from * once more; sc in each remaining dc, sc in top of turning chain. Ch 3, turn. Repeat last 2 rows (Rows 9-10) 2 (3) more times; then repeat Row 9 once more. Ch 1, turn. Repeat last 8 (10) rows (from Row 8) 4 (5) more times;

then repeat Row 8 once more. Ch 3, turn. There are 32 (33) sc at each side of center panel. Repeat Rows 9-10 alternately until total length is 13½ (16) inches, end with Row 9. Turn.

Armhole Shaping: Row 1: Sl st in each of first 4, (4), sts, sc in next dc; keeping continuity of pattern, work across to within last 4, (5), sts; do not work over remaining sts. Turn. *Row 2:* Skip first sc, sl st in next sc, ch 3, dc in next sc; work in pattern across to within last 2 sc, skip next sc, dc in last sc—dec made at each end. Turn.

Row 3: Skip first dc, sc in next dc; work in pattern across to within last dc and ch 3, skip last dc, sc in top of ch 3. Turn. Repeat last 2 rows (Rows 2-3) 1 (1), more time. At end of last row, ch 3, turn. There are 24 (25), sc at each side of center panel.

Work even (no more decs) in pattern until length is 4½ (5), inches from first row of armhole shaping, end with a sc row. At end of last row, break off and fasten.

Front: Work same as back. Block to measurements. Sew side seams. Starting at armhole edge, sew ¾ (¾)-inch seams for shoulders.

Lower Edging: Rnd 1: With right side facing, attach thread to end of a side seam at lower edge; working along opposite side of starting chain, sc in each ch around. Join with sl st to first sc. *Rnd 2:* Ch 1, sc in same sc as joining, * ch 3, sl st in top of last sc made for picot, sc in each of next 2 sc. Repeat from * around, end with sc in last sc. Join to first sc. Break off and fasten.

Next Edging: Rnd 1: With right side of front facing, attach thread to end of left shoulder seam, sc evenly along front and back neck edges. Join with sl st to first sc. *Rnd 2:* Ch 1, sc in same sc as joining, sc in next sc, ch 3, skip next sc for button loop, sc in next 3 sc, ch 3, skip next sc, * sc in next 2 sc, ch 3, sl st in top of last sc made for picot.

Repeat from * across to within 9 sc from next shoulder seam, (sc in next 2 sc, ch 3, skip next sc, sc in next sc) twice; sc in next sc; along back of neck continue edging of sc in each of 2 sc and a picot to end of rnd. Join to first sc. Break off and fasten. Sew buttons on back neck edge to correspond with button loops.

Armhole Edging: Rnd 1: With right side facing, attach thread to top end of side seam, sc evenly along entire armhole edge, having an even number of sts. Join. *Rnd 2:* Work same as Rnd 2 of Lower Edging. Break off and fasten.

Colorful Cover-ups

This handsome selection of cover-ups will keep your children in solid comfort indoors or out. The television slippers are ideal for warming up their toes by the fireplace and the helmet, scarf, and mittens are perfect for outdoor play.

Materials:

Television slippers — (shoe sizes 2-4, 5-7, 8-10) Win-Knit (Bear Brand, Fleisher's, or Botany, 4 ounce packs) or Softex (Bucilla, 4 ounce balls), 1 (1−1); size 10 knitting needles; and size F crochet hook.

Helmet and mittens — (sizes 2, 3, 4) Winsom (Bear Brand, Fleisher's, or Botany, 2 ounce skeins), 2; Win-Tot (Bear Brand, Fleisher's, or Botany, 1 ounce skeins), 4; size 6 knitting needles.

Striped scarf: Winsom (Bear Brand, Fleisher's, or Botany, 2 ounce skeins), color A−1, color B−1; Win-Tot (Bear Brand, Fleisher's, or Botany, 1 ounce skeins), color A−2, color B−2; size 5 knitting needles.

Gauge:

Television slippers — with two strands of yarn, Garter stitch − 7 stitches = 2 inches, 7 rows = 1 inch.

Helmet and mittens − 6 stitches = 1 inch, 15 rows = 2 inches.

Striped scarf − 9 stitches = 1 inch, 9 rows = 1 inch.

Finished Measurements:

Television slippers — Length of foot, 4½ (5½- 6½) inches. Instructions are for size 2-4, changes for sizes 5-7 and 8-10 are in parentheses.

Helmet and mittens — Instructions are for size 1-2, changes for size 3-4 are in parentheses.

Scarf — Instructions are given for 35-inch-long scarf.

Directions:

Television Slippers: With 2 strands of yarn, cast on 23 (27-35) sts for back edge. *Row 1* — right side − K. *Row 2* − K 8 (9-12), p 1, k 5 (7-9), p 1, k 8 (9-12). Repeat these 2 rows for 1¾ (2- 2¼) ins., end on wrong side. Dec. 1 st each side of next row and repeat decs. every 2nd row 1 (2-3) times; 19 (21-27) sts. Work even until 3½ (4-4¾) ins. from beg. or 1 (1½-1¾) ins. less than desired finished length, end on wrong side.

Toe — *Ribbing* − *Row 1* − K 1, * p 1, k 1; repeat from * to end. *Row 2* − P 1, * k 1, p 1; repeat from * to end. Repeat these 2 rows 1 (2-3) times. *Dec. Row* − right side − K 1, k 2 tog. 3 (3-5) times, work 5 (7-5) sts in ribbing,

SKP 3 (3-5) times, k 1; 13 (15-17) sts. Break yarn, leaving 16 in. ends.

Finishing—Thread yarn into tapestry needle and draw through sts slipping them off needle. Draw up tightly. Run yarn through sts again. Fasten. Weave tog. edges of toe, even edges of foot and shaped edges, leaving top dec. row free. Weave cast-on sts of back edges tog., weaving the k rib at edge of sole; run needle through the 5 (7-9) sts between K ribs and draw up tightly for heel. Fasten off.

Cord—With 1 strand of yarn, ch 15 (16-17) ins., fasten off. Run cord around ankle, running under every ridge, through the 3rd (3rd-4th) st below top edge. Tie in bow at front.

Helmet: Cast on 89 (97) sts for lower edge. *Pattern*—*Row 1*—* K 2, p 2; repeat from * to within 1 st of end, k 1. Repeat this row for pat. until 24 (26) rows—about 3¼ (3½) ins. from beg. *Dec. Row for Neck*—right side—P 1, * SKP, p 2 tog.; repeat from * to end; 45 (49) sts. *Ribbing*—*Row 1*—wrong side—K 1, * p 1, k 1; repeat from * to end. *Row 2*—P 1, * k 1, p 1; repeat from * to end. Repeat last 2 rows until 7 (9) rows of ribbing.

Inc. Row—right side—K 1, * inc. 1 st in next st as to k, inc. 1 st in next st as to p; repeat from * to end; 89 (97) sts. Beg. on wrong side, work pat. until 9 (11) rows above inc. row, end on wrong side.

Opening for Face—Work 37 sts, bind off in pat. 15 (23) sts, work pat. to end. Keeping first 37 sts at back of needle, work even for 19 (23) rows—About 2½ (3) ins. on last 37 sts, end on wrong side. Break yarn.

From wrong side join yarn at edge of opening and work other half of helmet in pat. for 20 (24) rows, end on right side; cast on 15 (23) sts, continue pat. on remaining 37 sts; 89 (97) sts. Work even for 19 (23) rows more.

Dec. next row same as for neck dec.; 45 (49) sts. Work ribbing as for neck for 5 (9) rows. *Next Row*—right side—K 1, * SKP; repeat from * to end; 23 (25) sts. P 1 row. Break yarn, leaving a 12 in. end. Draw end through all sts twice; draw up tightly and fasten off.

Finishing—Sew back seam. Steam lightly.

Mittens: *Cuff*—Cast on 33 (41) sts. Work pat. same as for helmet for 10 (12) rows. Dec. 16 (20) sts as for neck dec. of helmet; 17 (21) sts. Work ribbing same as for helmet for 5 rows.

Inc. 16 (20) sts as for helmet; 33 (41) sts. Work pat. for 3 rows; cast on 2 sts for thumb at end of last row.

Hand and Thumb—K 1, p 1 for thumb, place a marker on needle, work pat. to end. *Row 2*—Work pat. to marker, sl marker, k 1, p 1. Carry marker. *Row 3*—Inc. 1 st in each of the 2 thumb sts as to k and p, sl marker, work pat. to end. Work pat. as before, keeping thumb sts in k 1, p 1 ribbing, inc. 1 st each side on thumb every 2nd row until there are 12 (14) sts for thumb, end on right side with last thumb inc. row. *Next Row*—wrong side—Work to marker, sl thumb sts to holder.

Work on sts for hand until 23 (27) rows above inc. row after ribbing, end on wrong side. Dec. as for top of helmet; 17 (21) sts. Work 3 rows of ribbing. *Last Dec. Row*—K 1, * SKP; repeat from * to end; 9 (11) sts. Fasten off as for top of helmet.

Thumb—From right side, sl thumb sts to needle. From wrong side, join yarn and with care to keep pat. work 5 (7) rows of ribbing. *Next Row—For Small Size Only*—* SKP, repeat from * to end. *For Large Size Only*—K 2 tog. 7 times; 6 (7) sts. *For Both Sizes*—Fasten off leaving a 12 in. end. Finish same as top of helmet. Make 2nd mitten in same way.

Finishing—Sew side seam. Steam lightly.

Striped Scarf: *Pattern*—Multiple of 4 plus 3 sts. *First Stripe*—With A, cast on 47 sts. *Row 1*—wrong side—K 1, p 2, * k 2, p 2; repeat from * to end. *Row 2*—P 1, k 2, * p 2, k 2; repeat from * to end. Repeat these 2 rows for 5 ins., end with row 2—about 44 rows. Break A.

2nd Stripe—With B, work same as first stripe. Repeat first and 2nd stripes alternately until there are 3 A and 3 B stripes. Repeat first stripe again. Bind off in pat.

Fringe—Wind B 139 times around a 1½ in. cardboard. Cut 1 end. Knot 3 strands in every 2nd st on each end of scarf—23 knots on each end. Trim ends evenly. Block, see page 84.

Rough-and-Ready Rough Rider

This matching pullover, cap, and mittens feature a cable knit design that is a classic knitting pattern. Appropriate for many occasions, this is a perfect outfit for both boys and girls. Because it can be laundered in the washing machine and still retain its original good looks, it will make a hit both with mothers and children.

Instructions are given for size 1−2, and changes for size 3−4 are in parentheses.

Materials:
Pullover, cap, and mittens—Win-Knit (Bear Brand, Fleisher's, or Botany, 4 ounce packs) or Softex (Bucilla, 4 ounce balls). Pullover 2 (2), cap 1 (1), mittens 1 (1). Size 6 and 4 knitting needles, and size F crochet hook.

Gauge:
Pullover and cap—size 6 needles—5 stitches = 1 inch, 7 rows = 1 inch; mittens—size 4 needles, —6 stitches = 1 inch, 8 rows = 1 inch.

Measurements for blocking:
Pullover—width at chest: 22 (24) inches; width of back at underarm: 11 (12) inches; width of sleeve at underarm: 8¼ (9¼) inches.

Directions:
Pullover: Pattern—Row 1—Cable Twist Row —right side—K 3, p 1, k 3; * p 1, sl next 3 sts to crochet hook and hold at back, k next 3 sts, k 3 sts from hook—cable twist—p 1; k 3, p 1, k 3; repeat from * twice.

Row 2—P 2, k 1, p 1, k 1, p 2; * k 1, p 6, k 1; p 2, k 1, p 1, k 1, p 2; repeat from * twice. Row 3—K 1, p 1, k 3, p 1, k 1; * p 1, k 6, p 1; k 1, p 1, k 3, p 1, k 1; repeat from * twice. Row 4—K 1, p 5, k 2; * p 6, k 2, p 5, k 2, repeat from * twice, end last repeat k 1.

Row 5—Same as row 3. Row 6—Same as row 2. Row 7—K 3, p 1, k 3, * p 1, k 6, p 1; k 3, p 1, k 3; repeat from * twice. Row 8—P 7, * k 1, p 6, k 1, p 7; repeat from * to end. Repeat these 8 rows for pat.

Back—With size 4 needles, cast on 59 (63) sts. Row 1—wrong side—K 1, * p 1, k 1; repeat from * to end. Row 2—P 1, * k 1, p 1; repeat from * to end. Repeat these 2 rows for ribbing for 1½ ins., end with row 1. Inc. Row—right side—Work 13 (15) sts, * inc. 1 st in next

st, work 13 sts; repeat from * twice, end last repeat work 17 (19) sts; 62 (66) sts. Next Row— With size 6 needles, p 5 (7), place marker on needle, p 7, * k 1, p 6, k 1, p 7; repeat from * twice, place marker on needle, p 5 (7). Sl markers every row. Begin pattern. Row 1—K 5 (7), sl marker, work as for pat. row 1 to 2nd marker, sl marker, k 5 (7). Row 2—P 5 (7), sl marker, work as for pat. row 2 to 2nd marker, p 5 (7).

Continue pat. on 52 sts between markers, working 5 (7) sts at each side in St. st until 6¼ (8) ins. above ribbing, end with pat. row 3 (7). Mark for underarm.

Armholes—Continuing pat. between markers, bind off 2 (3) sts at beg. of next 2 rows. Work 1 row even. Dec. Row—SKP, work to within 2 sts of end, k 2 tog. Work 1 row even. Repeat dec. row; 54 (56) sts. Work even until 4 (4½) ins. above marker, end with pat. row 7. Shoulders—Bind off 5 sts at beg. of next 4 rows. Bind off 7 (8) sts at beg. of next row. Next Row— Bind off 7 (8) sts, work 9 sts, k 2 tog., work 9; 19 sts.

Back Neck Ribbing—With size 4 needles, work ribbing as on lower edge for 3¾ ins. for Turtle Neck. Bind off very loosely in ribbing.

Note:—For regulation neck, work ribbing for ¾ in. Bind off loosely.

Front—Work same as back until 2½ (2¾) ins. above underarm marker, end with pat. row 4 (2) at left armhole edge.

Divide for Neck—Work 21 (22) sts, sl to holder for left side, work 12 sts, sl to holder for neck, work 21 (22) for right side. Right Side—Work 1 row even. Dec. Row—SKP, work to end. Repeat these 2 rows 3 times, keeping pat.; 17 (18) sts. Shape shoulder as for left side of back when armhole is same length.

Left Side—Beg. at armhole edge, sl 21 (22) sts to size 6 needle. Join yarn at neck edge and work 1 row even. Dec. Row—Work to within 2 sts of end, k 2 tog. Finish to correspond to right side. Do not break yarn.

Front Neck Ribbing—With size 4 needles, pick up and k 15 (17) sts on left side of neck; sl 12 sts from holder to free size 4 needle

(continued on next page)

and work 5 sts, k 2 tog., work 5 sts, pick up and k 15 (17) sts on right side; 41 (45) sts. *Row 1*—P 1, * k 1, p 1; repeat from * to end. Continue ribbing for same number of rows as back neck ribbing. Bind off.

Sleeves—With size 4 needles, cast on 32 (36) sts. Work k 1, p 1 ribbing for 2½ (3) ins. *Inc. Row*—right side—Work 14 (16) sts, inc. 1 st in next st, work to within 2 sts of end, inc. 1 st in next st, p 1; 34 (38) sts. *Next Row*—With size 6 needles, p 6 (8), place marker on needle, p 7, k 1, p 6, k 1, p 7, place marker on needle, p 6 (8). Sl markers every row. Beg. pat. *Row 1*—Cable Twist Row—K 6 (8), sl marker, k 3, p 1, k 3; p 1, work cable twist on next 6 sts, p 1, k 3, p 1, k 3; sl marker, k 6 (8).

Continue pat. in this way on the 22 sts between markers, until 7 rows above ribbing, and working 6 (8) sts at each side in St. st, end with pat. row 6. *Inc. Row*—right side—Inc. 1 st in first st, work as for pat. row 7 to within 2 sts of end, inc. 1 st in next st, k 1. Repeat inc. row every 8th row 4 times, continuing pat. between markers and working increased sts in St. st; 44 (48) sts. Work even until 6¾ (8½) ins. above ribbing, end with pat. row 5 (3).

Bind off 2 (3) sts at beg. of next 2 rows. Dec. 1 st each side *every 2nd row* 5 (6) times; *every row* 3 times. *Next Row*—SKP, work 9 sts, k 2 tog., work 9 sts, k 2 tog. Bind off remaining 21 sts.

Finishing—Sew ends of neck ribbing tog. Finish and block, see page 84.

Cap: With size 4 needles, cast on 14 sts for top. P 1 row. *First Inc. Row*—right side—Inc. 1 st in each st to within 1 st of end, k 1; 27 sts. *Ribbing*—Row 1—wrong side—P 1, * k 1, p 1; repeat from * to end. *Row 2*—K 1, * p 1, k 1; repeat from * to end. Repeat row 1.

2nd Inc. Row—right side—Repeat first inc. row; 53 sts. Repeat rows 1 and 2 twice, row 1 once again. *3rd Inc. Row*—Work 3 sts in ribbing, inc. 1 st in each st to within 4 sts of end, work 4 sts; 99 sts. *4th Inc. Row*—wrong side—P 4, * k 1, p 3, inc. 1 st in next st as to p, p 1, k 1, p 7; repeat from * 6 times, end last repeat p 4; 106 sts.

Pattern—Row 1—Cable Twist Row—right side—With size 6 needles, p 1, k 3; * p 1, sl next 3 sts to hook, hold at back, k next 3 sts, k

3 sts from hook—a cable twist, p 1, k 3, p 1, k 3; repeat from *, end last repeat k 3, p 1. *Row 2*—P 1, k 1, p 2; * k 1, p 6, k 1, p 2, k 1, p 1, k 1, p 2; repeat from * end last repeat p 2, k 1, p 1.

Row 3—K 2, p 1, k 1, * p 1, k 6, p 1, k 1, p 1, k 3, p 1, k 1; repeat from *, end last repeat k 1, p 1, k 2. *Row 4*—P 3, * k 2, p 6, k 2, p 5; repeat from *, end last repeat p 3. *Row 5*—Same as row 3. *Row 6*—Same as row 2. *Row 7*—P 1, k 3, * p 1, k 6, p 1, k 3, p 1, k 3; repeat from *, end last repeat k 3, p 1. *Row 8*—P 4, * k 1, p 6, k 1, p 7; repeat from *, end last repeat p 4. Repeat these 8 rows for pat. twice, repeat rows 1, 2, 3, and 4 again—about 5½ in. from beg.

Dec. Row—right side—With size 4 needles, k 2, k 2 tog., p 1, k 2, k 2 tog., k 2, p 1, * k 7, p 1, k 2, k 2 tog., k 2, p 1; repeat from * to within 4 sts of end, k 2 tog., k 2; 97 sts. Repeat rows 1 and 2 of ribbing 3 times, end on right side.

Dividing Row—Work 31 sts, sl to holder for left side; bind off 35 sts in ribbing, work to end; 31 sts for right side. *Right Side*—Row 1—Work to within 2 sts of end, k 2 tog. *Row 2*—P 2, work ribbing to end. *Row 3*—Same as row 1. *Row 4*—Work even in ribbing. Repeat rows 1 and 2 once; 28 sts. *Row 7*—Bind off 12 sts, work to within 2 sts of end, k 2 tog.; 15 sts. *Row 8*—Work even. *Row 9*—SKP, work to within 2 sts of end, k 2 tog.; 13 sts. Repeat rows 8 and 9 three times, keeping rib pat.; 7 sts. Mark for beg. of chin strap.

For Boy Only—Work even until 1 in. from marker. Bind off.

For Girl Only—Mark chin strap with button-hole as for left side.

For Both Boy and Girl—Left Side—Beg. at back edge, sl 31 sts to size 4 needle. Join yarn at front edge. *Row 1*—SKP, work to end. *Row 2*—Work ribbing to within 2 sts of end, p. 2. Work next 4 rows to correspond to right side; 28 sts. *Row 7*—SKP, work 14 sts, bind off remaining 12 sts; 15 sts. Join yarn in last st on needle. Repeat rows 8 and 9 of right side 4 times; 7 sts. Mark for beg. of chin strap.

For Boy Only—Work even until 3¼ ins. from marker, end on wrong side. *Buttonhole Row*—K 1, p 1, SKP, yo, k 1, p 1, k 1. Work 3 rows even. Bind off. *For Girl Only*—Make short chin strap on left side. *Finishing*—Thread yarn in tapestry needle and run through cast-on sts at top of cap, draw up tightly, run yarn through sts again. Fasten off. Sew back edges of cap tog. Work buttonhole in blacket st. Block, see page 84. Sew a button on short chin strap desired length from end.

Mittens: *Cable Pattern*—*Row 1*—*Cable Twist Row*—right side—P 1, k 3, p 1, sl next 3 sts to hook, hold at back, k next 3 sts, k 3 sts from hook, p 1, k 3, p 1. *Row 2*—P 1, k 1, p 2, k 1, p 6, k 1, p 2, k 1, p 1. *Row 3*—K 2, p 1, k 1, p 1, k 6, p 1, k 1, p 1, k 2. *Row 4*—P 3, k 2, p 6, k 2, p 3. *Row 5*—Same as row 3. *Row 6*—Same as row 2. *Row 7*—P 1, k 3, p 1, k 6, p 1, k 3, p 1. *Row 8*—P 4, k 1, p 6, k 1, p 4. Repeat these 8 rows for pat.

Left Mitten—Cuff—With size 4 needles, cast on 31 (33) sts. *Row 1*—wrong side—P 1, * k 1, p 1; repeat from * to end. *Row 2*—K 1, * p 1, k 1; repeat from * to end. Repeat these 2 rows for ribbing for 2 (2½) ins., end with row 2, increasing 1 st each side of last row for size 3-4 only; 31 (35) sts.

Hand Inc. Row—wrong side—P 15 (18), place marker on needle, p 4, k 1, p 3, inc. 1 st in next st as to p, p 1, k 1, p 4, place marker on needle, p 1 (2); 32 (36) sts. *Next Row*—K 1 (2), sl marker, work as for row 1 of cable pat. on next 16 sts, sl marker, k 15 (18).

Next Row—P 15 (18), sl marker, work as for row 2 of cable pat. on next 16 sts, sl marker, p 1 (2). Sl markers every row. Continue cable pat. on 16 sts between markers, and St. st on sts at each side until 1¼ (1½) ins. above cuff, end on right side. Break yarn.

Next Row—With a piece of contrasting yarn, p 6 (7) sts for thumb; sl these sts back to left needle. Join yarn, leaving a 9 in. end, and p these 6 (7) sts. Work to end of row. Work even, continuing pat., until 3½ (4) ins. above cuff, end on wrong side, dropping markers in last row.

First Hand Dec. Row—K 1, * sl 1, k 2 tog., pass sl st over the k 2 tog., work 10 (12) sts, k 3 tog. *, k 15 (17); 28 (32) sts. Work 1 row even, continuing pat. on 8 sts of cable rib only. *2nd Dec. Row*—* K 1, SKP, work 8 (10) sts, k 2 tog., k 1; repeat from * once;

24 (28) sts. Work 1 row even. *3rd Dec. Row*—* K 1, SKP, work 6 (8) sts, k 2 tog., k 1; repeat from * once; 20 (24) sts. *Next Row*—P 10 (12) sts, leave remaining 10 (12) sts on needle. Break yarn, leaving a 16 in. end. Weave sts tog.

Thumb—Remove contrasting yarn. Beg. at edge, pick up 6 (7) sts of lower part and 6 (7) sts of upper part; cast on 1 st with end of yarn attached to upper part; 13 (15) sts. Mark for beg. of thumb. Join yarn. *Row 1*—K 6 (7), k 2 tog., k 5 (6); 12 (14) sts. P 1 row, k 1 row until 1¼ (1½) ins. from beg. of thumb, end with p row.

First Thumb Dec. Row—K 1, * k 2 tog., k 1; repeat from * twice, end k 2 tog. (k 2 tog.; k 2); 8 (10) sts. P 1 row. *2nd Thumb Dec. Row*—K 2 tog. 4 (5) times; 4 (5) sts. Break yarn, leaving a 9 inch end. Draw yarn through all sts twice. Fasten off.

Finishing—Sew edges of thumb tog. Sew edges of hand and cuff tog. Steam, see page 84.

Right Mitten—Cuff—Work same as left mitten.

Hand Inc. Row—wrong side—P 1 (2), place marker on needle, p 4, k 1, p 3, inc. 1 st in next st as to p, p 1, k 1, p 4, place marker on needle, p 15 (18). *Next Row*—K 15 (18), sl marker, work as for pat. row 1 of cable pat. on next 16 sts, sl marker, k 1 (2). Work to correspond to left mitten until same length to beg. of thumb, end on right side.

Next Row—Work to within 6 (7) sts of end; with a piece of contrasting yarn, p remaining 6 (7) sts for thumb, sl these sts back to free needle and p them with regular yarn. Work to correspond to left mitten until same length to first dec. row; end on wrong side.

First Hand Dec. Row—K 15 (17), repeat between *'s of first dec. row of left mitten; k 1; 28 (32) sts. Finish hand to correspond to left mitten.

Thumb—Remove contrasting yarn. Beg. at edge, pick up 7 (8) sts of upper part, picking up the extra st at edge; pick up 6 (7) sts of lower part; 13 (15) sts. Mark for beg. of thumb. Join yarn. *Row 1*—K 5 (6), SKP, k 6 (7); 12 (14) sts. Finish to correspond to left mitten.

Girls' Knit Dresses

◀ Knitted jumpers and poor-boy dresses have, over the years, became recognized as classics in children's wear. And no wonder—their straightforward good looks and wearing comfort are appreciated anytime.

Why not outfit your girls with the jumper dress with its striped pullover and/or the striped poor-boy dress shown here? Either is just right for nursery school activities.

Instructions are given for size 1-2, and changes for size 3-4 are given in parentheses.

Materials:
Jumper dress and striped pullover—Winsom (Bear Brand, Fleisher's, or Botany, 2 ounce skeins). Jumper dress: Color A—3 (3). Pullover: Color A—2 (2), color B—1 (2). Win-Tot (Bear Brand, Fleisher's, or Botany, 1 ounce skeins). Jumper dress: Color A—5 (6). Pullover; Color A—3 (4), color B—2 (3). Size 7 needles, size 5 needles for neck and sleeve ribbing, size E crochet hook.
Striped poor-boy dress—Perlette (Bucilla, 2 ounce skeins). Color A—3 (4), color B—1 (1). Size 4 knitting needles, and size 2 knitting needles for neck ribbing.

Gauge:
Jumper dress and striped pullover—size 7 knitting needle—11 stitches = 2 inches—15 rows = 2 inches.
Striped poor-boy dress—size 4 needles—7 stitches = 1 inch—9 rows = 1 inch.

Measurements for blocking:
Jumper dress and striped pullover—jumper dress—width at chest: 24 (26½) inches; width of back at underarm: 12 (13½) inches; width at lower edge: 37½ (42) inches; *pullover*—width at chest: 22 (24) inches; width of back at underarm: 11 (12) inches; width of sleeves at underarm: 8¾ (9½) inches.
Striped poor-boy dress—width at chest: 22 (24) inches; width of back at underarm: 11 (12) inches; width of sleeve at underarm: 8¼ (9½) inches.

Directions:
Jumper Dress: Instructions are for dress 15½ (17½) ins. long from top of shoulder when buttoned, to lower edge. Adjustment in length may be made above ribbing at lower edge.

Shoulder straps are made first and dress is worked from top to lower edge.

Back—Right Shoulder Strap—Cast on 17 sts. *Row 1*—wrong side—P 1, * k 1, p 1; repeat from * to end. *Row 2*—K 1, * p 1, k 1; repeat from * to end. *Row 3*—Repeat row 1. *Row 4*—*Buttonhole Row*—K 1, p 1, SKP, yo, work 9 sts in ribbing, yo, k 2 tog., p 1, k 1.

Rows 5 and 6—Repeat rows 1 and 2. *Row 7*—wrong side—Work 6 sts in ribbing, p 5, work 6 sts in ribbing. *Row 8*—Work 6 sts in ribbing, k 5, work 6 sts in ribbing.

Repeat rows 7 and 8 until 25 rows from beg., end with a row worked on wrong side—about 3½ ins. Leave sts on needle. Break yarn.

Left Shoulder Strap—Cast on 17 sts on free needle and work same as right strap, end on wrong side. Both straps are now on same needle.

Joining Row—Work 17 sts, cast on 21 (23) sts for neck edge, casting onto same needle holding sts just worked, join and work across 17 sts of right strap; 55 (57) sts. *Next Row*—Work 6 sts in ribbing, p 5, work 33 (35) sts in ribbing, p 5, work 6 sts in ribbing. *Next Row*—Work 6, k 5, work 33 (35) sts, k 5, work 6. Repeat last 2 rows twice. *Next Row*—wrong side—Work 6, p to within 6 sts of end, work 6. *Next Row*—Work 6, k to within 6 sts of end, work 6.

Repeat last 2 rows 5 (7) times, end on right side. Cast on 6 (8) sts at end of row for underarm. Mark for underarm. *Next Row*—Work 12 (14) sts in ribbing, p to within 6 sts of end, work 6 sts; with free needle and separate strand of yarn, cast on 6 (8) sts and work these sts for underarm; 67 (73) sts. *Next Row*—Work 12 (14) sts in ribbing, k to within 12 (14) sts of end, work 12 (14) sts in ribbing.

Continue ribbing at each side for 4 rows more. P 1 row, k 1 row. *Next Row*—P 17 (18), place marker on needle, p 33 (37), place marker on needle, p 17 (18). *First Inc. Row*—K 1, inc. 1 st by knitting a st in the next st in row below, then k next st, * k to within 1 st of marker, inc. 1 st as before, sl marker, inc. 1 st as before; repeat from * once, k to within 2 sts of end, inc. 1 st as before, k 1; 73 (79) sts. Sl markers every row. Continuing St. st, repeat inc. row every 10th row 5 (6) times; 103 (115) sts.

(continued on next page)

Work even until 10 (11½) ins. from underarm marker or ¾ in. less than desired length, end with a k row. Work ribbing for 5 rows. Bind off in ribbing.

Front—Left Shoulder Strap—Cast on 17 sts. Work as for right back strap, omitting buttonholes and working *only 17 rows*—about 2½ ins. from beg. Complete to correspond to back.

Finishing—Sew side seams. Join yarn at right underarm edge at seam. From right side, work 1 sc in each of next 4 (6) cast on underarm sts, draw up a loop in next st and in first row on armhole edge, yo and through all 3 loops on hook—a decreasing sc, 1 sc in *every 2nd row to corner*, 3 sc at corner, 14 sc on cast-on edge of shoulder strap, 3 sc at corner, 1 sc in *every 2nd row on neck edge*, ending with a decreasing sc in last row and first cast-on st of back neck edge, 19 (21) sc on cast-on sts of neck edge.

Continue sc around shoulder straps, armhole and neck edge in this way. Join with sl st to first sc. Fasten off. Block, see page 84. Finish buttonholes in blanket st. Sew 2 buttons on each front shoulder strap.

Turtle Neck Pullover: *Note:* Back begins with neck ribbing and is knit from neck to lower edge. Neck ribbing for sleeve and front is knit all in one piece, then front and sleeves are worked separately. Raglan seams are sewn together.

Back—With size 5 needles and A, cast on 23 (25) sts loosely for turtle neck. *Row 1—wrong side when turtle neck collar is turned over—right side of back*—P 1, * k 1, p 1; repeat from * to end. *Row 2*—K 1, * p 1, k 1; repeat from * to end. Repeat these 2 rows for ribbing for 3½ ins., end with row 1 on right side of back.

Note: Carry color not in use loosely along edge of work. With size 7 needles beg. Raglan Yoke. *Stripe Pat.—Row 1*—With size 7 needles and B, p. *Row 2—Inc. Row*—With B, k 1, inc 1 st in next st, work to within 3 sts of end, inc. 1 st in next st, k 2; 25 (27) sts. *Row 3*—With

A, p. *Row 4*—With A, repeat row 2—inc. row; 27 (29) sts. Repeat these 4 rows for pat. 8 (9) times more, repeat rows 1 and 2 again; 61 (67) sts. *Next Row*—With A, p. Mark for end of yoke. *Next Row*—With A, k.

Continue stripes as on yoke, work even until 5¼ (6¼) ins. from marker—or 1 (1¼) ins. less than desired length, end on right side with 2nd row of B stripe. Break B. *Next Row*—With size 5 needles and A. p 2 tog., p to end; 60 (66) sts. Work k 1, p 1 ribbing for 1 (1¼) ins. Bind off in ribbing.

Front And Sleeve Neck Ribbing—With size 5 needles and A, cast on 43 (45) sts loosely. Work same as for back neck ribbing until there is 1 row less than on back, end with row 2.

Inc. And Dividing Row—right side of front—Work 9 sts, inc. 1 st in next st, sl these 11 sts to holder for right sleeve; work 22 (24) sts, inc. 1 st in next st, work 10 sts. Break yarn. Sl last 11 sts to holder for left sleeve leaving 23 (25) sts on needle for front. Join B in last st on needle. With size 7 needles work raglan yoke and finish front same as for back.

Right Sleeve—Beg. at right edge of ribbing, sl 11 sts to needle, join B at yoke edge, work raglan yoke same as for back; 49 (53) sts. Mark for end of yoke. *Dec. Row*—With A, SKP, k to within 2 sts of end, k 2 tog. Continuing stripes, repeat dec. row every 2nd row once; every 8th (10th) row 5 times; 35 (39) sts. Work even until 12½ (14¾) ins. from neck ribbing or until desired length to cuff, end with 2nd row of B stripe. Break B.

Next Row—With size 5 needles and A, p 2 tog., p to end; 34 (38) sts. Work k 1, p 1 ribbing for 2½ (3) ins. Bind off in ribbing.

Left Sleeve—Beg. at yoke edge, sl 11 sts to needle, join B in last st on needle, work same as for right sleeve.

Finishing—Sew seams matching stripes, joining sleeves to raglan yoke of front and back. Sew underarm and sleeve seams. Sew side edges of collar tog. with seams on wrong side when collar is turned over. Block, see page 84.

Striped poor-boy dress: Instructions are for dress 16 (18) ins. long from lower edge to center of back of neck ribbing. Make any necessary adjustment in length before beg. stripes. *Note:* mark 2nd row of each piece for right side.

Back—With A, cast on 86 (94) sts. *Pattern*— *Row 1*—wrong side—P 2, * k 2, p 2; repeat from * to end. *Row 2*—K 2, * p 2, k 2; repeat from * to end. Repeat these 2 rows for pat. until 6 (8) ins. from beg., or until 10 ins. less than desired length to center back of neck, end on wrong side with row 1. Drop A.

First Stripe—*Row 1*—right side—With B, k. With B, work pat. for 3 rows. *Note*—Carry color not in use loosely along edge.

2nd Stripe—*Row 1*—*Dec. Row*—right side— With A, k 2 tog., k to within 2 sts of end, SKP: 84 (92) sts. *Row 2*—With A, p 1, * k 2, p 2; repeat from *, end last repeat p 1. With care to keep pat., work 2 rows. Drop A. *3rd Stripe*— With B, and with care to keep pat., work same as first stripe. Drop B.

4th Stripe—With A, repeat dec. row. Work 3 rows even in pat.; 82 (90) sts. Drop A. Repeat 3rd and 4th stripes twice; 3rd stripe once again having 5 B and 4 A stripes; 78 (86) sts. Break B. With A, k 1 row, work 2 rows even in pat. Mark for underarm.

Armholes—With care to keep pat., bind off 3 sts at beg. of next 2 rows. Work 1 row even. *First Dec. Row*—right side—K 2 tog., work to within 2 sts of end, SKP. Work 1 row even. Repeat last 2 rows once. *3rd Dec. Row*—P 2 tog., work to within 2 sts of end, p 2 tog. Work 1 row even. Repeat last 2 rows once; 64 (72) sts. Work even until 4¼ (5) ins. above underarm marker, end on right side. *Shoulders*—Bind off in pat., 5 (7) sts at beg. of next 2 rows, 6 sts at beg. of next 4 rows; 30 (34) sts.

Back Neck Ribbing—Continue ribbing with size 2 needles for 1 in. only, end on wrong side. Bind off loosely in ribbing.

Front: Work same as for back until 3 (3½) ins. above underarm marker, end on right side. *Divide for Neck*—Work 21 (23) sts and sl to holder for right side, work 22 (26) sts and sl to holder for neck, work remaining 21 (23) sts. *Left Side*—Dec. 1 st at neck edge every row 3

times, every 2nd row once, *at same time,* when armhole is same length as at back, shape shoulder same as for right side of back. *Right Side*— Beg. at armhole edge, sl 21 (23) sts from holder to size 4 needle. Join yarn at neck edge, dec. 1 st and complete to correspond to left side, reversing shaping.

Front Neck Ribbing—From wrong side, sl 22 (26) sts of neck to size 2 needle. From right side, beg. at left shoulder, with free size 2 needle, pick up and k 14 sts evenly spaced along left neck edge, work 22 (26) sts in pat., pick up and k 14 sts along right neck edge; 50 (54) sts. *Row 1*—wrong side—K 2 (0), * p 2, k 2; repeat from *, end k 2 (0). Continue ribbing for same number of rows as on back. Bind off as for back.

Sleeves—With A, cast on 58 (66) sts. Work pat. same as for back until 2 (3) ins. from beg., end on right side with pat. row 2. Bind off 3 sts at beg. of next 2 rows. Dec. 1 st each side every 2nd row 4 (6) times in same manner as for armholes. Bind off 2 sts at beg. of next 10 rows. Bind off remaining 24 (28) sts in ribbing. Finish and block, see page 84.

Knit Abbreviations

k . . . . knit
p . . . . purl
st(s) . . . . stitch(es)
St. st . . . . stockinette stitch
sl . . . . slip
psso . . . . pass slipped stitch over
inc . . . . increase
dec . . . . decrease
tog . . . . together
pat . . . . pattern
yo . . . . yarnover
rnd(s) . . . . round(s)
* or **—Repeat whatever follows the * or ** as many times as specified.
( )—Do what is in parentheses the number of times indicated.

Hairpin Lace Hoods

There's neither a generation gap nor an age limit when it comes to wearing the refreshing matching hoods shown above. This particular crochet pattern adds a refreshing touch to almost any winter wardrobe. You'll need 80 loops for the child's hood and 100 loops for the adult size. The hairpin fork or staple, which is used for the hairpin lace crochet pattern, usually comes in several sizes — ½, 2, and 3 inches wide.

Hairpin lace (originally, the process called for crocheting with an ordinary straight hairpin) is very simple to make and works up quickly. After learning the basic steps, you can make numerous attractive variations.

You can achieve several effects with hairpin lace. For a soft, fluffy look, use wool yarn and a large fork. This combination is ideal for afghans, baby wear, carriage covers, and stoles, as well as these hoods. With fine cotton thread, you can make lace edgings and insertions of great delicacy. And with heavy cotton, linen, or jute threads, you can make coarse lace for your curtains, mats, pillows, or trimmings.

The word crochet is derived from the French word *croche* meaning hook. Originally, one of a number of lace-making tools, the hook came to be used alone to fashion a multitude of designs such as the one featured here.

Because crocheting is so fascinating and versatile, it has become a well-loved hand art. Hook and thread plus agile fingers can produce an endless variety of designs.

New threads and new stitches, or rather variations of old ones, enable you to make new creations for both the young and older generations.

These mother-daughter hoods vividly express this point. Their use of bold color and heavier thread give them a modern effect.

Materials:
Knitting worsted (Coats & Clark's Red Heart, 4-ounce skeins), 2; hairpin lace staples, 4-inch and 1½-inch sizes; and a size G crochet hook.

Gauge:
On a 4-inch staple: 10 loops = 3 inches; when joined, 5 groups of 2 loops each = 3 inches.

Directions:
Wide hairpin lace strip (make three): Using 4-inch staple, work as follows:
Step 1: Make a loop at end of yarn. Step 2: Insert hook in loop and wind yarn around right prong of staple. Step 3: Yarn over hook and draw through loop at center. Step 4: Raise hook to an upright position with hook end down; pass hook through staple and turn staple to the left. Step 5: Insert hook in front loop of left prong. Step 6: Yarn over hook and draw loop through (two loops on hook), yarn over and draw through two loops.

Repeat Steps 4 through 6 until they're on each side of strip: 80 loops for child's hood or 100 loops for adult's hood. Break off, leaving a 6 inch end; pass this end through loop and tighten.

Note: While working, if staple is filled, remove all but the last four loops from staple and continue as before. Mark the end of each strip for future reference.

Narrow hairpin lace strip (make two): Using 1½ inch staple work same as wide strip.

To join strips: Be sure to have marked end of each wide strip in line with start of each narrow strip. Insert hook through first two single loops of narrow strip, draw the first two double loops of wide strip through the two single loops on hook, * insert hook through next two single loops on narrow strip and draw through the two double loops on hook, draw next two double loops on wide strip through the two single loops on hook. Repeat from * until all loops are joined.

Using the 6-inch end, fasten last loop securely. When joining remaining strips, be sure that the marked ends of strips are in line with the start of the adjacent strip. Join two narrow strips between three wide strips as before.

Fold piece in half matching the end of strips. For back seam, starting at ends of strips, link two double loops to two double loops. Fasten last loop—this is top point. For front edge, slip first two double loops onto hook, * pull next two double loops through the two double loops on hook. Repeat from * across. Fasten last loop.

Pompon (make 15): Cut two cardboard circles, each 1½ inch in diameter. Cut a hole ½ inch in diameter in center of each circle. Cut ten 1-yard strands of yarn. Place circles together and wind the strands through center opening and over the edge until hole is filled. Cut yarn around outer edge between circles. Double a 12-inch length of yarn; slip it between circles and tie securely around strands. Remove cardboard and trim pompon evenly. Sew 13 pompons to lower edge.

Drawstring: With double yarn, make a 45-inch chain. Run chain through hood three inches from lower edge. Fasten pompon to each end.

Artist's Vinyl Apron

There's a little bit of the artist in each of us, but children especially love to grab a paint-brush, dip it (or their fingers) in a paint pot, and express themselves artistically.

But before they begin, outfit them with this vinyl apron. Then, just stand aside and watch your budding Picasso create his masterpiece without a worry about splashes and spills.

Materials:

⅔ yard 54-inch-wide piece of vinyl fabric (you can purchase this in the variety stores, where it is sold for use as table covers), 5 yards of double-fold bias tape, 2 yards rickrack, thread, and snap fasteners.

Directions:

Begin by cutting out the paint apron according to the drawing. Double the vinyl fabric and cut the sash. Then, sew the bias tape to the sides, bottom, and neck of the apron.

Double-fold bias tape is intentionally folded off-center for binding. Place the wider side under the fabric so that when you stitch from the right side you will catch both edges of tape.

With the wrong sides together, sew the bias tape to the sash as follows: Begin sewing bias 9½ inches from one end of the sash. Continue around the end, the full length of the other side, around the other end, and 9½ inches up the remaining side. (The 11 inches remaining will attach to the upper end of the paint apron.)

Open the double thickness of sash and insert the apron ⅝ inch. Sew the sash to the apron, then continue sewing the folded bias tape over this seam to complete the sash.

Then, beginning at the sash, place the rick-rack 2 inches from the edge of the apron. Curve the rickrack in slightly so that it will be centered 2½ inches from the edge at the shoulder. Follow straight down the front to four inches from the bottom, curving at the corners.

Add snap fasteners at both ends of the sash (use three sets, spaced at 2-inch intervals for adjustability as children grow). Use the snap fasteners that can be attached by placing a wooden sewing thread spool over the snap section and pounding with a hammer.

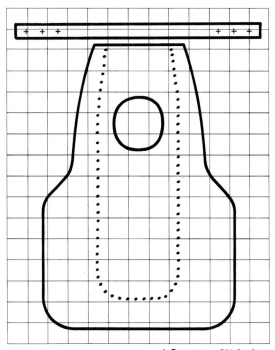

1 Square = 2½ Inches

Appliqued Cowboy Shirts

The West, with its colorful past, will come alive for your children when they wear these tailored blue shirts embellished with applique designs. Team them with blue jeans, and your children will be the hit of the playground.

And besides the fact that these shirts are fun to decorate, they are washable and permanent press.

Materials:

Blue chambray polyester and cotton permanent-press work shirt (one size larger than a child normally wears, as many children prefer to wear the shirt as a jacket); fabric with bold motifs, such as faces, birds, houses, animals, letters, flowers, and signs; dacron stuffing; bits of lace, trim, and ribbon; thread; and sharp scissors.

Directions:

First, plan the design or scene you want to use, and choose fabric with the appropriate motifs.

Choose one large design, such as the face that is featured on the shirt at the left in the photo, or create a scene of your own by arranging a few smaller motifs, such as the flower and butterflies on the shirt pictured at the right.

With a pair of sharp scissors, cut out the motifs ⅛ inch outside the edge of the designs. (This allows for a wider stitch without covering up any of the picture itself.) Lay out the scene on the shirt, being careful to center the design on the back of the shirt. Arrange and rearrange the pieces until you achieve a pleasing balance.

For a three-dimensional look, place a thin layer of stuffing under each design and baste the piece in place; use the same color thread you will use later on when you sew the picture in place. (Basting is very important and should not be eliminated, as the shirt and the applique designs tend to pucker if they are only pinned on before the final stitching.)

Set the sewing machine at the widest and finest zigzag stitch you have. It is important that the stitches be very close together to achieve a firm bond and to conceal the raw edges.

Stitch around each design carefully. If the machine skips over any area, continue on and go back over that area when you are finished. Now, remove the basting thread.

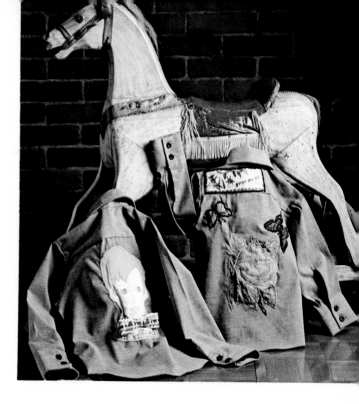

Quilt the designs either by hand or by machine. (This will help to hold the layer of stuffing in place so it will not get lumpy when the shirt is laundered.) To achieve a subtle effect, hand-quilt, with a single strand of the same color thread that you used to sew the design on the shirt. Or, you may prefer to use a contrasting color. Outline the large areas with a short running stitch (see the outline of the boy's hair in the applique on the shirt pictured at the left in the photo).

Do not quilt around the eyes, mouth, or nose, since this tends to depress the face, giving it a cadaverous appearance. Do quilt the shirt below the face, however.

To machine-quilt, narrow the zigzag stitch and go over the outlines. In the flower shirt, the rose applique is separated from the leaves with machine-quilting.

Give the appliqued shirts added dimension by adding special touches. Make a bow tie of woven cotton tape and sew it in place below the face. Add butterfly antennae on the other shirt by machine-stitching a narrow zigzag.

Materials:

Sleeveless jumper — Orange, gold, yellow, blue, and green medium-width rickrack; yellow baby rickrack; green jumbo rickrack; and black embroidery floss for the lion's features. (Make a sleeveless dress from your favorite pattern, or purchase a readymade garment.)

Jumpsuit — 2 yards of brush fringe in a bright color, and 2 yards of decorative braid in a complementary color. (Make a jumpsuit from your favorite pattern, or purchase one readymade.)

Directions:

Sleeveless jumper: First, measure and mark the front of the jumper for the placement of the lion's face, daisies, and rickrack border. For this design, you will need to make 9 orange baby mums, 2 full baby mums and 2 skimpy baby mums in gold, 2 blue daisies, 2 orange daisies, and 1 blue double daisy. Make all of these blossoms of medium-width rickrack, and all of the centers of yellow baby rickrack. Make 4 green leaves, 2 gold leaves, and 1 orange leaf from medium-width rickrack.

Make the baby mums by cutting two 12-inch lengths of rickrack (orange and gold) and interlocking the strips by hooking the "V's" together. Stitch in one point and then cut the next point along one edge. Next, draw the thread up snugly. Coil the piece into the shape of a flower and tack it through the center.

Make the daisies for the dress from a 12-inch length of jumbo rickrack for the outer petals and a 6-inch length of yellow baby rickrack for the flower centers.

To make the outer petals, stitch in and out of each point along the upper edge of the rickrack, building up points on the needle. Draw the thread up snugly, and seam the raw ends on the wrong side of the flower. Cut away the excess seam allowance. Stitch through each folded point around the inner circle on the wrong side. Space the petals evenly and end off. Then, turn to the right side.

To make the flower centers, you must have an even number of points along the upper edge, with the cut ends in a downward direction. Cut away excess, if necessary.

Tantalizing Trims

Add a third dimension to your child's favorite sleeveless jumper by attaching a lion surrounded by flowers to the front. This is just one example of how the decorative trims that are available today can work magic on your child's wardrobe. Used skillfully, colorful rickracks in different widths can bloom into garden flowers with just a needle and thread.

And fringe adds texture and color to any garment instantly; use it along with decorative braid and an ordinary play outfit becomes a fashionable jumpsuit.

Both of these trim ideas will adapt well to either handmade or readymade garments.

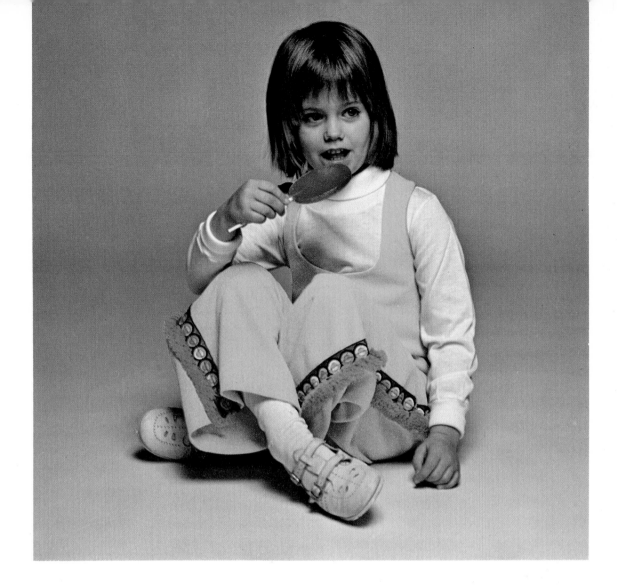

Stitch in one point and out the next point along the upper edge, building up all the points on the needle. Pull the thread through, leaving three inches of thread free at the knotted end. Tie the thread together from both ends so that it forms a tight circle.

Make the rickrack leaves by cutting one "W" (three points) length of jumbo or medium-width rickrack for each one.

Fold the "W" in half and clip away the free points. Seam together the lower "V" (four stitches). Open; then fold in the right end. Take one stitch. Fold in the left end. Take one stitch on each side of the leaf and knot the thread. Then, turn to the right side.

Apply the lion's face as follows: place the orange mums in a circle to outline the face. Use the large gold mums for the paws and the skimpy gold mums for the cheeks. Mark the mouth and eyes and embroider them in black. Use an orange leaf for the nose and gold leaves for the ears. Stitch the rickrack stems, add the flowers and leaves as shown in the photograph, and finally stitch on the green rickrack grass line.

Jumpsuit: If you are trimming a readymade jumpsuit, topstitch all of the trim, using the side seams as a stitching guide.

If you are making the entire outfit, machine-baste the heading of the fringe along the seam line. Then, stitch the seams, Finally, machine- or hand-stitch the decorative braid to the front side of the seam.

Paper Doll Dress

Little girls and paper dolls go together like sugar and spice. And this parade of hand-in-hand paper dolls is just as popular today as it was many years ago. If your little girl is eager to express her own individuality, let her cut out her own paper doll pattern.

You can use any basic dress pattern and add these applique designs, or you can simply add them to a readymade dress. If the dress has a full gathered skirt, applique a border of small dolls all around the hem. If you want to speed up the project, just make two larger dolls. If the dress has no waistline, arrange the dolls from the neckline to the hem.

This type of pattern can also be applied to pant cuffs, skirts, vests, aprons, or even some accessories. Although this dress uses gingham for both the dress and the paper doll shapes, you might prefer using prints, stripes, polka dots, or other combinations for your girl's dress.

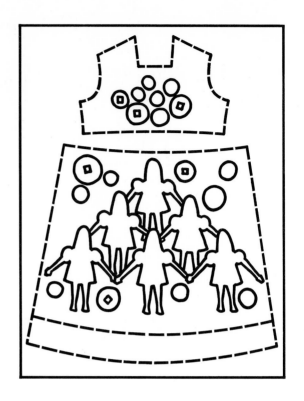

Materials:
Fabric scraps, a handmade or readymade dress, and matching thread.

Directions:
First, enlarge the doll pattern to the desired size. (The dolls shown here are 8 inches tall and are appliqued on a size 6 dress.) Next, pin the pattern to the fabric and trace around the edge of the pattern with a pencil. Cut out the doll shapes, leaving a ½-inch allowance all around for turning under.

Pin the doll shapes to the dress front as shown in the drawing at the right or follow one of the suggested arrangements at the lower right. (If you are using the trim on a handmade dress, it is best to applique the designs before sewing the garment together. Be sure to make allowance for the hem of the dress.)

Cut out circles of fabric. Position them at random or follow the placement on the pattern. (A broken line on the pattern indicates the variable seam line of the dress.) Using the whip stitch, sew the dolls and circles in place.

Rooms to grow in

Youngsters in the three-to-six age group are inquisitive by nature, so it is important that you decorate their room imaginatively. This chapter contains a collection of special touches such as decorated window shades and walls, sleeping bags, clothes holders, toy totes, and even a growth chart. These are the little extras that will enrich your child's world.

Under the Bunk Top

◀ It's a Barnum and Bailey world for the youngster who inhabits this brightly colored room. The bold red bunks are highlighted with sleeping bags created from twin-size sheets. The tried-and-true primary colors — red, yellow, and blue — prove to be center-ring winners in the decorating scheme.

The room incorporates a large circus poster featuring the "big" cats on the cheerful yellow wall, a smiling clown rug next to the bed on the bright red floor, and a wild, stuffed toy lion that blends with the poster's theme.

A canvas caddy is featured at the end of the bed. It serves as a partition as well as an ideal holder for pajamas, comb and brush, or any other bedroom accessories.

A vinyl floor covering was selected for easy upkeep, and the furniture pieces were chosen for their bright colors as well as for their sturdy construction. The blue and red wallpaper border, which complements the yellow wall and emphasizes the color scheme of the bed linens, completes the "Big Top" effect.

Materials:

For one youth bed-size sleeping bag: Two twin-size sheets (72x80 inches), two sheets of 68x70-inch polyester quilt batting, 90 inches of ¾-inch-wide Velcro closure tape for easy entry, 2½ yards of seam binding, and yarn for tying.

Directions:

Cut each sheet into a piece that measures 68x70 inches. To assemble the slumber bag, place the lining sheet face down on the floor, and place the two layers of polyester quilt batting over it. Next, cover this with the other sheet, right side up. Pin the four layers together, making sure that the layers are smooth and the edges are even. Baste all around the edge, 1 inch from the edge, and through the center lengthwise and crosswise. Machine-stitch 1 inch from the outer edge. Trim the quilt filling out of the seam allowance to ½ inch.

Place the slumber bag on the floor with the lining side up. Fold the seam allowances of the outer section toward the lining side on the stitching line. Starting from the center seam, at the bottom left-hand side, pin the hook side of the Velcro tape on the cut edges of the seam allowances with the tape ½ inch from the fold. Clip the tape at the corner and continue pinning it up the side of the bag, ending 10 inches from the top. Pin the loop side of the Velcro to the other side in the same manner.

Carefully baste the tapes in place. Then, machine-stitch along both edges of the Velcro. Above the closure tape and across the top of the bag, cover the seam edges with seam binding, mitering the corners. Stitch along both edges of the binding.

Place the opened slumber bag on the floor, smoothing out all the layers. With a long needle threaded with yarn in a harmonizing shade, take a small stitch through all four layers (the needle should go straight down and straight up) and tie a knot on top. Clip the yarn ends about ½ inch from the knot. Make ties over the entire sleeping bag about 6 to 8 inches apart.

Pajama Bags/Pillows

These comical characters have dual personalities. They'll house your child's pajamas and serve as "cushy" pillows, too. This captivating doll will be a delight in any little girl's room. Her extra-long legs make her almost "come alive" when she's seated on a shelf or wrapped around a bed post. The snail sets its own pace as a pajama holder-pillow combination. And, the beetle bug could find a bed in either a boy's or girl's decor.

Materials:
Gingham girl doll—1¼ yards 36-inch cotton print for legs, body, and skirt ruffle, ⅓ yard 36-inch cotton in solid color for face and arms, a small piece of black felt for eyes, a small piece of pink felt for cheeks and mouth, a 12x27x2-inch piece of foam rubber, ⅓ yard

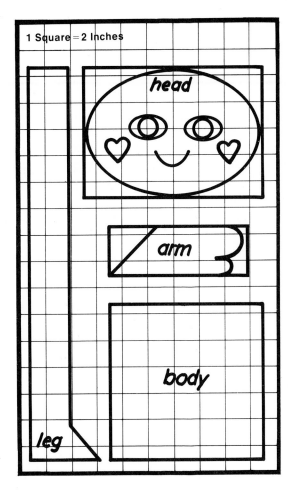

1 Square = 2 Inches

head

arm

body

leg

an opening, and turn right side out. Insert the foam rubber and hand-stitch the opening closed. Using the sketch, cut the fabric for the head, body, arms, and legs. (Use 1¼ yards gingham for the legs, body, and skirt ruffle; ⅓ yard solid-color cotton for the face and the arms.) Sew the arm seams on the wrong side. Turn the arms right side out and stuff with batting.

Stitch the leg seams on the wrong side. Turn the legs right side out and stuff the toes with batting. Insert 20 large plastic hair curlers in the legs (or stuff the legs with quilt batting or nylon hose, if desired).

Insert the zipper into the body back. Pin the arms and legs into the seam allowance. Stitch the body front and back together, leaving the neck open. Turn and insert the muslin-covered foam. Stitch the eyelet trim to the bottom of the ruffle by hand.

Sew the two headpieces together. Leave the neck open to allow for inserting the foam. Turn and insert the foam; hand-stitch the opening closed.

Next, add the features and the yarn hair (cut in 28-inch lengths). You'll need 22 strands of heavy yarn or 40 strands of lightweight yarn. Tie the yarn together at the top of the head with contrasting color. Spread the yarn over both sides of the face and tie. Hand-stitch to the top and the sides.

Stitch the face to the body at the neck by hand. Cover the seam by stitching washable trimming in place.

Snail: To make the snail, cut two 15-inch circles of fabric. Trim the top section with rickrack. With the right sides together, stitch around the circles. Leave a 9-inch opening for the head and for adding the zipper or snaps.

Cut the head from felt. Sew the pieces together, leaving an opening for stuffing. Stuff and stitch closed. Then, stitch the head to one side of the body opening. Machine-stitch the seam binding on the inside edge of the opening, and add a zipper or snaps. Attach the felt eyes and nose. Add the yarn top-knot.

Beetle Bug: To make the beetle bug, cut two 10x12-inch ovals from the striped fabric. Trim the top piece with contrasting striped fabric and braid, then sew the two body pieces together, leaving an opening on the left side of the back where the snap fasteners go. Add the stuffed legs, eyes, and mouth—all fashioned from felt.

muslin to cover foam, polyester batting for arms and toes, one skein of yarn for hair, scraps of yarn in contrasting colors, 20 large plastic hair curlers for legs, one 7-to-9-inch invisible zipper, 37 inches of trim for the skirt ruffle, 27 inches of trim for top of skirt, 15 inches of trim for neckline, and 18 inches of trim for eyes.

Snail— ½ yard flowered cotton fabric, rickrack, zipper or snaps, felt, and yarn for hair.

Beetle Bug—a 20x12-inch piece of striped cotton fabric, scraps of contrasting striped fabric, braid, snaps, felt, and polyester filling.

Directions:

Gingham girl doll: To make the gingham doll, cut the body and the head from the piece of foam rubber. Cover the foam pieces with muslin, cut according to the pattern pictured above. Seam the muslin on the wrong side. Leave

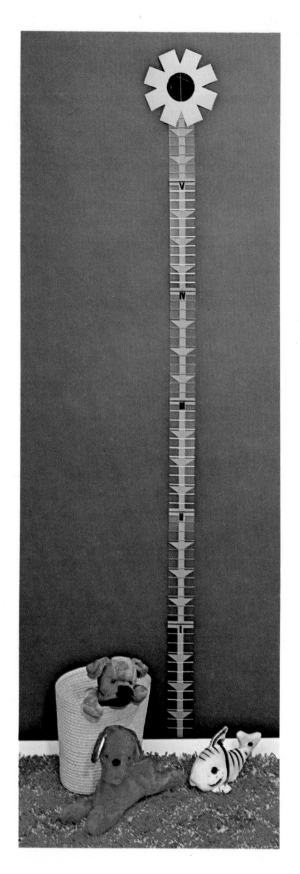

Sunflower Growth Chart

Add some sunshine power to your child's room with this unique sunflower growth chart. Easy to create with tape and clear plastic, the chart won't take up any floor space and it will make an eye-catching wall decoration.

Materials:

Plastic-coated ¾-inch-wide cloth tape in green and orange, plastic-coated 2-inch-wide cloth tape in yellow and black, double-faced tape, ¾-inch masking tape, one 21x20-inch sheet of acetate (.05 gauge), pencil and black felt-tip marker, brown wrapping paper, wax paper, ruler and yardstick, and a compass.

Directions:

Cut six strips of acetate, each 3 inches wide and 11¹⁵⁄₁₆ inches long. Place a ¾-inch-wide strip of green tape lengthwise through the center of each acetate piece to serve as the stem of the sunflower.

Next, place two acetate sections end to end, allowing ²⁄₁₆-inch space between. To hold the sections in position, tape them to the work surface temporarily with masking tape. Apply ¾-inch-wide green tape evenly across the edges of the two acetate sections; remove the pieces from the work surface and continue the tape around the back, overlapping slightly. Join all the acetate sections in the same manner. The spaced joining of acetate sections makes a "hinge" at each 12-inch interval, which allows you to fold the chart for storage.

Check each joining with the yardstick as you go so the center of the "hinge" falls in 12-inch divisions on the yardstick. Fold each hinge, face side out, and draw a line along the fold with a felt marker to indicate the foot marks on the chart.

With the ruler, pencil off 1-inch division lines across a 12-inch length of paper to use as a pattern. Tape the pattern to the work surface with masking tape. Work with one 12-inch acetate section at a time, placing it over the pattern and taping it to the work surface.

Cut very narrow strips of yellow and orange tape (about ⅛ inch wide), and, following the pattern marks shown under the acetate, apply the strips across the width at 1-inch division lines. Alternate the yellow and orange colors on each section of the stem.

For the leaves on each section, cut as follows: Place the wax paper over the section and onto it. Trace the outer edges of the acetate, two sides of the center green stem, and across the 1-inch orange or yellow strip. Remove and place the length of the ¾-inch-wide green tape on the marks now on the waxed paper, lining the tape up with the orange/yellow strip. Turn the waxed paper over (the marks will show on the underside).

Draw diagonal lines on the back of the waxed paper from the outer top-edge marks to bottom points at both sides of the stem marks. Trim the tape on these diagonal lines. Peel off the wax paper and apply tape to the acetate across the stem. Cut Roman numerals from the black tape, one through five, and apply them just below the appropriate 12-inch black hinge marks.

For the flower, cut four 8½-inch lengths of 2-inch-wide yellow tape. Crisscross them equal distances apart on the acetate sheet for the flower bloom. Cut out according to the flower shape formed with the tape.

For the center, place two 3½-inch lengths of 2-inch-wide black tape side by side on wax paper. Draw a 3-inch diameter circle over the two pieces, with the compass point placed in the center, and cut out. Remove the paper from the circles. Place each half-circle in the center of the flower, spacing them ⅛-inch apart so the yellow stripe shows in the center and is vertical with the stem.

Attach the flower to the top of the stem with the double-faced tape, positioning so the bottom of the petals comes at the 5½-foot mark on the chart. Also use the same tape to hang the chart.

When hanging the chart (on a door or baseboard top, etc.), measure off 12 inches from the floor and mark. Line up the bottom 12-inch division line with this temporary mark. Trim any excess from the bottom so the chart will read accurately wherever hung.

Sleep and Play Bed

There'll be plenty of room for play as well as rest for your youngster with this dual-purpose bed idea. Complete with bright pillows and fun stuffed toys, this design might encourage your three-year-old to be neat and make his own bed. Or else he can rough it up and use the area as a soft place to roll and tumble. Best of all, this bed doesn't occupy as much space as furniture, and it's a breeze to build!

Material:
2x4s and ¾-inch plywood for bed frame, one mattress (your choice of size), and carpeting.

Directions:
First, on a frame of 2x4s make the 12-inch-wide and 12-inch-high open rectangle of ¾-inch plywood. Make the rectangle slightly larger than the mattress you plan to use.

Build the wooden rectangular box directly onto the floor. Cover the box with carpeting that either matches or contrasts with the floor covering. As an option, cover the mattress with a sturdy upholstery fabric, then unroll a sleeping bag for your child to use at night.

Raggedy Ann Lives Here

If your little girl's world revolves around that lovable storybook character, Raggedy Ann, why don't you use fabric with this theme to decorate her room. Then, expand on the fabric design; enlarge the flower motifs, cut them out of felt, and let them "grow" on the painted wall.

Materials:

Cotton fabric patterned in a juvenile print, felt, paint, double-faced tape, and stapler or wall covering adhesive.

Directions:

First select an accent color from the fabric print and paint the wall (or walls). (Royal blue was used here.)

After the paint is dry, use double-faced tape to apply a garden of flowers fashioned from felt. Duplicate on a larger and bolder scale the flowers found in the fabric print.

You can, if you wish, make the round centers of the felt flowers so they'll hold a small round mirror. The stem of the flower also can serve as a growth chart (see page 108).

Paint your bed base in royal blue to match the felt flowered background, or in the accent color selection.

Next measure and cut the fabric in strips for the wall allowing for matching the patterns. Then follow these steps for applying the fabric strips to the walls.

First, spread the fabric on the floor and apply double-faced pressure-sensitive tape about ¼ inch from the edge on all four sides. Do not remove the backing. Next, hold the fabric to the wall at the ceiling height and use a plumb line to create a vertical line on the side of the fabric. Draw a line on wall with a pencil.

Then, starting at the top, remove about 12 inches of backing and press the fabric firmly in place, using the line as a guide. Continue to remove the backing, about 12 inches at a time, by pulling it toward you. Secure that part of the fabric and remove another 12 inches at a time, by pulling it toward you. Secure that part of the fabric and remove another 12 inches of backing. Repeat the process for the other side, pulling the fabric taut to eliminate air pockets.

Use the same print fabric for a window shade and cafe curtain. To make a laminated shade, purchase an iron-on or press-on shade kit that contains the shade backing and complete instructions. Select a firmly woven, light-to-medium-weight fabric. Follow the directions carefully.

Shades also can be made by bonding two fabrics together with an iron-on bonding web that fuses fabrics permanently and adds body.

With either the kit or the fusing web, work on a large, flat work area. Cut perfectly straight lines. The floor is the best work surface.

To make a shade using the bonding web, choose a fabric that is firmly woven and is light-to medium-weight. The finished shade should be the exact width of the shade roller. Measure the width of the shade roller. Cut the shade fabric 1 inch wider than the width of the roller and 20 inches longer than the length of the window. Cut the backing the same width, but only 5 inches longer than the window; cut the fusing web the same size as the backing, and piece together.

Next, press the shade and the backing to be sure both fabrics are wrinkle-free. For best results in fusing the shade and the backing fabrics, use a work surface equal to the total shade surface.

Protect the work surface with several layers of an old sheet or blanket. Place the window shade and the backing material on the work surface, with the wrong sides together and the fusing web between the two layers.

Follow the package directions for the proper heat setting and timing for the fusing web. First, partially fuse the two fabrics together, smoothing out any bubbles or wrinkles that form. Working from the center out, permanently fuse the two layers together. Do not remove the shade from the work surface; allow it to cool and dry completely before handling. Check the width of the shade, and mark the trimming lines along each side of the backing. The lines must be perfectly straight and parallel. Trim with sharp shears, and tack or staple the shade to roller.

For the cafe curtain, make a 2-inch hem at the top and the bottom and shirr the panel onto suspension-type rods.

Circus Wagon Window

◀ Jump on the decorating band wagon by adding this amiable lion to a window shade in your child's room. This treatment will give the window dimension as well as an atmosphere that will delight your youngster. If your outside view isn't overly stimulating, simply pull down the shade. Its refreshing colors create cheer, even without natural light filtering in.

Materials:

Cloth window shade (do not use a solid plastic shade), ¼ yard white fabric, ¾ yard yellow fabric, ¾ yard print fabric, ¼ yard print fabric for base, 8 yards ribbon, 1½ yards yellow adhesive-backed paper, 4x4-foot piece of ¼-inch plywood, scrap of 1x3, red semigloss paint, and window shade hardware.

Directions:

Cut the gingerbread trim for the window top and bottom out of ¼-inch plywood, following the drawing. Cut two plywood wheels 12 inches in diameter. Paint window trim and wheels red. Attach circus wagon cutouts to wall around window trim. Nail a strip of 1x3 to the wall below window trim and attach wheels to it.

Cut "gilt" trimming from yellow adhesive-backed paper, and apply it to plywood cutouts and wheels. Enlarge pattern pieces and trace around them on fabric. To keep raw edges of material from fraying, coat back of fabric with clear acrylic or clear nail polish to the edges of the motifs before cutting them out.

Attach the designs to the window shade with glue (the type that remains flexible) or fusible bonding material. If you choose to paint the designs on the window shade instead, trace around the patterns and paint them with textile paint, allowing each color to dry before starting another. (Start with the lightest color, then advance to darker hues.)

To enhance the circus atmosphere still further, add a decorative shade pull. Use a brass ring, which has a distinctive circus flavor, or you can choose a plastic or tasseled version.

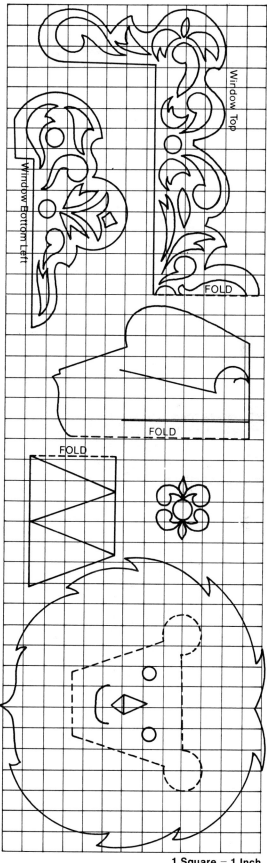

1 Square = 1 Inch

Toy Chest In Disguise

With this unique toy chest, there will be no more horsing around when it comes to picking up toys. Your children actually will enjoy leading this filly (she's mounted on casters) from room to room in search of toys. And when they find one, they can pull the horse's tail and the "lid" will drop down to accommodate playthings.

Ideally, toy boxes should serve a dual purpose in your child's room whenever possible. They should be practical for holding toys. However, since toy boxes are going to take up a certain amount of space in the room, rather than being hidden in a closet or under a bed, it is a good bonus when they can also serve to decorate the room.

In this case, the horse is a triple crown winner since the children can also use her as a toy which is sturdy enough to ride upon.

Materials:
One ¼-inch dowel, 4x4-foot piece of 1-inch plywood, one pair of hinges, one cupboard latch, four easy-rolling casters, felt for the saddle and the cinch, black adhesive-backed paper for the eyes and nostrils, primer, paint, yarn for the reins and bridle, and sisal rope. (The amount of the rope and the yarn you'll need depends on the weight and the length desired.)

Directions:
To start, build the sides, top, bottom, and one end from the piece of plywood. (See the drawing at the near right for the dimensions.)

Cut out the head, and drill ¾-inch holes for the mane and for the tail in the box door. Drill holes for the dowels in the head; mark and drill on the box top and the end.

Dowel the head to the box (A) (see the drawing), put the dowels in the head, then in the box; glue to secure the dowels in place.

Next push the dowels through the box into the head (B) according to the location shown in the drawing of the horse.

After the glue is completely dry, coat the horse with a primer. When the primer coat is dry, hinge the door to the back of the horse. Add cupboard door latches at both top corners and paint a finish coat. When dry, add casters to the bottom of the box.

Cut sisal rope into 14-inch pieces for the mane; unravel and thread through holes, knotting at the top. Comb with a big-toothed comb and trim evenly. Cut a 16-inch piece for the tail; thread through the hole and knot inside the door. Comb and trim the mane.

Cut out eyes and nostrils from black adhesive-backed paper. Add reins and bridle that you make from braided lengths of heavy yarn.

Cut out the blanket and cinch from green felt (see sketch). Glue the two pieces together; slip over the body for the saddle.

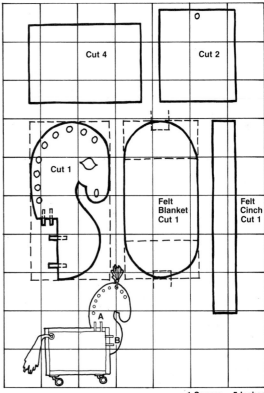

1 Square = 5 Inches

Peek-a-Boo Storage

◀ For a different kind of open storage, here is a well-rounded solution to an old problem— where to put the toys. This unit not only is designed to accommodate all shapes and sizes of toys, but it also adds visual punch to a room because of its ingenious design and happy colors.

If you wish to take advantage of funny-gapped waste space—underneath a dormer window or a stairway—you'll find this cubicle-type of storage unit is easy to build. And, you'll find that it's easier to keep toys stored neatly in these tightly defined spaces than it is when you arrange them on large open shelves.

This storage unit offers other possibilities, too. One circular opening, with its divisions, can provide your child with a four-room doll house in which to display a collection of miniature furnishings. When children get older, they can display school mementos and sports trophies here.

Materials:
¾-inch plywood for the shelves and dividers, ¼-inch plywood for the end and cutout front, and paints in bright primary colors.

Directions:
Measure the width and height of the area under the dormer or stairway. Then, divide the width in half to get the depth of the storage cubicles. Plan the radius of the cutouts an inch smaller than the squares. Install shelves in bookcase form with long vertical boards and short horizontal dividers. Make the shelves of ¾-inch plywood faced with ¼-inch plywood. For the graphic effect, cut a sheet of ¼-inch plywood to fit the space. Cut circles and half-circles into the plywood with a saber saw.

Paint the inside partitions bright shades to contrast with the outside coloring. The shelves featured here were painted pink, orange, and yellow for that extra punch. Paint the exterior of the storage unit the same color as the adjacent walls in the room.

Newel-Post Coat-Tree

If you are going from pillar to post about how to get your children to hang up their clothes, try this child-size, newel-post coat-tree. Since it is freestanding, it can be placed in any area.

Materials:
One newel-post (an old one retrieved from a stairway that is being torn down or a new one from a lumber company), four colorful enamel clothes hooks, a round wooden base turned on a lathe or any heavy, flat-surfaced base, and shiny enamel in bold colors.

Directions:
If you use an old newel-post, strip it down to the natural wood. Sand the post to a smooth finish to avoid any splinters and to ensure a professional-looking glossy finish. Paint the post in an assortment of brightly colored enamels.

Next, screw four vivid-colored, enamel clothes hooks into the four sides of the post, as shown in the photograph.

Finally, glue the post to the base. It is important that the base be sturdy and weighted. Paint the base to match one of the colors.

Laughing Song

*When the green woods laugh with the
 voice of joy,
And the dimpling stream runs laughing by;
When the air does laugh with our merry wit,
And the green hill laughs with the noise of it.*

William Blake

Things for Children
7 through 12 years

These are the years when time literally flies. Almost before you realize it, small children are approaching the teen-age years. Besides the physical changes that occur—growing in spurts and gaining permanent teeth to replace the baby ones—new interests and attitudes also develop. Their circle of friends is automatically expanded because they spend many of their waking hours in school. And, having learned to read, they are able to explore vast new territories through the pages of books alone.

Although family activities, such as camping, skiing, boating, and games at home, may occupy much of their leisure time, children in this age group also enjoy organized club and group activities.

Athletic and artistic skills begin to emerge, too. Some, such as bike riding, jumping rope, playing tag, and play-acting, will develop naturally. Others, such as music, dancing, swimming, tennis, and arts and crafts, will be stimulated by formal training.

And all of a sudden, children long for their own retreat, and a sleep/playroom that is decorated with their hobbies, interests, and color preferences in mind becomes the haven where they enjoy studying, listening to music, and entertaining their friends.

Games and hobbies

This chapter presents new and creative approaches to a wealth of family games and playthings that have been favorites for many generations. All of the projects are relatively easy to accomplish, and they are guaranteed to keep your children happily engaged hour after hour. Some of the items are ones to which the entire family can lend its time and talents.

Character Dolls

◀ The old-timey corn husk and apple dolls shown here and on page 122 get back to the basics — a reminder that all toys at one time were hand-crafted rather than mass-produced as most of them are today. They don't rely on gimmickry for their popularity, either. Rather, they're enjoyed for what they are — simple, natural creatures. And talk about character — they have a hundred times more than their plastic counterparts. Your children won't believe their eyes when they discover that the apple doll, as the apple ages, actually changes in appearance.

The nostalgic value of these dolls makes them ideal candidates for a doll collection. And, they also can double as a table centerpiece.

Materials:
Corn husk dolls — husks from mature corn, fabric dye recommended for home use, various sizes of plastic foam balls, and chenille stems.
Applehead doll — apples, vegetable peeler, sharp paring knife, lemon juice, 12- or 14-gauge copper wire, masking tape, white glue, polyester batting, fabric and yarn scraps, and discarded nylons or panty hose.

Directions:
Corn husk dolls: To prepare the husks, soak them clean in mild detergent and rinse well. Dye the moldy or discolored husks for later use in making accessories. After dyeing, rinse the husks in cool water to remove the extra coloring.

Soak the husks in warm water to keep them pliable as you work. Spread an old bath towel on your work surface to absorb the extra mois-

ture. Select a large foam ball for the body and a smaller ball for the head. Cut them down a little for the different size dolls.

Form the arms and shoulders by rolling a chenille stem lengthwise in a corn husk. Turn the husk ends under and tie off with thread.

Position the arms between the head and the body plastic foam balls. Choose a husk long enough to extend from the front waist, over the head, to the back waist of the doll. Be sure the cleanest side is out, since it will form the face. Lay the middle of the husk over the head, twisting it several times at the back of the head to make the husk curve out around the face. (Twists will be concealed by hair or hat.)

Use thread to secure this outer husk covering, cinching it tightly at the neck and again around the waist of the body ball.

Use several husks to make the skirt. Place these with the pointed ends up at the waist, and turn the bottom ends under. Continue adding the overlapping husk layers until the skirt is full and firm. Anchor husks at the waist with thread; trim to ½ inch above the waist. Cut the skirt to the desired length. Stuff the skirt with tissue paper to retain the shape; allow to dry overnight before removing the paper.

To make the shawl, split a husk lengthwise down the center. Drape the pieces over the shoulder, crisscross from front and back, and tie off at the waist. Use dyed husks for making the accessories. Dry the doll overnight away from direct heat. When dry, draw in facial features.

(continued on next page)

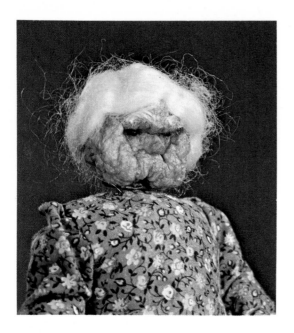

Applehead doll: Peel several apples, keeping the surface as smooth as possible. Remove the stem and the blossom ends (the top indentation will be covered by hair).

Use a paring knife to carve out the features. Make slits for the eyelids, round out the cheeks, and make the nose prominent since it will shrink.

Soak the heads in lemon juice for a few minutes to prevent the apples from darkening. For each doll, double a 24-inch piece of wire; push the ends down through the stem of the apple. To form the torso, tape together the wires extending below the head. Pull the wires apart as needed to form the legs. Fasten a 10-inch piece of wire across the vertical wire at the shoulder height for arms. Tie a string through the wire loop on the top of the head; hang the apple up to dry for four or five weeks.

When the head has reached the maximum shrinkage, lift the eyelids; insert the small beads or buttons for the eyes. Glue yarn scraps, cotton, or cotton floss in place for the hair.

Wrap the wire torso, arms, and legs with polyester batting until you have desired body shape. Secure the batting with small pieces of tape. Stitch together the nylon or panty hose scraps to form a body stocking casing. Fit the casing to the body and stitch securely. Make clothes from the fabric to fit the doll.

Chinese Checkers

This child-size version gives a fresh new look to the age-old game of Chinese checkers. The "marbles" are different, too; actually, they're table tennis balls. The board for this Chinese checker game also has a dual personality. It forms the top of a rug-hugging occasional table that encourages contestants to sit on the floor while a game is in progress, and it can be used as a bench between games.

Materials:
24-inch square of ¼-inch plywood for the table-top, 1x2s for frame, four 10-inch-long 2x2s for the legs, table tennis balls (at least a dozen), felt-tip markers, and flat latex paint.

Directions:
To build the table, frame the plywood with the 1x2s, then attach a leg inside each corner. Make the legs of 10-inch lengths of 2x2s.

Drill ½-inch holes in the tabletop to accommodate the table tennis balls. You'll have fewer holes in the star than you would for a regular Chinese checker game board with marbles. However, if you wish a full-size board, increase the overall dimensions accordingly.

Sand all the surfaces and cover with flat latex paint. Paint the balls in contrasting colors. Draw the six-point star pattern in pencil, then create the final star with felt-tip markers and paint.

Fabric Checkerboard

When they aren't jumping rope or playing a game of jacks, perhaps the members of your skinned-knee set will be ready to settle down to a quiet game of checkers, using color-coordinated flat bone buttons on a patchwork checkerboard. An extra bonus feature of this board is that the texture of the fabric keeps checkers from slipping so the game can take place even on the bed.

Materials:
18-inch square of ¼-inch hardboard or plywood, 1⅙ yard 36-inch-wide yellow and white polka-dot fabric, ⅛ yard 36-inch-wide blue and yellow flowered calico, 9 yards of medium rickrack, 1-inch buttons (12 blue and 12 orange), fabric glue, and protective coating.

Directions:
Center a 22-inch square of cotton print on the front of the 18-inch-square of ¼-inch hardboard or plywood board, then glue in place. Fold the excess over the back, miter the corners, and glue to the back of the board. Cut an 18-inch square of the same print, and turn the edges under ½ inch. Center on the back of the board and glue in place. Cut 32 2-inch squares of calico print. With a straightedge and a pencil draw a 16-inch square (centered) on the front of the board. Draw in 2-inch squares. Glue the calico squares to the board, forming the checkerboard pattern.

Cut 18 16-inch strips of rickrack. Glue the strips to the checkerboard along the edges of the calico squares, positioning the outside strips last for easier placement.

Allow the material to dry. Then, if desired, give the patchwork checkerboard a coat of protective coating for soil resistance.

123

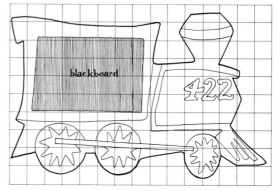

1 Square = 2 Inches

Train chalkboard: To make this chalkboard, cut the shape from insulation board, following the sketch above. Sand all of the edges, then undercoat the entire piece with liquid gesso. When the gesso is dry, trace the area for the chalkboard with a pencil; gouge out this area about $\frac{1}{16}$ inch deep. Paint the recessed area with chalkboard paint. (You can purchase chalkboard paint in black or green.) Gouge out to $\frac{1}{2}$-inch depth an area $1\frac{1}{2}$ inches high by 16 inches long along the base, following the pattern for the chalk holder. Paint the train with acrylics, following the colors in the photo.

Next, use a piece of molding strip that measures $\frac{1}{2}$x$1\frac{1}{2}$x16 inches for the chalk holder.

Crafty Cutout Toys

Children in this age group are eager to experiment with new crafts. They will enjoy helping their parents construct these projects in the family workshop. This diversified collection includes a chalkboard choochoo, a sun dial dart board, a Fatso beanbag toss game, and a llama note holder. The Fatso toss game would be perfect for a birthday party with a circus theme.

Materials:
Train chalkboard—insulation board, sandpaper, gesso, acrylic paint, molding strip ($\frac{1}{2}$x$1\frac{1}{2}$x16 inches), chalkboard paint, and clear enamel.
Dart board—insulation board, gesso, clear enamel, felt-tip pen or small brush, bright colors of paints, and suction darts.
Clown toss game—wood or insulation board, gesso, acrylic paints, clear enamel, felt, and beans (for the bags).
Llama tack board—insulation board, sandpaper, gesso, acrylic paints, and clear enamel.

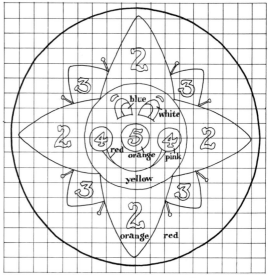

1 Square = 1 Inch

Cover this piece with a coat of clear enamel, then glue it in place over the painted wheels.

Dart board: Following sketch, at bottom of previous page, cut out a 14-inch diameter circle from insulation board. Use either a coping saw or a saber saw. Sand edges, then give board several coats of gesso to build up surface.

When dry, give the board a coat or two of clear enamel. Mark off the sections with a felt-tip pen or a small brush, then paint in the suggested colors in the sketch. Use acrylics. If small children will be playing with the dartboard, be sure to use suction darts. Otherwise, you can use regular darts. (If regular darts are used, give the board several more coats of clear enamel to build up a tough surface.)

1 Square = ½ Inch

Next, cut out fruit-shaped bags for the game from scraps of felt, according to the sketch. Using a blanket stitch and several strands of embroidery floss, stitch around each one, leaving a small opening for stuffing with beans or split peas.

After stuffing, sew the opening closed by hand, using a blanket stitch. Glue a felt tooth onto the clown, following the placement in the sketch.

1 Square = 2 Inches

Clown toss game *(it's designed to stand on the floor):* Following the sketch above, cut out the shape from a 20-inch-square piece of insulation board. Next, cut out the mouth opening and sand all of the edges. Apply a coat of gesso to build up the surface and for added strength. When it's dry, paint it according to the colors in the photo. When the paint is dry, finish with a coat of clear varnish.

1 Square = 3 Inches

Llama tack board: Cut the board from a piece of insulation board that measures 27x30 inches. (You can vary the size according to the space available for hanging.)

Sand the edges and coat the cutout with gesso. Then, give it two more coats. Paint it with acrylics, then give it a finish of clear varnish. Position pushpins or map tacks on the saddle.

Miniature Golf Course

Just imagine being able to play a round of golf, no matter what the weather is like. That's what you and your family can do with this Tom Thumb version of a roadside miniature golf course.

Made up of unlikely elements, the miniature course has traps and hazards that you can arrange and rearrange at will. Use regular golf balls and putters, and score as you would in a traditional golf game.

Materials:

Smooth-textured carpet tiles (green preferred, to simulate grass), stovepipe fittings, aluminum gutter screening, assorted pans and plastic bowls filled with pebbles and water, rubber tree protectors, salt boxes and juice cans, short lengths of $^{11}/_{16}$x2¾-inch cove molding and ¼-inch dowels, wooden block bases, paint, and cardboard.

Directions:

Arrange the smooth-textured carpet tiles to serve as greens and fairways. Saw the $^{11}/_{16}$x2¾-inch cove molding into various lengths to serve as connecting ball runs between the carpet tiles. Either glue or tape flat the cove molding around the outer edges of the carpet tiles to keep the balls in bounds.

Use a variety of household items, such as stovepipe fittings, plastic bowls, aluminum gutter screening, and rubber tree protectora for the holes and traps. Use salt boxes or juice cans with the ends removed for the golf holes. (See the drawings on the opposite page.)

126

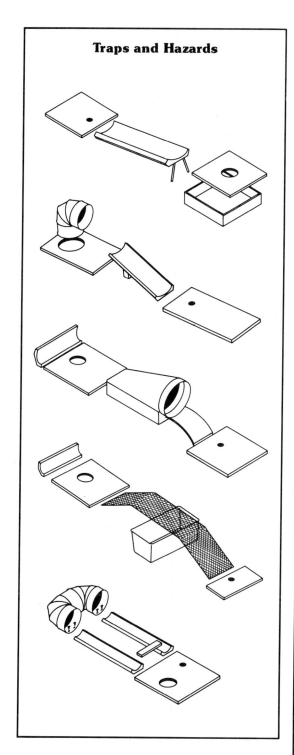

Traps and Hazards

Horse Racing Game

Here's an indoor game for two to six players. With each roll of the dice, a player advances down the track (one square for any number under six, two for any number over six). If he lands on a square with a hurdle, he must retreat two squares and wait for his next turn to start moving ahead again. The winner, naturally, is the one who crosses the finish line first.

Materials:
6 plastic horses, 6 ⅛-inch dowels, 1 ¼-inch dowel, 6 wooden block bases, a 22x38-inch piece of ¼-inch plywood or hardboard, narrow plastic tape or paint (white), juice can, and enamel.

Directions:
Use the 22x38-inch piece of ¼-inch plywood for the game board. Sand the edges, or frame it with wooden strips. Use a ¼-inch dowel for the finish line. Mark off six lanes of equal width and cover the lines with white tape or paint. Draw or paint horizontal lines 3 inches apart in each lane to form grid.

Make a hurdle for each lane from dowel scraps and position in a different square for each lane. Paint a juice can to serve as a dice cup. Glue toy horses to a piece of ⅛-inch dowel. Attach dowels to wooden block bases. Paint numbers on small cardboard squares and attach to dowel.

127

Shooting-Star Kite

Both adults and older children will enjoy making and flying this shooting-star kite. It is easy to launch by hand, or you can have a friend take it about 50 feet away, then toss it up as you pull in on the cord. This kite needs a steady brisk breeze to stay aloft, and with practice you can make it do various stunts.

Materials:

1 yard each of red, white, and blue 36-inch broadcloth; five grommets; a 36-inch piece of ³⁄₁₆-inch dowel; one 27-inch piece of ¼-inch dowel; ½-inch iron-on fusible webbing (available in most notions departments); and kite string.

Kite Flying Safety Tips

- Don't run backward with a kite.
- Never climb a tree to rescue a kite.
- Keep large kites away from crowds.
- Wear gloves when flying a hard-pulling kite in order to avoid line burns.
- Never use wire or metallic cord as line.
- Stay away from high wires and don't fly kites during electric storms.
- Keep kites from airplane landing paths.

Directions:

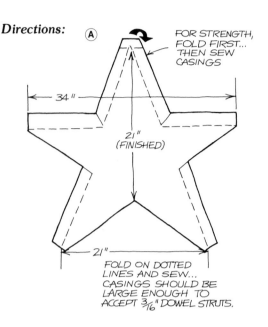

Using the dimensions given in drawing A, cut out the star shape from blue broadcloth, allowing an excess on the points indicated by the dotted lines (this will be folded over and zigzag stitched to form a casing for the three ³⁄₁₆-inch dowels). Be sure to fold the top point over first for added strength.

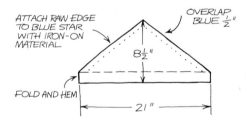

Using the dimensions in drawing B, cut out the three white broadcloth inserts and hem them along the bottom edge. Position the sides of the white pieces on the blue star, overlapping them ½ inch, and bond them together with ½-inch strips of iron-on fusible webbing.

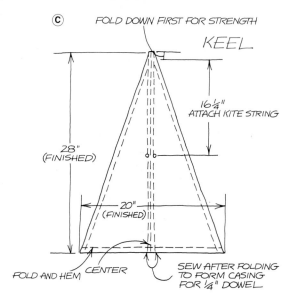

C FOLD DOWN FIRST FOR STRENGTH

KEEL

28" (FINISHED)

16¼" ATTACH KITE STRING

20" (FINISHED)

FOLD AND HEM CENTER

SEW AFTER FOLDING TO FORM CASING FOR ¼" DOWEL

FOLD ON CENTER LINE, SEW CASING, FOLD EDGES AND SEW DOWN CENTER LINE OF BLUE STAR

Cut the keel from red broadcloth, following the dimensions in drawing C. Hem on all three sides. Fold in half and stitch a casing down the middle to accommodate a ¼-inch dowel, folding under the top point first for added strength.

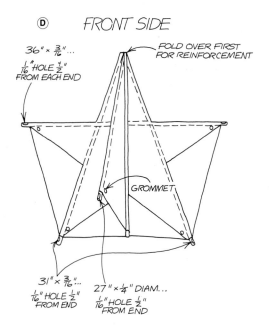

D FRONT SIDE

36" × 3/16"...
1/16" HOLE ½" FROM EACH END

FOLD OVER FIRST FOR REINFORCEMENT

GROMMET

31" × 3/16"...
1/16" HOLE ½" FROM END

27" × ¼" DIAM...
1/16" HOLE ½" FROM END

Fold the blue star in half, as shown in drawing D. Position the long edges of the keel together; pin them to the center line of the blue star, then machine-stitch.

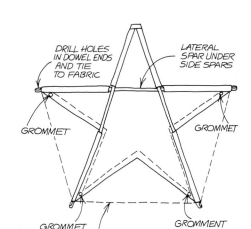

E REAR SIDE

DRILL HOLES IN DOWEL ENDS AND TIE TO FABRIC

LATERAL SPAR UNDER SIDE SPARS

GROMMET

GROMMET

GROMMET

GROMMENT

WHITE INSERTS IRONED ON FROM REAR SIDE

Fasten the grommets (small metal eyelets) by the casing on the keel and at the side and bottom points of the star as shown in drawing E.

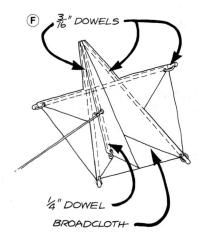

F 3/16" DOWELS

¼" DOWEL

BROADCLOTH

Insert the pre-drilled 3/16-inch dowels in the casings and attach them to the kite as shown in drawing F. Attach string.

Collapsible Doll House

Furnishing this easy-to-build doll house can be as exciting as a life-size decorating project. Use scraps of towels, washcloths, and sheets, to cover the walls, floors, and furnishings.

Materials:
One 4x4-foot piece of ¼-inch plywood, 6 small hinges, 6 feet of ¼-inch round molding, wood glue, four latch hooks and eyes, washcloths, and scraps of sheets or cotton fabric.

Directions:
Cut out the pieces of plywood, following the drawing. Drill a hole in each window section in order to place the jigsaw blade. Cut out windows. Next, cut molding into six 1-foot sections.

Draw a pencil line down the middle of the floor section (9 inches from either side). Glue two strips of molding ⅛ inch from either side of this line, making a ¼-inch track that will hold the center support wall. Draw a pencil line 8 inches from the bottom of each side section. Glue two molding strips ⅛ inch on either side of this line. Hinge the sides of the house to the floor section. Notch the support wall and the second floor.

Screw two eyes into each side of the back section edge, two inches from the bottom and two inches from the top. Screw the hooks into the side sections to line up with the walls. Hinge the roof pieces together along the 13-inch dimension.

To assemble the doll house, hook the back to the side sections with the hooks and eyes. Slide the support wall and the second floor together by sliding the notches into each other. Slide the support wall and the second floor section into place along the tracks, and set on the roof.

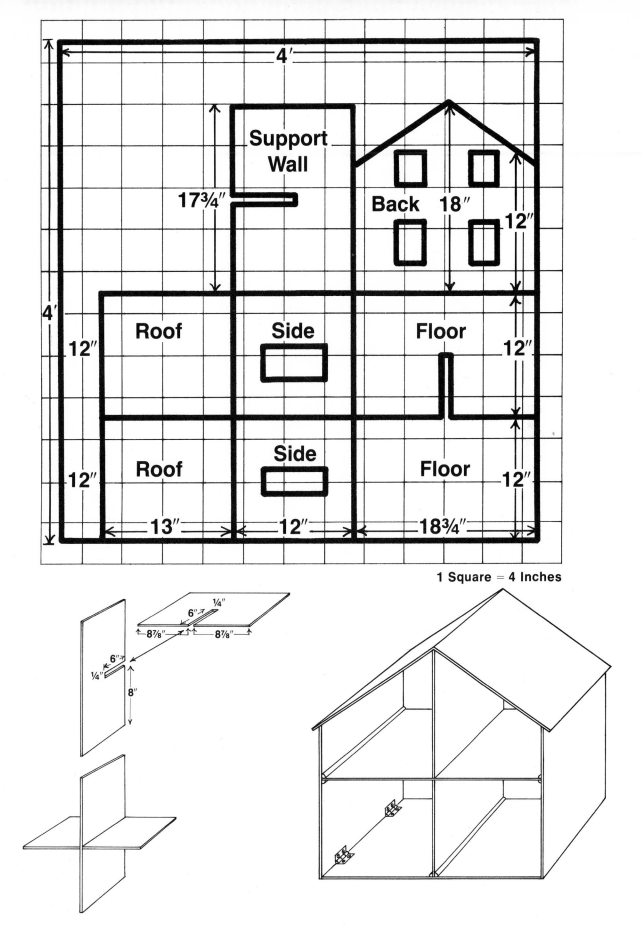

4'

Support Wall

17¾"

Back   18"   12"

4'

12"   Roof   Side   Floor   12"

Side

12"   Roof   Floor   12"

13"   12"   18¾"

1 Square = 4 Inches

¼"   6"
8⅞"   8⅞"

6"   ¼"
8"

Irresistible Puppets

With just a few scraps of brightly colored cotton fabric, lace, ribbon, and yarn plus the extension of your child's hands, puppets suddenly will come to life. This wide-eyed, smiling duo will soon become the stars of your youngsters' "let's pretend" world, and the children will spend hours creating dramatic roles for this calico girl and denim boy.

Today's puppets come in all shapes and sizes — from dinosaurs, clowns, and queens to witches, dragons, and cookie monsters. Each one of this loving twosome measures 18 inches tall.

For the outgoing child, puppetry provides another outlet for him to express himself. And, the child who is shy or withdrawn often becomes so absorbed in making these little people perform that he overcomes his shyness.

Materials:

⅓ yard 72-inch-wide pink felt, batting, white muslin, stuffing, one red bandanna, print fabric scraps, small amounts of ribbon and lace, 2 ounces each of ½-inch-thick orange and yellow acrylic yarn, fabric glue, 4½-inch-diameter wiggly plastic eyes, and small buttons.

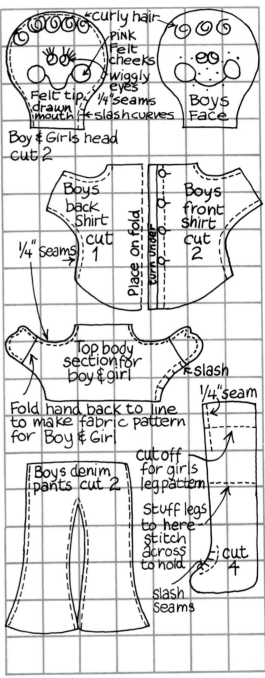

1 Square = 2 Inches

Directions:

Girl: First, enlarge the pattern pieces and cut two head pieces from pink felt, two from the batting, and two from the muslin. Lay one felt piece on top of the other, then place one piece of batting on either side of the felt. Pin one piece of muslin on each side through all of the thicknesses. Machine-stitch ¼-inch from the edge all around the head, leaving the neck edge open. Clip the curves and turn right side out. Hand-stitch the opening, leaving a space large enough for a finger to fit in it.

Next, cut out four pieces of pink felt for the legs. Stitch ¼-inch seams around the legs, leaving the top open. Clip the curves and turn to the right side. Stuff the lower leg and foot about 6 inches up from the seam on the foot. Stitch across the leg above the stuffing. Overlap the legs 1½ inches from the center top, and top-stitch to hold them in position (these will be attached to the waistline later).

Enlarge the body pattern pieces, following the drawing, and cut two pink felt bodies and hands. Cut two pieces of print fabric the same as the body, eliminating the hands. Machine-stitch the print fabric on top of the felt pieces. Place the body pieces right sides together, pin, and stitch, allowing ¼-inch seams. Leave the neck and waistline open. Clip the curves and turn to the right side.

Cut the 3x18-inch piece of white muslin for the slip. Sew 1-inch-wide lace trim on the bottom edge. Machine-stitch the sides together. Using the same fabric as the bodice print, cut a 3½x18-inch strip for the skirt. Sew ½-inch-wide lace trim to the bottom edge; sew the side seams. Place the slip section inside the skirt piece. On the raw edge, run a gathering stitch and pull up to fit the waistline on the bodice. Attach the legs.

To attach the head, insert the head piece 1 inch inside the neck opening, and sew the head and the neck together by hand. Glue on the lace trim to the neckline and the sleeves. Sew on small buttons to the bodice front, and tie a ribbon around the waist.

Cut 10-inch lengths of yellow yarn for the hair. Wrap each length of yarn around two fingers twice. Sew the loops together and then to the head about ¾ inches apart, covering the entire back of the head.

Laying the puppet flat, glue the eyes in place. Glue on the pink felt cheeks. When the glue is dry, draw on the eyelashes and mouth.

Boy: Follow the same instructions that you used for the girl's head and legs. Omit stitching the legs together at the center seam.

Enlarge the pattern for the bell-bottom pants, following the drawing. Cut out the pieces and sew them together; clip the curves, and turn to the right side. Slip the legs through the pants legs and sew together at the top through all of the thicknesses.

Cut two pink felt bodice and hand sections. Cut two red bandanna pieces from the girl's bodice pattern, but eliminate the hands. Stitch in the same manner as you did for the girl.

Machine-stitch the bodice together in the same manner as the girl's bodice. Stitch the pants and the legs to the center of the puppet's body. Attach the head to the body as you did with the girl puppet.

Next, enlarge the pieces for the shirt and cut the pieces from the red bandanna. Sew small buttons down the front of the shirt. Place the shirt on the boy puppet, and tack it to the body back to hold it in place.

Next, cut a 7x14-inch red bandanna triangle for the scarf. Hem under the raw edges and tie it around the boy's neck. Tack it at center front.

For the boy's hair, cut 8-inch lengths of orange yarn. Wrap the yarn around your finger twice. Sew it on in the same manner as you did for the girl, only higher on the neckline.

Add the facial features the same as you did for the girl, but omit the eyelashes and add a sprinkling of freckles.

Fashions and accessories

In the seven to twelve age range, youngsters have definite clothing preferences. Most conform to the "crowd's" dress code. They are particular about what goes together and how their clothes fit. This chapter presents many preferred items — sweaters, caps and scarves, bags, and jewelry. With this selection, your youngster will be among the "IN" crowd.

Pullover Tennis Sweaters

For fashion and an all-around comfortable fit, it's hard to beat tennis sweaters. What's more, they're always in style. Regardless of which of these versions you make — the V-neck or the round neck — the lucky recipient will wear it with pride.

Instructions are given for size 30 chest measurement, with 34 and 38 in parentheses. Knit abbreviations are given on page 95.

Materials:
Tennis pullover — V-neck — (In heavy and medium weights) — For heavy weight — Twin-Pak Win-Knit (Bear Brand, Fleisher's or Botany, 4 ounce paks). Color A — 3 (4, 5), color B — 1 (1, 1), and color C — 1 (1, 1); size 6 and size 4 knitting needles. For medium weight — Winsom (Bear Brand, Fleisher's or Botany, 2 ounce skeins). Color A — 6 (7,8), color B — 1 (1,1), and color C — 1 (1, 1); size 8 and size 5 knitting needles.
Tennis pullover — round neck — For heavy weight — Twin-Pak Win-Knit (Bear Brand, Fleisher's or Botany, 4 ounce paks). Color A — 4 (5, 5), color B — 1 (1, 1), and color C — 1 (1, 1); size 6 and size 4 knitting needles. For medium weight — Winsom (Bear Brand, Fleisher's or Botany, 2 ounce skeins). Color A — 6 (7, 8), color B — 1 (1, 1), and color C — 1 (1, 1); size 8 and size 5 knitting needles.

Gauge:
Tennis pullover — V-neck — For heavy weight — size 6 needles — Stockinette St. 5 sts = 1 inch; 7 rows = 1 inch; for medium weight — size 8 needles — Stockinette St, 5 sts = 1 inch; 7 rows = 1 inch. *Tennis pullover — round neck —* For heavy weight — size 6 needles — Stockinette St, 5 sts = 1 inch; 7 rows = 1 inch; for medium weight — size 8 needles — Stockinette St, 5 sts = 1 inch; 7 rows = 1 inch.

Directions:
Tennis pullover — V-neck:
Back — With smaller size needles and A, cast on 77 (87, 97) sts. *Ribbing — Row 1 —* wrong side — P 1, * k 1, p 1; repeat from * to end. *Row 2 —* K 1, * p 1, k 1; repeat from * to end. Repeat these 2 rows until about 2 ins. from beg., end on right side with row 2. Drop A.

Note: Carry A loosely along edge when not in use. *Stripe Pattern —* With B, continue ribbing for 4 (4, 4) rows. Break B. With A, work ribbing for 4 (4, 4) rows. Drop A. With C, work ribbing for 3 (3, 3) rows. *Inc. Row —* right side — Work ribbing for 11 (15, 19) sts.

Place marker on right needle for beg. of cable pat., † work 3 sts more, * inc. 1 st in next st by k an extra st in back of loop below next st, then k the next st, work 5 (5, 5) sts * repeat between *'s 1 (1, 1) times. Inc. 1 st in next st as before, work 3 (3, 3) sts. Place marker on right needle for end of cable pat. † — there are now between markers 22 (22, 22) sts. Work 17 (19, 21) sts. Place marker on needle for beg. of cable pat. Repeat between †'s once, place marker on right needle for end of cable pat.

(continued on next page)

Work remaining 11 (15, 19) sts, having on needle 83 (93-103) sts. Carry markers. Break C. *Cable Pattern—Row 1 and all uneven numbered rows—wrong side—*With larger size needles and A, p to marker, † sl marker, * k 1, p 6 (6, 6) sts *. Repeat between *'s twice; k 1, sl marker †, p to next marker, repeat between †'s once, p to end. *Rows 2, 4 and 6—*K to marker, † sl marker, * p 1, k 6 (6, 6) sts * repeat between *'s twice, p 1, sl marker †, k to next marker, repeat between †'s once, k to end. *Row 8—Cable Twist Row—*K to marker, * p 1, sl next 3 (3, 3) sts to hook, hold at back, k next 3 (3, 3) sts, k from hook 3 (3, 3) sts. A cable twist— p 1, k 6 (6, 6) sts, p 1, work a cable twist on next 6 (6, 6) sts, p 1 *, k to next marker, repeat between *'s once, k to end. *Row 10—* Same as row 2.

Repeat for pat. these 10 (10, 10) rows until about 13½ (14½-15½) ins. from beg., or desired length to underarm, end on wrong side.

Mark for underarm. *Armholes—*Bind off at beg. of next 2 rows 3 (4, 5) sts. *Dec. Row—*SKP, work to within 2 sts of end, k 2 tog., having 75 (83, 91) sts. With care to keep pat., repeat dec. row every 2nd row 3 (5, 7) times. Work even on 69 (73, 77) sts until about 7 (7½-8) ins. above underarm marker, end on wrong side.

*Shoulders—*Bind off at beg. of next 2 rows 6 (7, 8) sts. Bind off 8 sts at beg. of next 4 (4, 4) rows, ending on wrong side with 25 (27, 29) sts.

*Neck Ribbing—*With smaller size needles, k 1 row, end on right side. Drop A. Working in ribbing same as at lower edge, with C, work 4 (4, 4) rows. Break C. With A, work 4 (4, 4) rows. Break A. With B, work 3 (3, 3) rows. Bind off in ribbing.

*Front—*Work same as for back until 1 row less to underarm marker, end on right side. *Dividing Row—*Work and sl to holder for right side 41 (46, 51) sts. P 1 and sl to holder for center neck st, work remaining 41 (46, 51) sts. Mark for underarm. *Left Side—Armhole and Neck—*Bind off 3 (4, 5) sts, work to end. Work 1 row even.

*Next Row—*SKP—an armhole dec.—work to within 2 sts of end, k 2 tog.—a neck dec.—leaving 36 (40, 44) sts. With care to keep pat., dec. 1 st at armhole edge every 2nd row 3 (5, 7) times more. *At same time,* dec. 1 st at neck edge every 2nd row 4 times more, every 4th row 7 (8, 9) times and when armhole is same length as on back, shape shoulder same as for right side of back.

*Right Side—*From wrong side, sl from holder to larger size needle 41 (46, 51) sts. From right side, join yarn at neck edge and work 1 row. *Armhole and Neck—*Bind off 3 (4, 5) sts, finish row. *Next Row—*SKP—a neck dec.—work to within 2 sts of end, k 2 tog.—an armhole dec. —leaving 36 (40, 44) sts. Complete to correspond to left side reversing all shaping.

*Sleeves—*With smaller size needles and A, cast on 40 (44, 48) sts. Work k 1, p 1 ribbing for 2 ins. for cuff. Work stripe pat. same as at lower edge to inc. row. *Inc. Row—*right side— Work ribbing for 11 (13, 15) sts. Place marker on right needle for beg. of cable pat., work 3 sts more, inc. 1 st in next st as on back, * work 5 (5, 5) sts. Inc. 1 st in next st as before; repeat from * once, work 3 (3, 3) sts more. Place marker on right needle for end of cable pat., finish row, inc. 1 st at end having 44 (48, 52) sts. Carry markers.

*Cable Pattern—Row 1—*wrong side—With larger size needles, p to marker, repeat between †'s of pat. row 1 for back once, p to end. *Row 2—*K to marker, repeat between †'s of pat. row 2 for back once, k to end. Continue working cable pat. as established. Inc. 1 st each side every 8th row 8 (9, 10) times. Work even on 60 (66, 72) sts until about 11¾ (12¾, 13¾) ins. above ribbing for cuff, or desired length to underarm, end on wrong side. Bind off at beg. of next 2 rows 3 (4, 5) sts. Dec. 1 st each side of next row. Dec. 1 st each side every 2nd row, ending on right side 15 (17, 19) times more. Work 1 row even. Bind off 2 sts at beg. of next 2 rows. Bind off remaining 18 (18, 18) sts.

*Neck Ribbing—*From right side, beg. at left shoulder, with smaller size needle and A, pick up and k evenly spaced along left neck edge 44 (46, 48) sts. Place marker on right needle, sl 1 st from holder and k it for seam st. Place marker on right needle, pick up and k along right neck edge 44 (46, 48) st having 89 (93, 97) sts remaining.

Drop A. Carry markers.

Row 1—wrong side—With C, p 1, * k 1, p 1; repeat from * to end. *Row 2*—* K 1, p 1: repeat from * to within 2 sts of marker, SKP, sl marker, k seam st, sl marker, k 2 tog., ** p 1, k 1; repeat from ** to end, leaving 87 (91, 95) sts. *Row 3*—P 1, * k 1, p 1 *; repeat between *'s to within 2 sts of marker, SKP, sl marker, p seam st, sl marker, k 2 tog., p 1; repeat between *'s to end. Working rows of color same as on back, repeat rows 2 and 3 until same number of rows as on back, end on wrong side. Bind off in ribbing.

Tennis pullover—round neck:

Back—Work same as for back of tennis pullover with V-neck, see page 135. *Neck ribbing*—Work same as for neck ribbing of tennis pullover with V-neck, see page 136.

Front—Work same as back until about 4½ (5, 5½) ins. above underarm marker, end on right side. *Dividing row*—Work and sl to holder 30 (31, 32) sts for right side; p and sl to holder for neck 9 (11, 13) sts. Work remaining 30 (31, 32) sts.

Left side—*neck and shoulder*—*Dec. row*—Work to within 2 sts of end, k 2 tog. Repeat dec. row every 2nd row 7 (7, 7) times and when armhole is same length as back, end on wrong side. Shape shoulder same as for right side of back.

Right side—From wrong side sl from holder to larger size needle 30 (31, 32) sts. From right side, join yarn at neck edge. *Dec. row*—SKP, work to end. Complete to correspond to left side, reversing all shaping.

Front neck ribbing—From wrong side, sl from holder to smaller size needle 9 (11, 13) front neck sts. From right side, join A at left shoulder, pick up and k evenly spaced along left front neck edge 21 (21, 21) sts, k across front sts, pick up and k along right front neck edge 21 (21, 21) sts, having 51 (53, 55) sts in all. Drop A. Work stripes same as for back neck ribbing. Bind off loosely in ribbing.

Sleeves—With smaller size needles and B, cast on 53 (57, 65) sts. Work ribbing same as at lower edge for 4 (4, 4) rows. Break B.

With A work ribbing for 4 (4, 4) rows. Drop A. With C work ribbing for 3 (3, 3) rows. *Inc. row*—right side—With C, work ribbing for 8 (4, 14) sts. Inc. 1 st in next st as on back, * work 5 (5, 5) sts. Inc. 1 st in next st as before; repeat from * 5 (7, 5) times. *At same time*, when there are 19 (22, 25) sts on right needle, place a marker on right needle for beg. of cable pat., and when there are 22 (22, 22) sts on right needle after marker place 2nd marker on right needle for end of cable pat. After last inc. work in ribbing remaining 8 (4, 14) sts having 60 (66, 72) sts in all. Break C. Carry markers.

Cable pattern—*Row 1*—wrong side—With larger size needles and A, p to marker; repeat between †'s of pat. row 1 for back once, p to end. *Row 2*—K to marker, repeat between †'s of pat. row 2 for back once, k to end.

Continue working cable pat. as established until about 2½ ins. above inc. row, end on wrong side. Bind off at beg. of next 2 rows 3 (4, 5) sts. Dec. 1 st each side of next row. Dec. 1 st each side every 2nd row, end on right side 15 (17, 19) times more. Work 1 row even. Bind off 2 sts at beg. of next 2 rows. Bind off remaining 18 (18, 18) sts.

Knitting Tips

• Always buy enough yarn at one time, as the dye lots may differ somewhat in color.

• To measure your work, spread the article out on a flat surface to the required width before you measure the length at the center of the piece.

• When you are joining a new ball of yarn, always join at the outer edge. Make a slip knot with the new strand around the strand you are knitting with. Move the slip knot up to the edge of your work and continue knitting with the newly attached strand. (Knot will be concealed in seam of garment; one in center of row would show.)

• Always bind off in the same pattern as that in the garment and work very loosely so there will be "give" to bound-off edge.

Sleeveless Argyle

Fashion, just like history, repeats itself. And in the case of the argyle plaid, that's a fortunate event. The pattern shown here was popular even during Grandfather's boyhood when it made a hit on the golf course, and now it's back in vogue and is ideal for today's layered look. Equally as popular as argyle sweaters are socks and scarves in the same diamond patterns. Although some are mass-produced by machine, none of them can match the classic beauty of handknit argyle designs.

Directions are given for small sizes (4-6), with changes for medium (8-10), and large (12) sizes in parentheses.

Materials:

Wintuk Sport Yarn (Coats and Clark's Red Heart 3 ply "Tangle-Proof" pullout skeins), 3 (3, 4) ounces of No. 403 Lt. Oxford; 1 (1, 2) ounces each of No. 1 white and No. 905 red; and 1 ounce of No. 12 black for each size.

For both the small and the large sizes: 1 pair of No. 2 and No. 4 knitting needles. For the medium size: 1 pair of No. 1 and No. 3 knitting needles. Bobbins: 9 (11, 11).

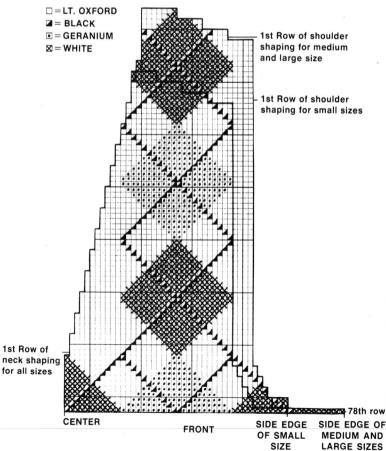

□ = LT. OXFORD
◨ = BLACK
▣ = GERANIUM
⊠ = WHITE

1st Row of shoulder shaping for medium and large size

1st Row of shoulder shaping for small sizes

1st Row of neck shaping for all sizes

CENTER

FRONT

SIDE EDGE OF SMALL SIZE

SIDE EDGE OF MEDIUM AND LARGE SIZES

78th row

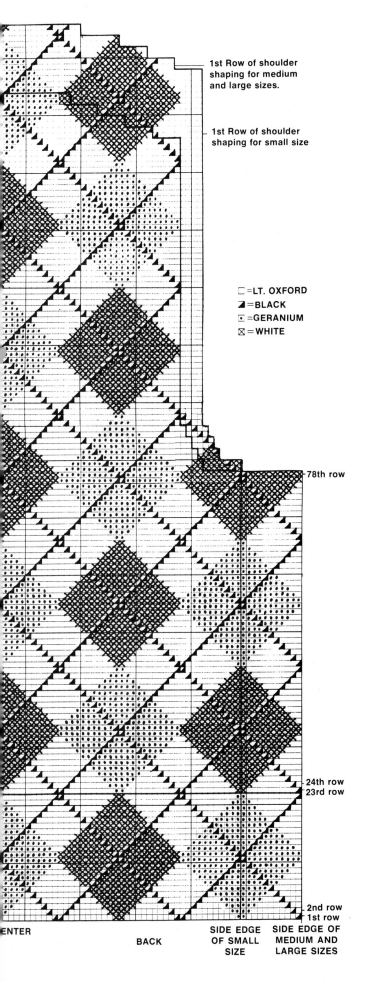

1st Row of shoulder shaping for medium and large sizes.

1st Row of shoulder shaping for small size

☐ =LT. OXFORD
◪ =BLACK
⊡ =GERANIUM
⊠ =WHITE

78th row

24th row
23rd row

2nd row
1st row

CENTER   BACK   SIDE EDGE   SIDE EDGE OF
                              OF SMALL   MEDIUM AND
                              SIZE   LARGE SIZES

Gauge:

No. 3 needles: 15 sts = 2 inches; 10 rows = 1 inch. No. 4 needles: 7 sts = 1 inch; 9 rows = 1 inch.

Blocking Measurements:

Sizes: small (4-6), medium (8-10), and large (12). Body chest size (in inches): (23-24) (26-28) and (30). Actual knitting measurements — chest: 25 (29, 31½); width across the back or front at the underarm: 12½ (14½, 15¾); length from the shoulder to the lower edge: 15½ (18, 19¾); length of the side seam (excluding the armbands): 9 (11, 12).

Directions:

Wind 3 (5, 5) bobbins with lt. oxford, 3 bobbins each with white and red for each size. Cut 8 (10, 10) strands of black, each 2 yards long.

Note: When changing colors, always twist the unused color around the other to prevent making holes. Pattern is worked in stockinette st (k 1 row, p 1 row). Charts on the left show one half of front and back. Starting at the side edge where indicated for desired size, follow each row to the center; to complete row, follow same row from center back to starting line. When necessary, break off strands and attach colors as needed.

Back: Starting at lower edge with No. 2 (1, 2) needles and lt. oxford, cast on 86 (110, 110) sts. *1st row — wrong side:* P 2, * k 2, p 2. Repeat from * across. *2nd row:* K 2, * p 2, k 2. Repeat from * across. Repeat last 2 rows for 2¾ (3¼, 3¼) inches, increasing 2 sts on last row on small size only — 88 (110, 110) sts. *Next row:* Purl.

Change to No. 4 (3, 4) needles and work in pattern as follows: Drop lt. oxford. *For medium and large sizes only: 1st row:* Attach black and k 1 black, drop black, pick up lt. oxford and k 9, * drop lt. oxford, attach red and k 2, drop red, attach another lt. oxford and k 9, drop lt. oxford, (attach black and k 1, drop black) twice; pick up lt. oxford and

(continued on next page)

k 9, drop lt. oxford, attach white and k 2, drop white, attach another lt. oxford and k 9, drop lt. oxford (attach black and k 1, drop black) twice; pick up lt. oxford and k 9.

Repeat from * once more; drop lt. oxford, attach red and k 2, drop red, attach another lt. oxford and k 9, drop lt. oxford, attach black and k 1. Starting with 2nd row on chart for back, follow chart until the 23rd row has been completed.

For small size only: 1st row — This is 23rd row on chart for back: Attach white and k 1, drop white, * pick up lt. oxford and k 9, drop lt. oxford, (attach black and k 1, drop black) twice; pick up lt. oxford and k 9, drop lt. oxford, attach red and k 2, drop red, attach another lt. oxford and k 9, drop lt. oxford, (attach black and k 1, drop black) twice; pick up lt. oxford and k 9 drop lt. oxford, attach another white and k 2.

Repeat from * once more, ending with k 1 white instead of k 2 white. *For all sizes:* Starting with 24th row, follow chart until the 78th row on chart has been completed.

Armhole shaping: Following chart, bind off 7 (11, 11) sts at beg. of next 2 rows.

For medium and large sizes only: Bind off 4 sts at beg. of next 2 rows. *For all sizes:* Dec. one st at both ends of every other row 4 (3, 3) times — 66 (74, 74) sts. Continue to follow chart to first row of shoulder shaping for designated size.

Shoulder shaping: Following chart, bind off 5 sts at beg. of next 8 (6, 6) rows, then bind off — (7, 7) sts at beg. of next 2 rows. Slip remaining 26 (30, 30) sts onto a stitch holder for back of neck.

Front: Work same as Back until armhole shaping has been completed. *Next row:* Follow chart on page 138.

Neck shaping: 1st row: Following chart for front, work across the first 31 (35, 35) sts, k next 2 sts tog. Slip remaining 33 (37, 37) sts onto a stitch holder to be worked later. Following chart, dec. one st at neck edge on every 4th row 12 (14, 14) times more. Complete to correspond with chart.

Attach yarn to first st at neck edge, k 2 tog. and complete to correspond with other side, reversing shapings.

Block to measurements. Sew the right shoulder seam.

Neckband: With right side facing, No. 2 (1, 2) needles and lt. oxford, starting at left shoulder, pick up and k 52 (60, 60) sts along left neck edge to center, pick up and k one st at center front (between last st and next st) — mark this st; pick up and k 52 (60, 60) sts along right neck edge, k across the sts on back stitch holder — 131 (151, 151) sts.

1st row — wrong side: K 2, * p 2, k 2. Repeat from * across to within marked center st, p the center st; k 2, p 2 to end of row.

2nd row: Work in ribbing as established to within 2 sts before marked st, p 2 tog., k 1 — center st; p 2 tog., complete row in ribbing as established.

3rd row: Work in ribbing as established to within 2 sts before center st, k 2 tog., p 1, sl 1, k 1, psso, complete row in ribbing. Repeat last 2 rows alternately 2 (3, 4) times more. Bind off loosely in ribbing.

Sew left shoulder seam.

Armbands: With right side facing, No. 2 (1, 2) needles and lt. oxford, pick up and k 140 (160, 160) sts along armhole edge. Work in k 2, p 2 ribbing for ½ (¾, 1) inch. Bind off loosely in ribbing.

Sew side seams.

Caring for Knits

● Fold knits loosely and store in drawers. Never hang sweaters on hangers.
● After a day's wear, air garment before storing it.
● Be careful not to snag yarn on sharp objects. If this does happen, work from underneath and pull snagged yarn to the wrong side with a crochet hook. *Never cut snagged yarn.*
● If pill balls accumulate on a sweater, brush them away with a dry sponge, using lengthwise strokes.

Crocheted Matchmates

You can perk up your girl's wardrobe with this crocheted pullover and matching cap. She can wear it as it is shown here, or over a tailored blouse for the layered look. Although this version has been accented in white, try your own adaptations for a variety of eye-catching and pleasing color combinations.

All you need to know are the simple single and double crochet stitches. Directions are given for size 6, with 8 and 10 in parentheses.

Materials:
Wintuk Sport Yarn (Coats and Clark's Red Heart, 2 ply, 2 ounce Tangle-Proof pull-out skeins). 4 (4, 4) No. 795 cerise; 1 (1, 1) No. 1 white: size F crochet hook; and a buckle.

Gauge:
9 sts = 2 inches; 5 rows = 2 inches.

Blocking Measurements:
Body chest sizes (in inches): 24 (26, 28). Actual crochet measurements—chest: 26 (28, 30); width across back of front at underarm: 13 (14, 15); length from shoulder to lower edge: 15 (16½, 18); length of side seam: 10 (11, 12); length of sleeve seam: 4 (5, 5½); width across sleeve at upper arm: 10 (11, 11½).

Directions:
Pullover: Starting at lower edge with white, chain 60 (64, 69) stitches having 9 ch sts to two inches. First row: Sc in second ch from hook and in each ch across. There are 59 (63, 68) stitches. Ch 1, turn.

Second row: Sc in each sc across. Ch 1, turn. Repeat second row twice more for border. Break off white, attach cerise and with cerise, ch 3 to count as 1 dc. Turn. Now work as follows: First row: Skip first st, dc in each st across.

Ch 3, turn. Second row: Skip first st, dc in each st across, dc in top of ch 3. Repeat second row for pattern. Work even in pattern until total length is 10 (11, 12) inches. Do not ch 3 at end of last row. Turn.

Armhole shaping: First row: Sl st in first 5 (5, 6) stitches. For underarm, ch 3, dc in each dc to within last 4 (4, 5) stitches. Do not work in remaining sts. Ch 3, turn.

Second row: Skip first dc, holding back on hook the last loop of each dc, dc in next 2 dc, yarn over and draw through all loops on hook— 1 dc decreased; dc in each dc across to within last 2 dc and turning chain, dec 1 dc as before, dc in top of ch-3.

Repeat last row 3 (3, 3) times more. Work even over remaining 43 (47, 50) stitches until length from first row of armhole shaping is 5 (5½, 6) inches. Do not ch 3 at end of last row. Turn.

Shoulder shaping: First row: Repeat first row of armhole shaping. Do not ch 3 at end of row. Turn. Second row: Sl st in first 5 (6, 6) stitches. Ch 3, dc in each dc across to within

(continued on next page)

141

last 4 (5, 5) stitches. There remains for back of neck 27 (29, 30) stitches. Break off and fasten.

Front: Work same as back until length from first row of armhole shaping is 3 (3½, 4) inches.

Neck shaping: First row: Skip first dc, dc in next 11 (12, 13) stitches. Do not work over remaining sts. Ch 3, turn. Dec one st at neck edge on next row and at same edge on every row three times more. Work even, if necessary, over remaining 8 (9, 10) stitches until length is same as back to first row of shoulder shaping, ending at armhole edge.

Shoulder shaping: First row: Sl st in first 4 (4, 5) stitches. Complete row as before. Break off and fasten. Skip the center 19 (21, 22) stitches. Attach yarn to next st and complete to correspond with other side, reversing shapings.

Sleeves: Starting at lower edge with white, chain 40 (45, 47) stitches, having 9 ch sts to two inches. Work as for back until border has been completed. There are 39 (44, 46) stitches. Break off white, attach cerise and with cerise, ch 3. Turn. Now work as follows: First row: Dc in first st—1 dc increased at beginning of row; dc in each st across, ending with 2 dc in last st—1 dc increased at end of row. Ch 3, turn. Working in dc rows as for back, increase one st at both ends of every second (third, third) row two (two, two) times more. Work even over 45 (50, 52) stitches until total length is 4 (5, 5½) inches.

Top shaping: First row: Repeat first row of armhole shaping of back. Ch 3, turn. Decrease one st at both ends of every row 1 (1, 2) times, then decrease 2 sts at both ends of every row until there remain 11 (12, 10) stitches. Break off and fasten.

Pocket: Starting at lower edge with cerise, chain 17 (17, 19) stitches. First row: Dc in fourth ch from hook and in each ch across. Ch 3, turn. Work even in dc rows for 2½ (2½, 3) inches. Break off cerise, attach white and ch 1, turn. With white, work in sc rows for one inch. Break off and fasten.

Belt: With white, make a chain four inches longer than desired size. Work even in sc rows for one inch. Break off and fasten.

Block to measurements. Sew side, shoulder and sleeve seams. Sew in sleeves, holding in to fit. Sew pocket in place as shown. Sew buckle on belt.

Neck border: With right side facing, attach cerise at one shoulder seam. First round: Sc evenly around, holding in to desired size. Join with sl st to first sc. Break off cerise, attach white. Next four rounds: With white, sc in each sc around. Join. At end of last round, break off and fasten.

Cap: Starting at center top with cerise, ch 2. Foundation round: Make 8 sc in second ch from hook. Join with sl st to first sc. First round: Ch 3, dc in joining, * 2 dc in next st—1 dc increased. Repeat from * around—16 dc counting ch-3 as 1 dc. Join to top of ch-3. Second round: Repeat first round—32 dc. Join as before. Third round: Ch 3, dc in joining, dc in next dc, * 2 dc in next dc, dc in next dc. Repeat from * around—16 dc increased. Join. Fourth round: Ch 3, dc in joining, dc in next 5 dc, * 2 dc in next dc, dc in next 5 dc.

Repeat from * around—8 dc increased. Join. Next round: Ch 3, skip joining, being careful that incs do not fall over incs. of previous round, dc in each st around, increasing 8 dc evenly spaced. Join. Repeat last round—(1, 2) times more—64 (72, 80) sts.

Break off and fasten. Attach white to joining. Following round: With white, sc in each st around, increasing 8 sc evenly spaced—72 (80, 88) sc. Join. Next round: Ch 3, skip joining, dc in each sc around. Join. Following round: Ch 1, sc in joining, sc in each dc around. Join. Break off and fasten.

Attach cerise to joining. Next round: Ch 3, skip joining, dc in each st around. Join. Repeat last round for 2½ (2¾, 3) inches. Last two rounds: Ch 1, sc in each st around. Join. Break off and fasten.

Scandinavian Knits

Regardless of children's preferences in winter sports, these turtleneck pullovers and caps make sporty matchmates. Directions for these sweater and cap sets are in sizes 6-7.

Materials:

Sweater and cap (left) — Red Heart Knitting Worsted, (Coats & Clark's): 12 ounces robin blue, 8 ounces each of white and skipper blue, No. 8 needles.
Sweater and cap (right) — 13 ounces white, 9 ounces robin blue, 7 ounces skipper blue, and No. 8 needles.

Gauge:

Sweater and cap (left) — 5 sts = 1 inch; 13 rows = 2 inches; *Sweater and cap (right):* 5 sts = 1 inch; 13 rows = 2 inches.

Measurements:

Sweater and cap (left) — Chest — 26 inches; side seam — 10 inches; sleeve seam — 12 inches; width across sleeve at upper arm — 11 inches. *Sweater and cap (right)* — Chest — 30 inches; side seam — 12½ inches; sleeve seam — 14 inches; width across sleeve at upper arm — 12 inches.

Directions:

Sweater *(Left): Back:* With robin blue, cast on 65 sts. *Row 1:* K 1, * p 1, k 1. Repeat from * across. *Row 2:* P 1, * k 1, p 1. Repeat from * across. Repeat Rows 1 and 2 alternately 3 more times — 8 rows in all. *Next row:* K across. *Following row:* P across. *Note:* When changing color, always twist the unused color around the other to prevent making holes and carry unused color loosely across wrong side of work to maintain stitch gauge.

Pattern is worked in stockinette st (k 1 row, p 1 row) as follows: *Row 1:* * K 2 robin, k 1 skipper blue, k 2 robin. Repeat from * across. *Row 2:* * P 1 robin, p 1 skipper, p 1 white, p 1 skipper, p 1 robin. Repeat from * across.

Chart at bottom of page 144 shows one repeat of pat. of design; repeat every row from A to B across all sts. Starting with Row 3 and changing colors as indicated by symbols, follow chart

(continued on next page)

until row 16 has been completed; then repeat rows 1 through 16 until total length is 10 inches ending with a p row. *Note:* Keep continuity of pat. through all shapings. (See chart at bottom of page.)

Armhole shaping: Bind off 3 sts at beg. of next 2 rows and 2 sts at beg. of following 2 rows. Dec. one st at both ends of every other row 3 times—49 sts remaining. Work even until length is 5 inches from first row of armhole shaping ending with a p row.

Shoulder shaping: Bind off 3 sts at beg. of next 6 rows and 4 sts at beg. of following 2 rows, Bind off rem. 23 sts loosely for back of neck.

Front: Work same as back until 3 inches above first row of armhole shaping, ending with a p row—49 sts.

Neck shaping: Work across 19 sts, slip remaining 30 sts onto a stitch holder. Work over sts on needle as follows: At neck edge, bind off 2 sts on every other row twice; dec. one st at same edge every other row twice—13 sts remaining. Work even until armhole measures 5 inches same as back, ending at armhole edge.

Shoulder shaping: At armhole edge, bind off 3 sts every other row 3 times; at same edge bind off remaining 4 sts. Slip sts from holder onto needle; bind off center 11 sts for front of neck; work across remaining 19 sts. Starting with "work over sts on needle" work same as other side of neck shaping.

Sleeves: With robin, cast on 35 sts. Work 8 rows of ribbing same as back. *Next row:* K across increasing 10 sts evenly across—45 sts. *Following row:* P across. Work in pat., same as back until Row 16 of pat. is completed.

Keeping continuity of pat., inc. one st at both ends of next row and every 10th row thereafter 5 times in all—55 sts. Work even until total length is about 12 inches ending with same row as back before armhole shaping.

Top shaping: Bind off 3 sts at beg. of next 2 rows and 2 sts at beg. of following 2 rows. Dec. one st at both ends of every other row 5 times; bind off 2 sts at beg. of every row until 11 sts remain. Bind off. Press pieces lightly through a damp cloth. Sew side and sleeve seams. Sew the right shoulder seam.

Collar: With right side facing, using robin pick up and k 80 sts evenly along entire neck edge. Work in k 1, p 1 ribbing for 6 inches. Bind off loosely in ribbing. Sew left shoulder seam including collar. Sew in sleeves.

Cap: With robin blue, cast on 95 sts. Work 23 rows of ribbing same as back of pullover. Then k 1 row, p 1 row. Work in pat. same as back until Row 16 of pat. is completed. Break off all but robin. Work 8 rows of stockinette st.

Top shaping: row 1: * K 2 tog., k 6, place a marker on needle. Repeat from * 10 times more, k 2 tog., k 5—12 sts decreased. *Row 2:* P across. *Row 3:* * K 2 tog., k to next marker, slip marker. Repeat from * across. Repeat rows 2 and 3 until 23 sts remain, ending with a p row.

Next row: K 1, (k 2 tog.) 11 times. Break yarn leaving an 18 inch end. Thread this end into a tapestry needle, draw through remaining 12 sts, pull up tightly and fasten securely on wrong side; with same yarn, sew back seam allowing for turn-up cuff.

Pompon: Wind 1 strand of each color 12 times around a 4 inch cardboard. Slip from cardboard and tie strands tightly around middle. Cut loops at each end and trim. Sew to top of cap.

Sweater (*right, page 143*): *Back:* With white, cast on 75 sts. *Row 1:* K 1, * p 1, k 1. Repeat from * across. *Row 2:* P 1, * k 1, p 1. Repeat from * across. Repeat rows 1 and 2 alternately 3 more times—8 rows in all. *Next row:* K across. *Following row:* P across. *Note:* When changing colors, always twist unused color around other to prevent making holes and carry the unused color loosely across wrong side of work to maintain the stitch gauge. Pattern is worked in stockinette stitch (k 1 row, p 1 row) as follows: *Wide Band—Row 1:* K 1 white, * k 1 robin, k 1 white. Repeat from * across. Break off white. *Row 2:* With robin p across.

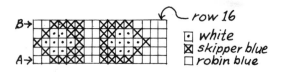

B→
A→

↰ row 16

⊡ *white*
⊠ *skipper blue*
☐ *robin blue*

Changing colors as indicated by symbols and starting with row 3, reading from right to left, follow chart below from A to B; then from C to B once; then from C to D (on even rows, read chart from left to right), until row 24 has been completed.

Break off skipper blue, attach white and work narrow band as follows: *Row 1:* Repeat row 1 of wide band. Break off robin. *Rows 2 through 10:* Starting with a p row, using white, work 9 rows of stockinette st. *Row 11:* Attach robin and repeat row 1. Break off white. *Row 12:* With robin, p across. Attach skipper. *Row 13:* * (K 1 skipper, k 3 robin) twice; k 1 skipper, k 2 robin. Repeat from * 5 times more; (k 1 skipper, k 3 robin) twice; k 1 skipper. *Row 14:* * (P 1 robin, p 1 skipper) 4 times; p 3 robin. Repeat from * 5 times more; (p 1 robin, p 1 skipper) 4 times; p 1 robin. *Row 15:* Repeat row 13. Break off skipper. *Row 16:* With robin, p across. Repeat rows 1 through 16 of narrow band until length is 12½ inches ending with a p row. *Note:* Keep continuity of narrow band pat. throughout all shapings.

Armhole shaping: Bind off 4 sts at beg. of next 2 rows and 2 sts at beg. of following 4 rows. Dec. one st at both ends of every other row twice—55 sts remaining. Work even until 5½ inches from first row of armhole shaping ending with a p row.

Shoulder shaping: Bind off 4 sts at beg. of next 6 rows and 3 sts at beg. of following 2 rows. Bind off remaining 25 sts loosely for back of neck.

Front: Work same as back until 3½ inches above first row of armhole shaping ending with a p row—55 sts.

Neck shaping: Work across 21 sts, slip remaining 34 sts onto a stitch holder. Work over the sts on needle as follows: At neck edge, bind off 2 sts once; then dec one st at neck edge every other row 4 times—15 sts remaining. Work even until armhole measures 5½ inches same as back ending at armhole edge.

Shoulder shaping: At armhole edge, bind off 4 sts every other row 3 times; at same edge, bind off remaining 3 sts. Slip sts from holder onto needle; bind off center 13 sts for front of neck, work across remaining 21 sts. Starting with "work over sts on needle" work same as other side of neck shaping.

Sleeves: With white, cast on 37 sts. Work 8 rows of ribbing same as back. *Next row:* K across increasing 16 sts evenly across—53 sts. *Following row:* P across. Work wide band same as back (only work from A to B; then from C to D) until row 24 of pat. is completed.

Work remainder of sleeve in narrow band pat. increasing one st at both ends when total length is 6 inches and *every* 2 inches thereafter 4 times in all—61 sts. Work even until total length is about 14 inches ending with same row as back before armhole shaping.

Top shaping: Bind off 4 sts at beg. of next 2 rows and 2 sts at beg. of following 4 rows. Dec. one st at both ends of every other row 5 times; bind off 2 sts at beg. of every row until 11 sts rem. Bind off. Press pieces lightly through a damp cloth. Sew side and sleeve seams. Sew right shoulder seam.

Collar: With right side facing, using white, pick up and k 84 sts evenly along entire neck edge. Work in k 1, p 1 ribbing. Sew left shoulder seam including collar. Sew in sleeves.

Cap: With white, cast on 97 sts. Work 10 rows of ribbing same as back of pullover. Work 4 rows of St st. Working as for narrow band of pullover, rpt rows 11 through 16; then rpt rows 1 through 16; then rows 1 through 10.

Top shaping: row 1: * K 2 tog., k 7, place a marker. Repeat from * 9 times more; k 2 tog., k 5-11 sts decreased. *Row 2:* P across. *Row 3:* K 2 tog., k to next marker, slip marker. Repeat from *—11 sts dec. Repeat rows 2 and 3 alternately until 31 sts remain ending with a p row.

Next row: K 1, (k 2 tog.) 15 times. Break yarn leaving an 18 inch end. Finish cap and pompon same as Norwegian design cap.

□·white ⊠ *skipper blue* □ *robin blue*

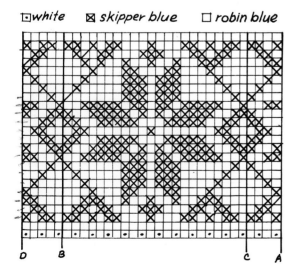

D   B   C   A

145

Skullcaps and Scarves

When they wear these colorful head-huggers, your children will be easy to spot against those stark, wintry backgrounds. The color and design possibilities of this handknit cap and scarf set are rainbow-wide, giving you plenty of latitude.

Another exceedingly attractive color combination is rust, beige, brown, and eggshell. The caps fit the 20 to 22-inch head size.

Materials:

Four-color skullcap—Wintuk sport yarn (Coats & Clark's Red Heart, 2 ounce skeins): 1 ounce each of four different colors. No. 6 needles.
Four-color scarf—Wintuk sport yarn (Coats & Clark's Red Heart, 2 ounce skeins): 2 ounces each of four colors, No. 10 needles.

Gauge:

Four-color skullcap—5 sts = 1 inch; 8 rows = 1 inch.
Four-color scarf—9 sts = 2 inches; 5 rows = 1 inch.

Directions:

Four-color skullcap: Starting at face edge with first color, cast on 111 sts. *Row 1:* K 1, * p 3, k 3, p 3, k 1. Repeat from * across. *Row 2:* P 1, * k 3, p 3, k 3, p 1. Repeat Rows 1 and 2 alternately for ribbed pat. Work in pat. until 16 rows have been completed.

Break off first color, attach second color and work 14 rows in pat. Break off second color; attach third color. First dec row: K 1, * p 2 tog., p 1, k 3, p 3, k 1. Repeat from * across—100 sts.

Next row: P 1, * k 3, p 3, k 2, p 1. Repeat from * across. Work 4 rows in rib as established. Second dec row; K 1, * p 2, k 3, p 2 tog., p 1, k 1. Repeat from * across—89 sts. *Next row:* P 1, * k 2, p 3, k 2, p 1. Repeat from * across. Work 4 rows in rib as established. Third dec row: K 1, * p 2, k 2 tog., k 1, p 2, k 1. Repeat from * across—78 sts.

Next row: P 1, * k 2, p 2, k 2, p 1. Repeat from * across. Work 2 rows in rib as established. Break off 3rd color, attach 4th color. Fourth dec row: K 1, * p 2 tog., k 2, p 2, k 1. Repeat from * across—67 sts. Work one row even. Fifth dec row: K 1, * p 1, k 2, p 2 tog., k 1. Repeat from * across—56 sts. Work 1 row even. Sixth dec row: K 1, * p 1, k 2 tog., p 1, k 1. Repeat from * across—45 sts. Work 1 row even.

Seventh dec row: K 1, * p 2 tog., k 2 tog. Repeat from * across—23 sts. Work 1 row even. Last row: * K 2 tog. Repeat from * across ending with k 1. Break off leaving a 12″ end of yarn. Thread a needle with this end and slip through remaining 12 sts. Draw tightly and fasten securely on wrong side. With same end sew back seam.

Four-color scarf: Starting at one narrow edge with first color, cast on 72 sts. * Work in st st (k 1 row, p 1 row) for 2½ inches ending with a p row. Break off; attach next color. Repeat from * until 2½ inches of each color has been made.

Continue in stripe pattern for 60 inches or desired length. Bind off. Pin out to 16 inches wide and the length worked, and press very lightly through a damp cloth. Allow to dry. Fold in half lengthwise and sew long edges together, then sew ends. Add fringe if desired.

Crocheted caps and scarves have long-lasting value. Unlike other articles of children's apparel, you don't have to worry as much about your child's growing spurts. Ideal for either sex, this combination of crocheted stripes combines well with various coat and jacket patterns and perks up the wardrobe of the sled set. These instructions are for an 18-inch head size.

Materials:
2-ounce skein white washable knitting worsted, 4-ounce skein blue knitting worsted, size F crochet hook.

Directions:
Cap: *Row 1:* Start at center of cap by making a loop of blue yarn (wind yarn 2 times around right index finger, slip off and grasp between left thumb and middle finger). In this loop make 8 sc. Pull up loose end to make a tight ring. Sl st in first sc. Ch 1.

Row 2: 2 sc in each sc, sl st in first sc of row. Ch 1. *Row 3:* Sc in each sc, increase with 2 sc in sc to keep work flat, sl st first sc. *Row 4:* Ch 3, dc in each sc, increasing where needed to keep work flat. *Row 5:* Ch 3, dc in each dc, increasing where needed.

If head size is larger than 18 inches, add another row of stitches before Row 6, increasing the total number of stitches in the row by four for each extra inch. Do the extra row the same way as Row 5. From this point on, add the extra stitches to every row.

Row 6: Repeat Row 5, using white yarn. *Row 7:* Change to blue, dc in each dc. *Row 8:* Repeat Row 6 (there will be about 65 dc in this round). *Rows 9-14:* Dc working even (don't increase), using blue. *Rows 15-20:* Sc in each st.

Rows 21-24: Ch 3, turn and working in opposite direction (this will make cuff right side out when flipped up), work 3 rows even in dc blue. *Row 25:* 1 row white dc, work even. To finish edges, 1 blue sc in each st. Fasten end with sl st. Make yarn pompon for top.

Scarf: *Row 1:* With blue, ch 27, 1 dc in 3rd st from hook, 24 dc in ch. *Row 2:* Ch 3, turn, 24 dc in each dc of last row. Repeat row 2 for rest of scarf, adding 2 white rows 7 rows from ends. Four-inch fringe requires 25 9-inch strands for each end.

Crocheted Cap and Scarf

Before the cold winds start to blow this winter, whip up this colorful scarf and cap set from washable knitting worsted. The cap design is a series of stripes topped by an optional puff of yarn. The cap also has a cuff that can be pulled low over young ears on those especially inclement days. The scarf is easy to make and is accented with a knotted fringe.

Tam and Shoulder Bag

◀ Classic crochet stitches take on a new look when you adapt them to fashion accessories. Try this "updated" tam and shoulder bag combination made of crocheted triangular units.

Materials:
Knitting worsted (4-ounce skeins), 1 each of red, aqua, light orange, gold, light lime; 25x50-inch piece of gold felt, 24 inches of ⅝-inch grosgrain ribbon, size H crochet hook, 2-inch wood drapery rings.

Gauge:
7 sc = 2 inches.

Directions:
Crocheted tam: *Triangle shape:* Make 5 for tam and 10 for bag. With lime, ch 4, sl st to 1st ch to form ring. *Rnd 1:* 12 sc in center of ring, sl st to 1st sc. *Rnd 2:* Ch 1, * skip next sc, work a cluster of 5 dc in next sc, skip next sc, 1 sc in next sc, repeat from * 2 more times, end off.

Rnd 3: Attach orange to back of 3rd dc in any cluster, skip next 2 dc spaces, * make a cluster of 7 dc in next sc space, skip next 2 dc spaces, 1 sc in next dc space, repeat from * 2 more times, end off.

Rnd 4: Attach aqua to back of 4th dc in any cluster, ch 1, 1 sc in same space, ch 2, 2 sc in same space, * 1 sc each in next 7 back spaces, 2 sc in next space, ch 2, 2 sc in same space, repeat from * around, sl st to 1st sc, end off.

Rnd 5: Work in both top loops, attach red in any ch 2 corner, ch 3, (counts as 1 dc) 1 dc in same space, ch 2, 2 dc in same space, * 1 dc each in next 11 sc spaces, 2 dc, ch 2, 2 dc in next corner, repeat from * around, sl st to top of 1st dc, end off.

Rnd 6: Work in top back loop only, attach gold in back loop of 1st ch in any corner, ch 1, 1 sc in same space, ch 2, 2 sc in next ch, * 1 sc each in next 15 spaces, 2 sc in ch back, ch 2, 2 sc in next ch back, repeat from * around, sl st to 1st sc, end.

Tam: with gold, picking up back loops only, whipstitch 5 triangle shapes together for top. Block.

Border and headband, Row 1: Attach gold, work in top back loops only, 1 sc in same space, 1 sc each in each space around, sl st to 1st sc, end off. *Row 2:* Work through both loops for rest of tam, attach red, work 1 sc in each sc around, sl st to 1st sc, end.

Row 3: Attach blue, work same as Row 2. *Row 4:* Attach red, * 1 sc in each next 10 sc, skip next sc, repeat from * around, sl st to 1st sc, end off. *Row 5:* Attach orange, 1 sc in same space, * skip 1 sc, 3 dc in next sc, skip 1 sc, 1 sc in next sc, repeat from * around, sl st to 1st sc, end off.

Row 6: Attach lime in 2nd dc of any cluster, 1 sc in same space, * 1 hdc in next dc, 1 dc in next sc, 1 hdc in next dc, 1 sc in next dc, repeat from * around sl st to 1st sc, end off.

Row 7: Attach red, work 1 sc in each space around, sl st to 1st sc, end off. *Row 8:* Attach aqua, * 1 sc each in next 5 sc, skip 1 sc, repeat from * around, sl st to 1st sc, end off. *Row 9:* Attach red, work same as Row 8. *Row 10:* Attach gold, * 1 sc each in next 10 sc, skip 1 sc, repeat from * around, sl st to 1st sc. *Rows 11, 12:* Ch 1, 1 sc each in each sc around, sl st to 1st sc, end off at Row 12 end. *Row 13:* Attach red, work same as Row 12. Attach pompon to center top.

Bag: Make two 5-triangle sections as for tam. *Row 1:* On 1st 5-triangle section, attach gold and work through both top loops, 1 sc in each sc around, sl st to 1st sc, end off. *Row 2:* Attach blue and repeat Row 1. Set this section aside. Work second 5-triangle section the same, except use red yarn in Row 2. Steam-block sections.

Lining: Using one finished section as a pattern, place on gold felt and trace around. Remove crochet and cut out two circles for lining. Pin lining together, with 9-inch opening at top. Stitch in ¼-inch seam around edges. Trim excess ¼-inch seam from opening. To assemble bag, place crochet sections wrong sides together. Using one side as center guide, measure 4½ inches down from both sides for top opening and mark with pins.

Pin bag together except at top. Whipstitch bag together with red. Place lining inside bag and sew in place around opening. With red, sew wood rings to each side of opening.

Shoulder strap: With aqua, ch 98. *Row 1:* 1 sc in 2nd ch from hook and in each ch across, end off. *Row 2:* Attach gold where aqua ended, ch 1, 1 sc in each sc across, end off. *Row 3:* Attach red where gold ended and repeat Row 2. Sew ribbon to underside of strap and sew ends to rings.

as 1 dc), 2 dc in center of ring, * ch 2, 3 dc in center of ring, repeat from * two more times ending with ch 2, sl st to top of first dc and end off. *Second round:* Attach aqua in any ch 2 space. Ch 3, 2 dc in same space, ch 2, 3 dc in same space, * 3 dc in next ch 2 space, ch 2, 3 dc in same space, repeat from * around, sl st to first dc, end off.

Third round: Attach pink in any ch 2 space. Ch 3, 2 dc in same space, ch 2, 3 dc in same space, * 3 dc in top of fourth dc in previous round, 3 dc in next ch 2 space, ch 2, 3 dc in same space, repeat from * around, sl st to first dc, end off. *Fourth round:* Attach red in any ch 2 space, ch 3, 2 dc in same space, ch 2, 3 dc in same space, * 3 dc in top of next fourth dc in previous round, 3 dc in top of next third dc in previous round, 3 dc, ch 2, 3 dc next ch 2 space, repeat from * around, ending with sl st to first dc, end off.

Fifth round: Attach gold in any ch 2 space. Work as for fourth round, adding one cluster of 3 dc on each side. *Sixth round:* Attach red in any ch 2 space, 1 sc in same space, ch 2, 1 sc in same space, * 1 sc in top of each space to next ch 2 corner, 1 sc, ch 2, 1 sc in same space, repeat from * around, sl st to first sc, end off.

Make back of bag in same way. To assemble squares, work first row in top back loops only. Hold two squares together, right sides out, attach red in any corner, 1 sc in each sc around three sides, ch 1. Second row: 1 sc in each sc around top opening, sl st to first sc. Third row: (beading row) Ch 4, * skip next sc, 1 dc in top of next sc, repeat from * around, sl st to third ch of first ch 4 to join.

Fourth row: Ch 3 (counts as 1 dc) 1 dc in top of each st around, sl st to first dc to join, ch 1. Fifth row: 1 sc in same space, * ch 3, sl st in second ch from hook (picot), skip next dc, 1 sc in top of next dc, repeat from * around, sl st to first sc, end off.

Drawstring ties: Make two with red. Ch 85, leave three inches of yarn on each end of ch. Run ties in and out of dc beading row, one each at opposite ends. Tie ends together, make two tassels 3¾ inches long and attach to ends.

Fringe: Cut two 10-inch strands for each sc space across bottom of bag. Fold in half and loop through sc. *Lining:* Fold felt in half and stitch ¼-inch seams on sides. Place inside bag and slip-stitch to sc row below drawstrings.

Granny Square Bag

This over-the-shoulder bag is ideal for today's younger generation. It has a picot edging on top and bright crocheted squares on both sides. Overall size without fringe is 9½x12 inches.

Materials:
2 skeins of red cotton rug yarn, 1 skein each of gold, aqua, pink, and lavender; 9½x20-inch piece of orange felt, size K crochet hook.

Directions:
Basic square: Starting at center with lavender, ch 4, join with sl st. First round: ch 3 (counts

Crocheted Shoulder Bag

Schoolday wardrobes will take on a bright, new look with this felt-lined, casual shoulder bag made of cotton rug yarn. It is so quick and easy to crochet that you'll probably decide to make several in a variety of colors. The bag measures 9½x12½ inches without the fringe.

Materials:
Two 70-yard skeins of cotton rug yarn, size K crochet hook, and felt for lining.

Gauge:
3 sc = 1 inch. Two rows = 1¾ inch.

Directions:
Ch 54, join with sl st in first ch. *Row 1:* Ch 4, * skip next ch, dc in next ch, ch 1 *, repeat around, sl st in 3rd ch of ch 4.

Rows 2-12: Sl st in center of next ch 1, ch 4, * skip next dc, dc in center of next ch 1, ch 1 *, repeat around, sl st 3rd ch of ch 4.

Top of bag and border: Ch 1, * 1 sc in top of each sc around, (54 sc) sl st to beginning ch 1, ch 1 *, repeat for 2 more rows. Fasten off.

Bottom edge: Tie on rug yarn. Hold the edges together and sc in each ch st across to close the bottom. Ch 1, turn, 1 sc in each sc across. Fasten off.

Fringe: Using double strands of yarn, each 12 inches long, knot 6-inch fringe in each sc across the bottom of the bag.

Twisted shoulder strap: This requires two persons to make. Tie one end of the yarn around a small dowel or pencil. Measure off 3 yards and loop the yarn around the center of a second pencil, then loop 3 yards of yarn back around the first pencil and then 3 yards back to the second pencil.

Do this 8 times. Each person holds the yarn right in front of the pencil as if the hand were a tube, and twists the pencil around with the other hand. Keep the yarn taut. When it starts to kink, stop twisting.

Hold the yarn in center with outstretched arm to keep it straight. Let one person hold the two pencils about 6 inches apart. The other person holding the yarn in the center now slides one hand up yarn and releases the yarn with the other hand every 2 inches to let it twist.

When it is twisted, remove the pencils and tie a knot in both ends of the twisted cord 4 inches up. Cut the looped ends open and trim off both ends to match. Sew the shoulder strap securely onto the sides of the bag.

Lining: Cut a 10x24-inch rectangle of felt. Fold the piece in half, and using invisible thread, stitch down the 12-inch sides. (Use a ¼-inch seam allowance.) Turn the lining inside out and press. Fold down the top edge ½-inch on the inside and zigzag-stitch in place. Place the lining inside the crocheted bag and whip-stitch to the top edge. Press the bag with a warm steam iron.

151

Colorful Child's Cape

Your little girl will delight in showing off this colorful felt cape. It's perfect for wearing with a dress, slacks, or skirt and sweater. The giant posey appliqued motifs give a children's art flavor to this swinging creation.

Felt is a perennial favorite for applique projects because it is easy to cut and stitch. And there are no raw edges that need to be hemmed.

Materials:

1¼ yards 72-inch-wide felt for cape and ¼ yard 72-inch-wide felt for border, or 2½ yards 36-inch-wide felt for cape and ½ yard 36-inch-wide

felt for border; wrapping paper for pattern; felt squares in assorted colors; and fabric protector.

Directions:

Using the sketch, enlarge and transfer the cape pattern to wrapping paper. Adjust the pattern pieces to the proper size, then cut out the four front pieces and the two back pieces from the felt. Cut the back pieces on the fold.

Cut out the flowers from the felt squares or felt scraps, using pinking shears for some of the edges of the flower centers; if desired. Cut the border as indicated on the sketch.

Sew the darts on the shoulder lines (two on the back piece and one on each side of the front opening). Machine-stitch the front and back

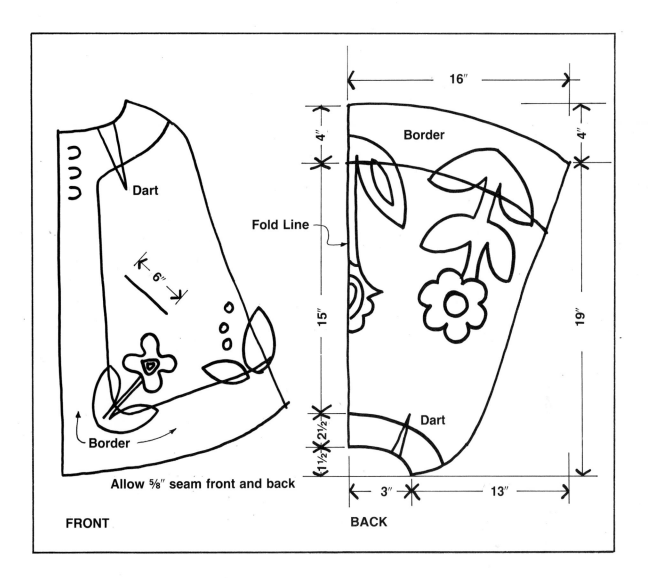

FRONT

Dart

6"

Border

Allow ⅝" seam front and back

BACK

16"

Border

4"

Fold Line

4"

15"

19"

Dart

2½"

1½"

3"

13"

pieces together, and top-stitch the border pieces. Stitch the flower motifs in place. Seam the front and back lining sections together.

Cut the arm opening on the side, and cut a strip of felt for facing each opening. (The piece used here is about 1½ inches wide and long enough to go around the opening.) Pin the right sides of the facing to the front pieces of the cape around the arm openings. Machine-stitch and turn facing to wrong side; tack in place.

Make three felt loops (each one about two inches long) of the same color as the border for button closures. Position the loops between the right front piece and the lining with the right sides together. Sew the cape and the lining together, leaving an opening at the bottom back. Trim the seams and turn to the right side; then steam press.

Slash the lining at the arm opening and fold ½ inch inside, slip-stitching down. Cover three buttons with felt; attach them to the cape.

When the cape is complete, spray with fabric protector to guard against stains.

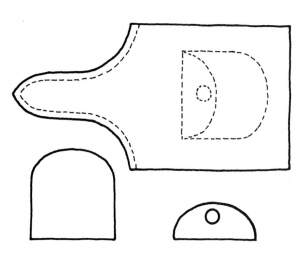

Big Pocket Tote Bag

This burlap tote bag is perfect for casual outings such as swimming or bike riding. The big pocket not only serves as handy storage for your keys and coins, it adds a tailored design to the bag. If you wish, accent the bag with a matching lining and scarf combination, as shown in the photograph.

Materials:

⅔ yard of burlap and ⅔ yard cotton suede fabric for the lining.

Directions:

First, cut the burlap material for the exterior and the cotton suede for the lining, following the pattern pieces in the drawing.

Fold under ½ inch all around pocket and press; hem top. Fold burlap down the center, and pocket down center. Then, align folds to center pocket. Double-stitch around pocket, using contrasting color thread.

With right sides together, stitch lining to pocket flap, leaving straight edge open. Turn right side out and make a machine-stitch button-hole. On the main bag pieces, match the lining front and the burlap front, right sides together, and stitch ¼ inch around the handle only. Clip the seam to ease the curve.

Repeat the process for the back part of the handle. Keeping the pieces right sides together, match the front lining and the burlap to the back lining and burlap. Stitch the burlap to the burlap inside out along the sides only, leaving the top and bottoms open.

The lining will still be loose at this point. Still keeping the right sides together, stitch the lining front to the lining back along the sides only.

The burlap will already be stitched inside the lining. Pull the lining over the burlap so the bag is completely inside out.

Stitch the two front burlap pieces and two lining pieces together along the bottom edge. Turn right side out. Topstitch the handle, double-stitching with contrasting thread the same color as the stitching on the pocket.

Turn the back flap over the front and secure it with a button. Sew the button on the pocket. The scarf is optional, but you can make it from a triangle of lining material hemmed with a zigzag stitch.

Butterfly Book Tote

The old leather strap formerly used by school children to carry books to and from school has been replaced by book totes such as this bright orange one. This practical design is easy to make and fun to decorate. Best of all, while providing a bright, cheerful look, the tote protects books on rainy days—an advantage the old belt strap wasn't able to provide.

Most woven fabrics are well suited for machine applique. Although cotton canvas was used for this book tote bag, you might want to use sturdy cotton fabrics such as gingham, light sailcloth, denim, corduroy, seersucker, or any fabric of a comparable weight.

Materials:

¾ yard of cotton canvas material, fabric scraps in assorted patterns, and fabric glue.

Directions:

Cut two 14x24-inch pieces of cotton canvas. Applique the butterfly motif to the top right side of one piece. (Use fabric scraps for the butterfly parts and a satin zigzag stitch. Before stitching, lightly glue the butterfly to the background to keep it in position and let dry.)

With the right sides together, stitch the two canvas pieces in a seam on the two long sides. Turn the bag right side out, and press and topstitch the long sides.

For the handles, cut two 2½x16-inch pieces of canvas. On the long edges, press under ¼ inch. Fold the handles in half lengthwise and topstitch along the edges, leaving the ends free. Topstitch along the folded sides also.

On the short ends of the canvas pieces, turn under a ½-inch hem and pin. Insert the handles between the ends of the canvas, about three inches from the outer edges and one inch down. Baste shut the edges of the canvas, catching in the handles. Then, topstitch the entire edge.

155

Bold-Look Backpack

Today, children are especially fond of wearing clothing and accessories with a touch of individuality. This probably accounts for the immensely popular practice of using brightly colored, decorative trims on shirts, jeans, blouses, and a variety of other items. Now, you can even send your child camping or hiking with his own personalized backpack. All it takes is an assortment of braids and fringes, a readymade backpack, and one evening of your time.

Materials:
2-inch-wide decorative braid; narrow-width flat braid; red super-large and yellow giant rickrack; (amounts of braid and rickrack will be determined by measurements of backpack) 6 inches red, 8 inches yellow, 11 inches green, and 14 inches orange brush fringe; and two 12-inch lengths each of yellow, green, purple, and orange ball fringe.

Directions:
Machine- or hand-stitch a strip of the 2-inch-wide decorative braid to the flaps of the backpack. Accent the decorative braid with a row of flat braid stitched at each side of the wide bands. Next, outline the flaps with super-large and giant rickrack (super-large on the largest flap, giant on the smaller flap).

For the short top tassel, cover a short piece of clothesline with brush fringe. Wind the 6-inch piece of red brush fringe around the top of the clothesline, and stitch it in place. Next, attach the 8-inch piece of yellow, then the 11-inch piece of green, and finally the 14-inch piece of orange. Wind and sew them to the piece of clothesline in the same manner, allowing the tassel to graduate in size at the bottom. Attach the tassel to the backpack.

For the long ball fringe tassel, use 12-inch lengths of yellow, green, purple, and orange. Button two strips together at a time by buttoning the ball of one strip into the loop on the heading of the other; repeat to the end of the strip. Fasten the four ball fringe strips together by laying one heading on top of another and stitching through the four layers. Stitch a row of rickrack down the center of each strip, and attach the long ball fringe tassels to the backpack clips.

Decorated Duffel Bags

All it takes for you to make drawstring bags similar to those shown here is a readymade bag and an assortment of iron-on trim. If you make a trip to your local Army surplus store, you'll find sturdy duffel or laundry bags in denim or duck that adapt well to this decorating treatment.

The iron-on trims and stencils make these useful accessories fun and easy to make, and they can be used for laundry, beach outings, toy storage, and overnight camping trips. Use the tiny heart-trimmed bag for small beach accessories.

Materials:

Girl's laundry bag — 3-inch alphabet stencils, 2½ yards polka dot band trim (Wright's), red, white, and blue Bondex, and denim laundry bag.
Boy's laundry bag — 2½ yards star band trim (Wright's), red, white, and blue Bondex, 3-inch alphabet stencils, and denim laundry bag.
Toy bag — 3-inch alphabet stencils, red, blue, or navy Bondex, and a muslin or duck bag.
Small denim bag — ⅜ yard denim, red Bondex, calico print scraps, fusible bonding material, and 2 yards red rayon macrame cord (Wright's).

Directions:

Girl's beach bag: Trace and enlarge the flower motif from the grid. Cut three flowers in red, three centers in white, and three leaves in blue. For the name, trace the stencil letters onto the Bondex back (wrong side for the letters) on white. With pencil, join the segments of the letters. Cut out the letters. Arrange the name and the flowers on the bag and iron on. Mark evenly and stitch the trim to the top and bottom of the bag.

Boy's beach bag: Trace and enlarge the star motif from the grid. Cut two in red and three in white. Cut the name in red. Finish it the same as the girl's bag above.

Toy bag: Trace and enlarge the toy motifs from coloring books or patterns. Make the letters the same as with the girl's bag. Arrange the motifs and letters on the bag and iron on.

For the small bag: Cut two denim rectangles 16¾x10¾ inches, one small heart in red Bondex, one large heart from calico, and one heart of fusible bonding material. Press the Bondex heart on top of the calico heart. With red thread, embroider around the calico heart.

Join the two rectangles on the two long and one short side. Turn the top edge under ½ inch and press. Turn again 3 inches and press. Run two rows of stitching ¾ inches apart to form casing. Open stitching of casing at each side seam to make the opening for the drawstring. Insert the macrame cords as drawstring by using the two cords so that each cord pulls against the other to pull in the top. Make the casing wide enough to accommodate both cords plus extra room for the shirring of the fabric.

When ironing on the Bondex, press with a low heat, as this is the quickest way to apply decorative trim. Do not use steam.

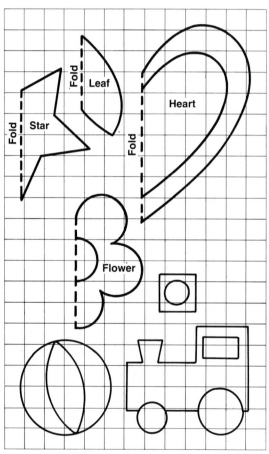

1 Square = ½ Inch

Leather Accessories

◀ There's a distinct Southwest flavor to this collection of cowhide mittens, belts, and beaded and feathered jewelry. These leather accessories add a flair to casual clothes.

Materials:

Leather mittens — 3 square feet of brushed cowhide, leather cement, utility knife, six brass rivets or paper fasteners, heavy-duty thread, permanent felt-tip markers, two 2½-inch squares smooth leather for the design, 12 inches of ½-inch dark brown leather strap, 1-inch brass rings, and paper or eyelet punch.

Leather pendants — *blue* — two 2½-inch squares of blue leather, three small orange feathers, 60 small dark brown beads, 14½-inch-long orange beads, 14 large brown beads, 4 ivory beads; *brown* — two 2½-inch squares of brown leather, 70 small silver beads, 38 small orange cubes, 80 ⅜-inch-long blue beads, 4½-inch long orange beads, 11 rooster feathers; for both — contact cement, dark brown waxed linen thread.

Leather belts — 1½-inch-wide soft leather strip, 1½-inch buckle, eyelets, utility knife, eyelet or leather punch, leather dye or permanent felt-tip markers, brass fasteners or rivets.

Directions:

Leather mittens: Make a paper pattern and cut out leather around it with a knife. Stitch pieces together by machine, using a long stitch and a heavy-duty needle (¼-inch seams). Cut smooth leather into squares and apply designs with markers. Cement to top as shown. Punch holes and add brass fasteners to ends of ½x3¼-inch leather strips and cement them close to squares. Wrap another leather strip around ring and fasten; cement on top, flush with the square.

Blue leather pendant: Round the leather as shown and sew beads to the front. String large brown beads and ivory ones on ends of the feathers. String several small beads, allowing some thread to show (make four 2-inch strands). Glue the three feathers and four strands to inside of back leather square. Glue front to back, wrong sides together. Punch holes at top for string. Using double waxed thread, knot at one hole and string with brown and orange beads, knotting occasionally (middle 10 inches are just knots), to make it about 24 inches long. Fasten to other hole.

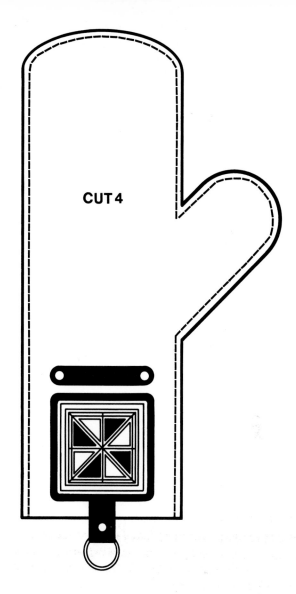

CUT 4

Brown leather pendant: Sew orange and blue beads to front. String various beads on ends of the feathers and blue feathers to inside back square. Glue back to front, wrong sides together. Punch holes at top for string. String necklace from back to front on waxed thread with silver, blue, and orange beads until strand is 24 inches long. Knot through holes with silver bead on back.

Leather belts: Cut leather to waist measure, adding 5 inches for eyelet and 4 inches to fold over buckle. Round the eyelet end, then adjust best for proper length and cut off excess.

Mark the holes for the eyelets and punch out. Add eyelets. Paint on the designs with dye or markers, or applique designs with leather scraps. Attach the buckle and loop with reinforced machine stitching or use rivets or fasteners.

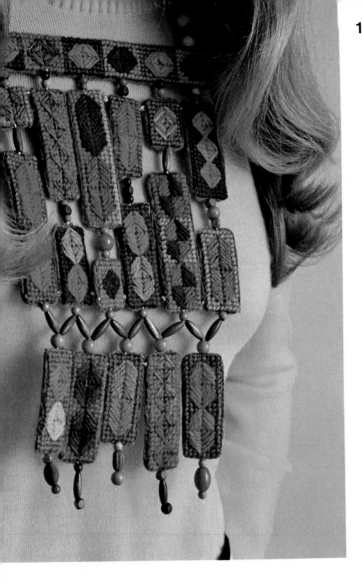

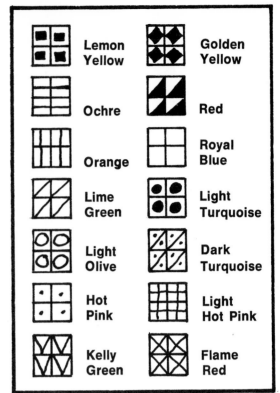

■■ / ■■	Lemon Yellow	(symbol)	Golden Yellow
(symbol)	Ochre	(symbol)	Red
(symbol)	Orange	(symbol)	Royal Blue
(symbol)	Lime Green	(symbol)	Light Turquoise
(symbol)	Light Olive	(symbol)	Dark Turquoise
(symbol)	Hot Pink	(symbol)	Light Hot Pink
(symbol)	Kelly Green	(symbol)	Flame Red

Needlepoint Necklace

This contemporary bib-type design necklace is a combination of colorful yarn and beads, plus simple needlepoint stitches. It is a perfect topping for young girls' sweaters.

Materials:

10x13-inch piece of needlepoint canvas (10 mesh to the inch); tapestry yarn in hot pink, light hot pink, red, flame red, orange, lemon yellow, golden yellow, ochre, light olive, lime green, kelly green, light turquoise, dark turquoise, and royal blue; an assortment of beads in colors that match yarns, or all one color, if you prefer; blunt-end tapestry needles, and fabric glue.

Directions:

Work the needlepoint motifs on the 10x13-inch piece of canvas, following the color symbols in sketch 1, and the patterns on sketch 3. For the stitch detail, see sketch 2.

Make the inner diamond by starting with *upper left section*. Make a long diagonal stitch from lower left to upper right over three meshes. Repeat this as many times as shown. Make the same stitch over two meshes, then over one mesh at center. Repeat for the *upper right section*, beginning at upper left to lower right.

Repeat for *lower left section*, beginning at center to cross one, then two and then three meshes, moving from upper left to lower right. For *lower right section*, start at center crossing one, two, and then three meshes from upper right to the lower left.

Work the background of each rectangular piece in the traditional half-cross stitch with colorful yarn. The section at the top is a horizontal bar 60 mesh across and 8 mesh deep. Work this piece and all of the rectangles, leaving at least one inch of canvas between them for cutting and finishing the necklace.

When the needlepoint is complete, cut the worked rectangles apart, leaving ½ inch border of canvas around each piece. Clip all of the corners and fold the edges under; press until flat, using a steam iron and pressing cloth. Cut pieces of cardboard into corresponding sizes to fit each piece of needlepoint. Glue the cardboard to the back of each piece; weight them down until they are dry. To hide the thick cardboard edges, glue yarn in any color around each edge. Pin the yarn so it stays in place until all of the pieces dry thoroughly.

When they are completely dry, lay out all of the pieces, following sketch 4. String beads and clasps as desired for each side of the neck. Attach one to each top corner of the top bar. Knot the thread and snip. With beads, string the rectangular shapes together, using as many beads as necessary to achieve spacing. Make sure the bottoms of the second row of rectangles line up. Attach a third row of rectangular pieces, as shown in 5A.

If you wish a different effect, use two strands of beading cord, and wherever desired, separate the cords by putting beads on each strand, then joining them together again as shown in sketch 5B.

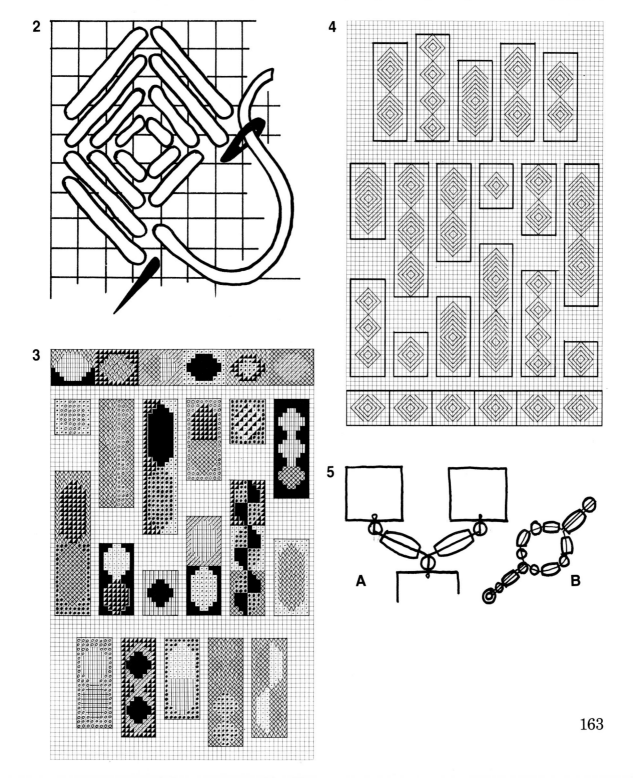

Personalized Sleep/Playrooms

Everyone yearns for a private retreat of his own, and children are no exception. As they grow older, they become increasingly aware of their surroundings and take particular delight in a room that has been decorated with their interests in mind. The ideas in this chapter will help you create something new and different for your child's room.

Calico Castle

◀ You've all heard the old saying, "A man's home is his castle," but here's a "calico castle" that will warm the heart of your junior miss. Although this "ivory tower" is steeped in Victorian tradition, its uniqueness stems from the lavish use of cotton fabric that features polka dots and small patterns in vivid colors. Everything in the bedroom/playroom takes its cue from these colors and patterns.

This room provides sleeping comfort, a place to study, and an area to play. A little girl will be proud to entertain her playmates here.

Materials:
Printed cotton fabric with a permanent-press finish (the amount will depend on the area you plan to cover and the size of the bedspread you make), high-gloss enamel for the recessed area, solid-color fabric that matches the paint color for the ruffle and tieback bows, and an assortment of plain and print cotton fabrics in small amounts for the decorative pillows.

Directions:
If you are planning a total redecorating project, be sure to do all of the painting first. Paint the ceiling first, then the woodwork and window trim, and finally the walls in the recessed niche. Match paint colors to fabrics.

Next, install the cushioned vinyl flooring. For the striped pattern inserts, work out a plan on paper first, taking into consideration the furniture placement and the size of the room.

Now, it's time to tackle the fabric-covered walls. This project will be simplified greatly if you choose fabric that requires no matching, such as the one pictured here.

The first step is to measure the area to be covered. Measure the distance from the top of the baseboard to the bottom of the ceiling molding. To this measurement, add 6 inches (3 inches each at the top and the bottom). Allow 1½ to 2 times the width to achieve necessary fullness. For example, to cover a wall 8 feet high and 9 feet wide, you will need 5 panels (each 8½ feet long) of 36-inch fabric or a total of 14⅛ yards.

Trim off the selvage on both sides of each strip and stitch a narrow hem along both edges (do not join panels together). Turn under ½ inch at both top and bottom and press; then, turn under 2½ inches at both ends and press again. Stitch close to the edge, then make another row of stitching to form a 1½-inch casing. Make all of the panels of fabric in this same manner. Attach them to the walls simply by sliding them onto expandable spring-tension rods both at top and bottom. When it comes time for major house-cleaning, all you have to do is slide the panels off the rod, launder them, and mount them again.

For the tieback draperies that frame the alcove, simply make a pair of unlined draperies and trim them with a 6-inch-wide ruffle of solid color fabric cascading down the center fronts. Allow for ample fullness, and hold them back with tiebacks adorned with huge bows.

The bedspread is easy to make, too. Make the top of the spread to fit the top of the bed, and attach a gathered flounce that extends almost to the floor. Use scraps of fabric and trim plus your ingenuity to concoct a collection of eye-catching decorative pillows.

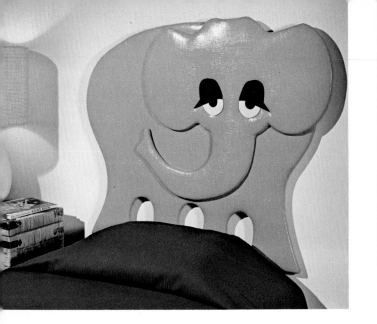

Elephant Headboard

When you build this headboard, which resembles a playful pachyderm, you're bound to get squeals of delight from the child whose bed it protects. What could be more fun for a child than to enter the room and see this giant of the jungle stalking across the bedroom wall.

Materials:

4x6-foot piece of ½-inch plywood, 2 yards of vinyl fabric, polyester batting, and two 1x2s.

Directions:

Draw a pattern for the elephant body and head on wrapping paper (make the body approximately 36 inches high by 39 inches wide). Trace the pattern pieces onto the sheet of ½-inch plywood and cut with a jigsaw or a saber saw.

To upholster the headboard, first cover the body and head plywood cutouts with layers of polyester batting. Next, wrap vinyl-coated fabric over the synthetic batting; bring it over the edges and around to the back, then staple the fabric onto the backs. Cut the eyes out of plywood, and paint them. Screw through the eyes, head, and body, fastening all three layers together at the same time.

From behind the headboard, attach two 1x2s vertically to attain the desired height and to allow for fastening them to the bed frame.

Gingham With a Flair

For those of you who want something other than the conventional headboard, here's a regal canopy for the princess in your family. The graceful, sweeping lines of the canopy also complement the gentle curves and delicate scale of the desk and chair at the bedside.

Plump pillows and a menagerie of animals harmonize with the overall feminine theme. A shelf on the adjacent wall supports hooks for clothes.

Materials:

One twin-size, fitted, checked permanent-press sheet, three double-size flat sheets, two twin-size flat sheets (one of the same color and one of a contrasting color), and polyester stuffing for the pillows.

Directions:

Use the fitted sheet for the bedspread and one double-size sheet to make the gathered flounce. Use the other two double-size sheets to create the canopy-style headboard. Make a casing at the top of the canopy panels and shirr them onto a curved curtain rod mounted high on the wall. Make fabric tiebacks to secure the canopy-headboard in graceful folds.

Make a collection of stylized animals from the two twin-size sheets, stuffing them with polyester batting. Arrange some of these cuddly pets on the bed, and mount several on the wall for a three-dimensional effect.

Gymnast's Exercise Mat

This patchwork mat has a dual personality. For those active times, it's the ideal place to let off steam. And for quieter moments, it provides a comfortable place for relaxing.

Materials:

4 yards red print fabric (#1 in diagram), 1½ yards navy fabric (#2), 1 yard navy and red print (#3), 1 yard blue and white check (#4), ½ yard navy and white print (#5), ½ yard orange print (#6), ¼ yard orange gingham, scraps of red and black polka dot fabric, 2 packages polyester batting, and four ½-inch plastic drapery rings.

Directions:

Cut #1 backing fabric to 44½x60½ inches, and cut two 4½x36½-inch and two 4½x60½-inch border pieces. From scraps, cut three 4½x8½-inch pieces and 18 triangles (cut from nine 4½-inch squares) for acrobats. All seam allowances are ¼ inch, and the acrobat blocks are 16 inches. Each figure has a 6-inch head, 6 triangles (cut from 4½-inch squares) for arms, 2 triangles for polka dot bow tie, 6 triangles and one 4½x8½-inch piece for body and legs, and 10 triangles and 2 squares of blue and white check for background.

To construct each block, stitch appropriate triangles together to make squares, then stitch squares together to make strips. Stitch strips to form blocks. The body rectangle in the center spans two strips. Applique head later (2 background triangles are under it). Stitch the blocks together. Press.

Cut two 2½x32½-inch and two 2½x52½-inch pieces from solid navy and seam the strips to the block section. Next, seam the red print border pieces to the navy. Applique head pieces by turning under ¼ inch and stitching the edges.

Cut the quilt batting to 44½x60½ inches. Lay the patchwork piece over it, right side up. Lay the backing piece on the patchwork, right sides together. Baste through all three layers along edges. Machine-stitch around edges, leaving about 16 inches free for turning. Turn right side out, and slipstitch opening closed.

Using 6 to 8 stitches per inch, machine-quilt around the outline of the acrobats and the red border. Tie mat with thread or yarn. Hang up with four plastic drapery rings.

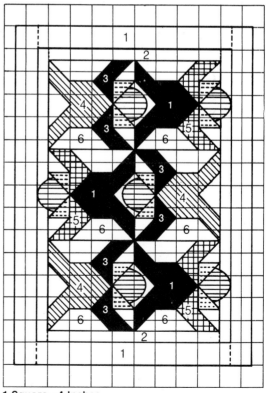

1 Square = 4 Inches

167

Batik Headboard

It will be smooth sailing at bedtime when you make a headboard that flaunts an unorthodox ark loaded with animals, and a whale beside it to act as a convoy across the stormy sea.

The unique headboard employs batik, a technique for dyeing fabric. This centuries-old process was developed in the Far East, where craftsmen still use ancient methods to produce intricate designs. The headboard measures 26x 38 inches and the batik motifs are outline-quilted. Animals have batik fronts and solid fabric backs.

Materials:

2½ yards of 45-inch unbleached muslin for batik and 1¼ yards for backing of ark scene; 4-ounce containers of cold water permanent textile dyes in yellow, orange, red, blue, and black; wax substitute or paste resist; brushes; polyester stuffing; fabric scraps for backs of animals; nylon fastening tape; ¼-inch cording for border; and a wooden drapery rod and brackets.

Directions:

Note: If you're a novice at batik, buy extra muslin and experiment until you like the results. If dyes are almost colorless before developing, test colors before applying to final project.

Enlarge and trace designs on paper with a permanent black felt-tip marker. Place pattern under muslin and trace on designs with pencil (hold up to window, if necessary). Draw bottom of ark twice (once as scene's background, once as front pouch).

Using a small, fine brush or batik tjanting tool, draw outlines and major details with black dye. If your dye calls for developing in the sun, do so. Otherwise, iron the fabric on the wrong side. (See sketch C.) Each time the directions call for setting dyes, follow this same procedure.

Note: *"Resist" means paste resist or wax substitute.*

Cut apart muslin so background is a separate piece and each animal is, too. Brush resist on all areas that are to remain white (sky, ark window, eyes, and above giraffe's head). (See sketch A.) Let dry completely.

Paint the lightest color next, *just* to areas you want that color—yellow for whale, giraffe, lion, background; blue for fox; pink for rabbit. (See sketch B.) Let dry and set dyes. Brush resist over those areas and dry.

Apply next darker color same way, cover with resist, and dry (orange for giraffe, rabbit, bird, and sun; green for fox and sea; pink for lion). Coat again with resist and let dry.

Bend each piece gently to make cracks in resist to make crackles. Brush diluted black dye over entire area and dry. Remove resist in water. Add details with black felt-tip marker.

Lay ark background on top of layer of batting and muslin backing, and machine-quilt through all three layers. Stitch along waves, boards in ark, window, sun, and house. Cover cording with 1½-inch-wide bias fabric and sew between layers of the quilting, using a zipper foot. At top, stitch on 4-inch-wide tabs to hold rod.

Cut fabric for backs of animals, allowing ¼-inch for seams. Stitch on stiff cording for whiskers, mane, and whale's spout. Seam animal fronts to backs, right sides together; leave an opening at bottom to stuff. Clip curves and corners, turn to the right side, and stuff. Slipstitch opening closed.

Stitch boat pouch to backing (not quilted ark) along top edge. Fold and insert batting. Quilt along outside planks, porthole, and waves. Pin pouch to ark and slipstitch firmly at sides and bottom. Machine-stitch top of boat just below house. Sew on two strips of nylon fastening tape to whale and ark pouch.

Mount brackets and wooden drapery rod on the wall to support the batik headboard.

A

B

C

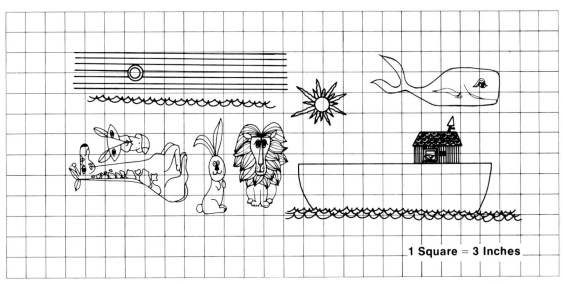

1 Square = 3 Inches

Headboard-Wall Unit

Every little boy likes to have a good spot to display his hobbies and collections. This built-in wall storage unit, which doubles as a headboard, will be the perfect showcase.

Materials:
2x4s and blue and white paint.

Directions:
First, paint the headboard wall blue. Next, plan the wall arrangement. Work out your design on paper first, drawing it to scale and keeping in mind the dimensions of the furniture in the room. Twin beds are 39 inches wide, and the twin campaign chests shown here measure 30 inches wide, 16 inches deep, and 30 inches high. The variations you can use for the wall arrangement are endless. The number of shelves you install will depend on the size and number of items you wish to display.

Cut the 2x4s to suit the shelf arrangement you desire, then paint them white. Install the uprights first, then the shelves. Toenail them to the wall. *Note:* "Toenailing" means driving a nail through one piece of wood at an angle to another piece. If you can't drive a finishing nail all the way without hitting and marking the wood, use a nail set to finish the job.

Add bright red, washable bedspreads and let your child display his treasures proudly.

Wall-To-Window Cats

A youngster who's mad about cats will love this very colorful room with its feline theme wallpaper and accessories. The wall covering sets the pace, and everything else in the room takes its cue from it.

Materials:

A room-darkening window shade, wallpaper cutouts (cats in this case) that you can apply to the window shade, fringe braid, ring pull, adhesive, textile paints, masking tape, and stenciling materials (paper, knife, and brushes) if you decide to stencil instead of applique.

Directions:

Select the various motifs of the wallpaper design that will be transferred to the shade. Cut out the various cat sizes from the wallpaper. Then, arrange them on the window shade.

Always use an adhesive that remains flexible when dry so that you can roll up the shade when necessary. Applique the lower quarter of the shade only, the section not frequently rolled up. This will prevent it from wrinkling.

Use mainly the larger figures, since they will give a greater impact to your window treatment. If you would rather create your own artwork, draw on your own design with stencil materials. Paint the design in bright colors of textile paint that match the room in hue and theme.

Add a border of wide fringe at the bottom of the shade and a row of decorative braid. Use the same braid to trim the cafe curtains. Use a large shade pull.

Work-of-Art Walls

The flower-filled train wall mural in this youngster's room gains impact from the paisley-like wallpaper pattern sprinkled across the ceiling. This is just one example of the visual tricks wall coverings can play, and it's guaranteed to delight the room's young occupant.

Materials:

Wallpaper mural and paisley print wallpaper.

Directions:

To hang the ceiling wallpaper, select a pattern to go with the wall (in this case the paisley print matches the "smoke" of the train mural) and hang the ceiling paper before you hang the wall mural.

To hang the mural, first select the focal point where the mural is to be hung so it will be compatible with the bed location.

Pencil a vertical line at the midway point of the wall. If the mural has an even number of panels, mark the width of the panels from this line to the left and right and draw new verticals. Mark the panel widths to each corner of the wall. If there are an odd number of panels, measure half the panel distance left and right from the center vertical, then continue measuring the full panel widths of the mural left and right to the corners.

Before hanging, draw a horizontal line where the top of the mural design should start. Be sure it ends above the top of the bed so that the image becomes a dramatic background.

171

Nail and glue the 2x2 16-inch legs to the measured table base. Use a square to keep the angles perpendicular, as shown above.

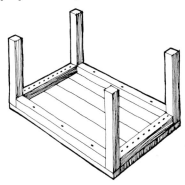

Place the leg/base on top of the loose 1x4s; glue and nail base to 1x4s, as shown above.

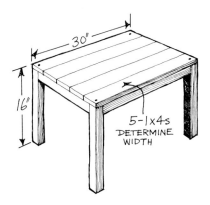

For stability, drill a long screw through the tabletop into each leg, as shown above. Countersink screws, and fill holes with wood putty. Sand the entire project, prime, and paint with a shiny, high-gloss enamel.

Table and Coat Rack

You can do a lot to improve the appearance of your child's room when you construct built-to-last furniture such as this table and coat rack.

Besides being sturdy, functional, and easy-to-build, they add a contemporary flavor to a child's room. Even the home handyman with only modest carpentry skills will have no difficulty following these directions. All you need is a small amount of lumber and the basic hand tools.

Materials:
1x4s, 2x2s, 1x2s, dowel, nails, glue, screws, 4 long screws, paint, primer, and wood putty.

Directions:
Table: Lay out 5 30-inch lengths of 1x4s on the floor to form the tabletop. Use these measurements to determine the size of the table base.

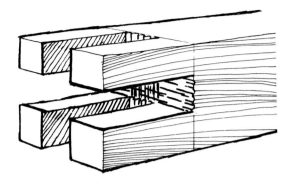

Coat Rack: Start by sawing two pairs of parallel lines at right angles on the bottom of a 48-inch 2x2. Make the cuts approximately 1⅝ inches deep. Next, drill into the center crosspieces and break out all of the sections except for the four corner pieces, as shown above. File the remaining rough areas smooth.

Then, drill angled holes into the upper portion of the 2x2 pole to accept 4-inch-long dowels. Attach the dowels to the post with glue. With a wood file, shape the top of the 2x2 to a round or semiround design.

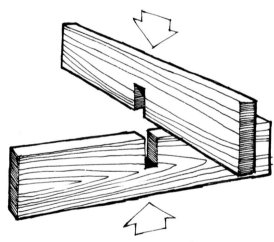

Next, cut slots into cross base (made from two 16-inch 1x2s) as shown above and glue the 1x2s together. Then, fit bottom section of the 2x2 post onto the 1x2 cross base. Finally, sand, prime, and paint the coat rack.

Barber Pole Lamp

This unique children's room idea not only adds a distinctive flair, it increases the general lighting as well.

Materials:

4-foot length of white polyvinyl chloride (plastic) 4-inch-diameter pipe, bulb socket, brass plate, 10-inch globe, metal collar, electric cord line switch or electric plug, ¾-inch plywood, and red adhesive-backed vinyl.

Directions:

Cut red vinyl into 4-inch-wide strips and attach to white plastic pipe vertical column in a spiral effect. Attach bulb socket, brass plate, and 10-inch globe to the top with a metal collar. Run the electric cord through the threaded tubing from top to bottom. Build 12-inch-square base of ¾-inch plywood, with a hole in the center to anchor the pipe base. Install a line switch on the cord.

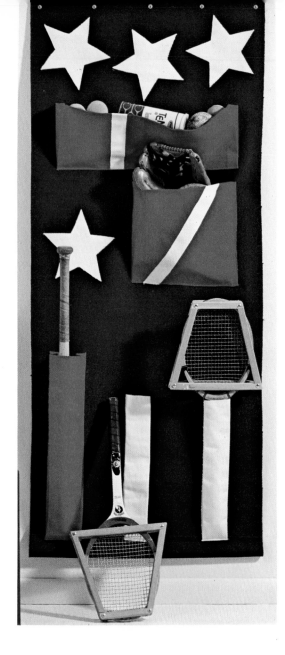

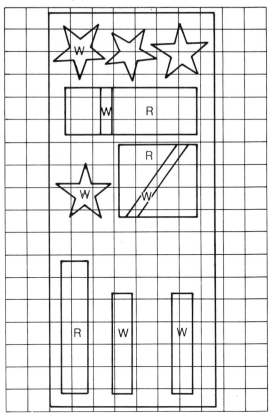

1 Square = 4 Inches

Four-Star Organizer

If you supply your youngsters with this practical, decorative wall organizer, you won't have to worry about tripping over sports equipment anymore. Just hang it in a conspicuous location and watch things return magically to their rightful storage place.

Materials:

2 yards of 29-inch-wide blue canvas, 1 yard of red canvas, 1 yard of white canvas, heavy-duty thread, 28-inch-long dowel, 1 inch in diameter. 5 ½-inch grommets, and fabric glue.

Directions:

Using the entire length of blue canvas, encase the raw edges with large zigzag stitching. Fold 2½ inches at the top and 3½ inches at the bottom. Pin in position; do *not* stitch.

From white canvas, cut out four 9-inch stars, 2 7x18½-inch strips, 1 2x8½-inch strip, 1 2x16½-inch strip; from red canvas, cut 12x33½-inch piece, 9x29-inch piece, and 3x17½-inch piece.

Position the white stars on the blue background and zigzag stitch them in place, using white thread. Attach the white stripes the same way.

To form the pockets, zigzag across top edges, turn under ½ inch, and press. Pin one side of pocket to blue background, right side up, and zigzag stitch reinforcing at corners. Pin other side in position, making a fold in the middle so the pocket will expand to hold equipment. Stitch in same manner as first side. Make a pleat in bottom of the pocket so bottom is flat, then zigzag stitch, reinforcing corners. The ball holder should measure 8x23 inches, the glove holder 12x13½ inches, the bat holder 4½x22½ inches, and the racket holders 3½x17 inches each. Press the folds flat.

Across the top, attach five grommets. Slip a dowel into the pocket formed by the bottom hem. Glue down corners of hems.

174

Denim Pocket Hamper

Anything made of denim has special appeal for members of the "blue jean world," and this jumbo pocket with its mock saddle stitching is bound to make a hit as a laundry bag.

Materials:
20x28-inch piece of ½-inch plywood, 1 yard of blue denim or an old pair of jeans, orange embroidery thread, and one button.

Directions:
To make this supersize pocket hamper, cut plywood into the pocket shape. Cut the blue denim about 6 inches larger than the plywood backing. Make a narrow hem along the top. Fit the denim over and around the edge of the board, allowing the pocket to bow out at the top and tapering to fit at the bottom. Mark and embroider the two lines of decorative embroidery stitching.

Staple the raw edges of the pocket to the underside of the backing. Cut the flap about 10 inches deep. Hem the raw edges along the bottom and sides. Add the mock saddle stitching and the button. Staple the top of the flap to the plywood backing. Mount on a closet door.

Wall Organizer

This wall organizer doubles as a contemporary wall hanging. The pockets provide convenient containers for art supplies for the young artist-in-residence, and the bath towel construction makes it a quick, easy-to-make project.

Materials:
One blue bath towel, one yellow hand towel, one red hand towel, one blue washcloth, one orange washcloth, and two cafe curtain rods.

Directions:
Turn under a 1½-inch hem at both ends of the blue bath towel and machine-stitch. Attach various-sized pockets in a patchwork scheme, and top-stitch around the three sides. Choose pocket sizes that will suit the items you wish to store in them.

Insert brass cafe extension rods through the hem casing and hang on the wall with hooks.

Little Extras

Any of these accessories will add zest to a child's room. The needlepoint pennant pillow that boasts "charge" will be a prized possession and center of attention in a youngster's room. And, the framed sampler and "smile" mirror are wall decorations that will encourage children to start the day with a spirit of optimism.

Materials:

Pennant pillow — ½ yard gros point canvas (four meshes per inch), 50 yards navy blue and 70 yards orange 3-ply Persian needlepoint yarn, 1-inch masking tape, ½ yard vinyl for backing, 2 yards ⅛-inch cording, polyester stuffing, tapestry needle, and 4 squares-per-inch graph paper.

Sampler — frame, white felt, felt scraps, and glue.

Needlepoint mirror — 9x12-inch piece of mono needlepoint canvas (12 squares per inch), 1 orange and 2 yellow 40-yard skeins of needlepoint yarn, 12 squares-per-inch graph paper, No. 18 tapestry needle, 9½x13-inch mirror, two each of 20½-inch and 9½-inch thin plastic or wood strips, one 9½x20¼-inch sheet of ½-inch plywood or hardboard, and epoxy.

Directions:

Pennant pillow: Draw design on graph paper, following diagram. Place needlepoint canvas over drawing and trace pattern with a waterproof felt-tip pen. Tape raw edges of canvas with masking tape. Stitch letters first, then background with running or cross-stitch. Then, block the piece in this manner: you will need a flat surface that is rigid, yet soft enough to push pins or tacks into. (A pine board or drawing board is ideal.) Place graph paper drawing on blocking board, then place needlepoint on it, right side up.

Now, canvas is ready to moisten. Use water at room temperature, and wet evenly but do not saturate. Place rustproof pushpins into the tape around the edges at a slightly outward slant. Stretch the canvas into its original shape as you pin it. Allow needlepoint piece to dry thoroughly before you remove it from blocking board.

Make two orange 4-inch tassels and attach them to ends of completed canvas. Using zipper foot, cover the ⅛-inch cording with backing fabric. Place blocked needlepoint face up on a flat surface, and pin strip of cording around the edges with the raw edge toward the canvas raw edge. Baste, making sure cording seam is inside

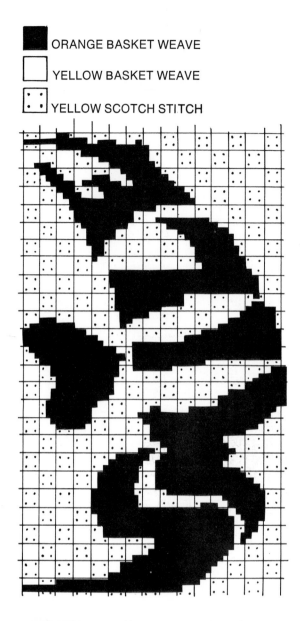

- ■ ORANGE BASKET WEAVE
- □ YELLOW BASKET WEAVE
- ⊡ YELLOW SCOTCH STITCH

several rows of needlepoint stitches, then machine-stitch in place. Cut vinyl backing piece to size, and stitch needlepoint and cording to the backing, right sides together; catch the tassels in the seam at the same time. Leave opening for turning. Trim seams and corners. Turn to right side, fill with polyester stuffing, and slip-stitch opening closed.

Sampler: For the background, cut a piece of white felt to fit the size of your picture frame. Cut out "Happiness is a friend like you" letters and a sprinkling of small hearts of felt in an assortment of colors. Arrange the pieces in a carefree, topsy-turvy fashion, and glue them in place with fabric glue. Mount the sampler on a piece of cardboard backing, and position it in the picture frame.

Needlepoint mirror: Bind the edges of the canvas with masking tape. Draw the design on the graph paper, following the diagram. Place the needlepoint canvas over the graph paper and trace the design with a light color waterproof pen.

Stitch the orange letters in basketweave stitch first. Next, stitch the background in light yellow yarn, alternating three-stitch squares each of basketweave and Scotch stitch. Fill in the background. Block the needlepoint piece according to instructions given for pennant pillow.

Stretch the needlepoint piece over one end of the plywood or hardboard backing and staple in place. Glue the mirror to the other end of the board with epoxy. Frame the mirror and needlepoint wall hanging with the plastic strips and attach hangers.

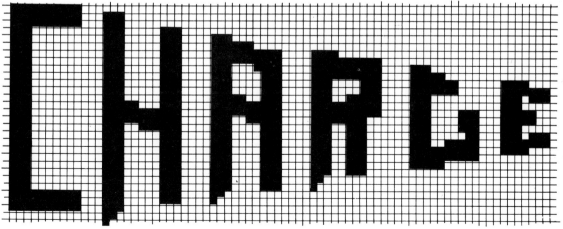

King of the Jungle

Children who love to read and hear stories about
the mysteries that lurk in the jungle and who
secretly yearn for the life of a big game hunter
will be proud to own this soft, furry, jungle
rug. Stretched out in all its glory, the shaggy
beast measures 35x41 inches from paw to
paw, not including the generous, curving 25-
inch tail. It is equally at home on the floor or
sprawled atop a youngster's bed.

Because it's made of washable rug yarn, you
can launder the whole rug. You crochet the
backing first, then hook on the yarn fur.

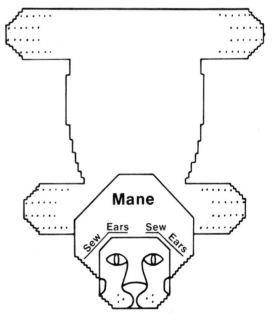

Materials:
Four 70-yard skeins of black washable rug yarn, 17 skeins of antique gold rug yarn, large tapestry needle, and size J crochet hook.

Gauge:
3 stitches = 1 inch. Size: 35x41 inches (paw to paw, minus 25-inch tail).

Directions:
Wind into balls 7 skeins of gold and ½ skein of black. Beginning at the hind legs with gold yarn, ch 76, turn. *Row 1:* 2 sc in 2nd ch from hook (increase 1), sc across, 2 sc in last ch 1 (increase 1). Ch 1 and turn after each row. *Row 2:* In all of the even-numbered rows, pick up the top hook facing you only.

There should be a ridge between the two rows on the side away from you into which you hook the fur. Sc across, increase 1 at the beginning and at the end of row. *Row 3:* In all odd-numbered rows, pick up the loop away from you. The ridges should be on the side facing you. Sc across, increase 1 at the beginning and end of row.

Repeat rows 2, 3, then sc 6 rows without increasing. Decrease in the 1st 2 and last 2 sts of the next 5 rows and end off. To decrease, * hook through the far or near loop of the next st, yo hook, draw loop through, hook through loop of next st, yo hook, draw the loop through, yo hook, draw the yarn through 3 loops on the hook. *

Body: Skip 16 sts, sc 43 across in far loop. Continue to the next to last body row, increasing and decreasing as per chart. End off. *Front legs:* Ch 15, sc across body, ch 16, turn. Begin the next row in the 2nd ch from the hook. Repeat as for hind legs. End off.

Head: Skip 12 sts, sc 39 across. Continue, shaping the head as per chart, end off.

Tail: With gold yarn, ch 3, sl st to join. Sc 6 over ring. Do not join. Beginning with ch, (7 sts around) sc in far loop of sts until the tail is 20 inches long. 2 sc in next st, sl st next 3 sts. End off.

Ears: Make 2. *Row 1:* With gold yarn, ch 2, sc 4 into 1st ch, ch 1 to turn after each row. *Row 2:* Sc 2 into loop facing you of each st row 1. *Row 3:* * Sc into far loop of next st,

2 sc next far loop *. Repeat from ** to end. *Row 4:* * Sc into near loop next 2 sts. 2 sc next near loop next 2 sts, 2 sc near loop *. Repeat from ** to end. *Row 5:* * Sc into far loop of next 3 sts, 2 sc in next far loop *. Repeat from ** to the end. End off, leaving about 15 inches of yarn for sewing.

Nose: With black yarn, ch 7. In the 2nd ch from hook, do 2 sc. Sc across, 2 sc in last ch, ch 1, turn. Decrease in every 2 sts across, ch 1, turn (there should be 4 sts). Decrease in every 2 sts again (2 sts). Decrease to 1 st, end, leaving about 24 inches of yarn to sew on the nose and make the mouth.

Eyes: With black yarn, ch 2, 3 sc in 1st ch, turn. Sc in 3 sc and in turning ch (4 sts across), ch 1 turn. Sc across, ch 1, turn. Decrease across (2 sts), ch 1, turn. Decrease to 1 st, end, leaving about 15 inches to sew on eyes and make the side of the nose. Make 2. With gold yarn, embroider the centers of the eyes in 2 satin sts.

Fur: Open ½ skein of black yarn, cut ends, divide each half into 4 bundles. Repeat with 10 skeins of gold yarn. Open the ends of 3 remaining skeins of black and divide each half into 3 bundles for the mane and tail. Use 2 strands of yarn throughout (except on whiskers) and hook it in every other st of raised ridges on backing. To hook, fold 2 strands in half, insert the latch hook into the ridge, pull the folded loop through, push the hook through the loop and catch the ends of the strands, pull the strands through the loop and tighten.

Body: This is done in gold yarn except for the back at the paw tips, which are done in shorter black strands. In the second ridge, hook 6 black tufts, counting from tips of paws. Skip 3 rows of ridges and repeat 3 times for a total of 4 rows of 6 black tufts. The mane and 5 inches from the tail tip are in longer black strands. The rest of the tail is gold.

Sew the eyes, ears, nose on. Embroider the nose and mouth. Make 3 yarn whiskers on each side of the nose. Sew the tail firmly to the center back.

Things Children Can Make

Up to this point in the book, most of the items presented are for adults to make for children. This section, however, features projects that are suited to the skills and talents of youngsters from 7 to 12 years of age. Some of these can be accomplished without the help of an adult, while others are intended to be joint efforts by parents and children.

Mini-Village Scene

◀ What appears to be a picturesque village nestled in a field of waving grain is actually a miniature version resting on the playroom carpet.

The charm of this quaint village scene can be captured and duplicated with little effort and an assortment of ordinary materials. No expensive tools are necessary, as it is primarily a cut-and-paste project.

Materials:

Discarded milk cartons, paper towel core, cardboard, small scraps of felt in a variety of colors, bias tape, rickrack, baby rickrack, middy braid, soutache braid, Venice lace, two lace daisy medallions, and fabric glue.

Directions:

Cut the milk cartons for the barn, house, and house/shop, using three 1-gallon containers for the barn, two ½-gallon containers for the house, and one ½-gallon and a 1-quart container for the house/shop. Cut cardboard gables, following the illustration. Glue the buildings together. Use a paper towel core for the silo.

Cover the buildings, including the silo, with felt. Use two colors of felt for the barn for extra impact. Draw windows and doors on the buildings as desired. Cover the lines with bias tape, middy braid, soutache braid, and baby rickrack. Add the lace daisy medallions to the barn gables. Use fabric glue to attach the trim to the buildings.

Measure and cut the cardboard for the roofs, allowing a ½- to ¾-inch overhang on all sides. Cut the silo roof and chimney, following the drawing. Cover these pieces with felt. Glue the trim to the edges, using rickrack, bias tape, and Venice lace edging. Repeat the roof design of the house/shop on the chimney and glue it to the shop roof. Glue roof on silo.

To complete the tranquil scene, purchase several miniature artificial trees to cluster around the buildings. Run your railroad track and trains right through the village and it will spring to life immediately.

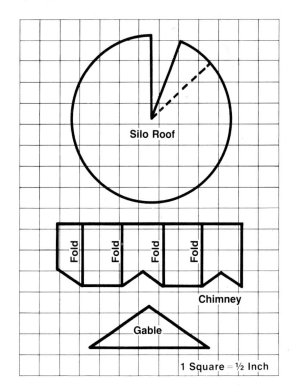

1 Square = ½ Inch

Container Gardens

Children love to watch things grow. And very few things afford a better chance to observe this phenomenon than plants. To nurture interests, urge your youngsters to make these container gardens and care for them.

Materials:

Dairy-box gardens—Milk, cottage cheese, or yogurt containers, drainage rocks, potting soil, and seeds.

Fruit jar terrarium—Pint fruit jar, ¾-inch plywood, ½x½-inch strip of wood, and plants.

Smiling egghead—Eggshell, stiff paper, potting soil, grass seed, and felt-tip pen.

Directions:

Dairy-box gardens: Cut quart or ½-gallon milk cartons lengthwise. Or, make a planter from an upright quart container, using a cut-off ½-gallon box as a plant saucer. Or, start with an upright quart and cut off the top; cut window flaps in each side. Line the interior with clear plastic wrap, fastened with transparent tape. You can also use round cottage cheese and yogurt cartons and trim them.

Trim the outsides of the boxes with fabric scraps, adhesive-backed plastic, wrapping paper, or bright bandanna print kerchiefs.

Put drainage rocks in the bottoms of the planters, add potting soil, and plant with seeds. If you'd rather start with plants, use small terrarium-size plants. Water when the surface of the soil is dry.

182

Use a trimmed milk carton for a letter-growing project (see drawing above). The idea is to sow seeds (cress or birdseed) in the shape of letters of the alphabet; naturally, this will be the initials of the youthful gardener's name.

Mark the letters in the soil, and sow seeds thickly along the marks. Cover lightly with more soil. After the seeds are in place, keep the soil moist, but not soggy. Once the seeds sprout, remove the seedlings that are outside the boundaries of the initials.

Fruit jar terrarium (*see drawing below*): Make a 4x7-inch ¾-inch plywood platform to hold fruit jar. Cut two 7-inch lengths of ½x½s; glue two strips to top of base to form cradle.

Place a pint fruit jar on its side and rest it in the cradle. Add potting soil until the jar is about a quarter-full. Dampen the soil. Gently reach into the jar and set two or more terrarium-sized plants into the soil. (If it's difficult to get your hand in the opening, use tweezers to hold plants.) Press down around roots, then screw on the lid. Set terrarium away from the sun; water it about every two months.

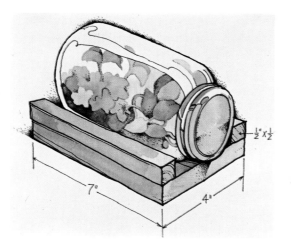

Smiling egghead (*above*): First, hard-cook an egg, then carefully cut off the top of the egg (draw a penciled line around the top to use as a cutting guide). Next, use a felt-tip marking pen to draw on the facial features or whatever design you choose. Then, hollow out the edible hard-cooked portion of the egg (do this gently so you don't crack the shell).

Staple a strip of colored construction paper together to form a supporting base for the egghead. Place the decorated eggshell in an upright position on the base, fill it with potting soil, and then plant grass seed. Keep the soil moist, and watch for the tender, green shoots to peek out of the egghead.

183

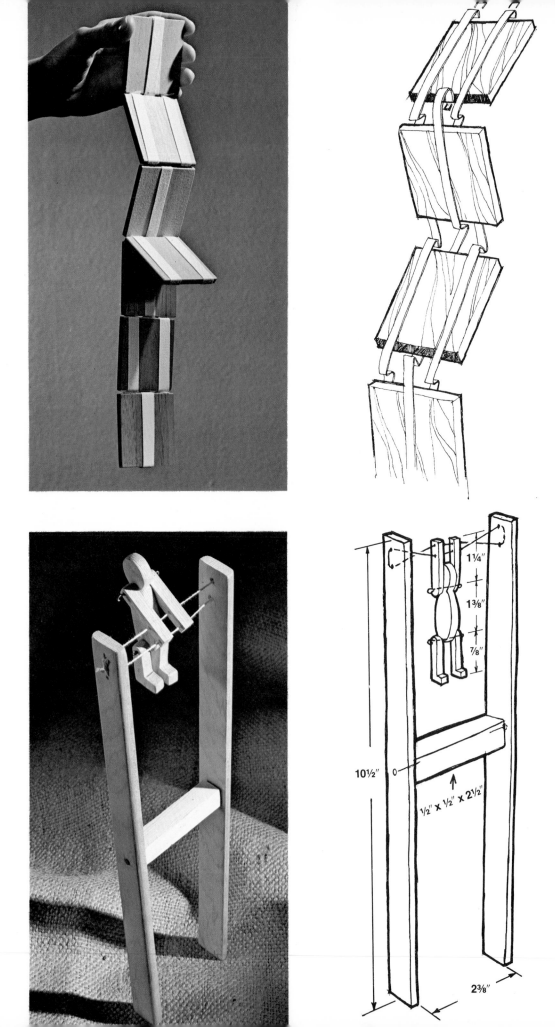

1¼″

1⅜″

⅞″

10½″

½″ x ½″ x 2½″

2⅜″

Old-Time Toys

These all-time favorites never lose their play appeal. With the somersault clatter blocks, you grasp an end block, tilt it forward and backward, and the blocks somersault down the tapes. With the monkey on a swing, you squeeze the handles and watch the monkey do his tricks.

Making these wooden toys is almost as much fun as playing with them, and it can be a rewarding parent-child experience.

Materials:
Somersault clatter blocks — ¼-inch plywood scraps and a package of twill tape.
Monkey on a swing — ¾-inch screen molding, scraps of ½x½-inch pine board, 20-gauge iron wire, and string.

Directions:
Somersault clatter blocks: Cut seven 2½-inch-square blocks of ¼-inch plywood and sand them smooth. Loosely weave two strips of twill tape around blocks, stapling tape at top of each block, as shown in drawing. Then, weave the center tape through the blocks in the reverse direction, stapling at the bottom of the blocks.

Monkey on a swing: First, cut the two 10½-inch upright handles from ¾-inch screen molding. Drill two holes for string ½ inch apart, starting ¼ inch from the top of each handle.

Slightly round the ends of the 2½-inch strip of ½x½-inch pine, which connects the handles. Connect the pine piece to the handles with two nails driven in 4¾ inches from the top.

Cut the monkey from screen molding, making the arms 1¼ inches long, the body 1⅜ inches long, and the legs ⅞ inches long. Drill small holes in the arms, body, and legs in order to connect them with 20-gauge iron wire. Drill two holes ½ inch apart in each of the monkey's "hands," and thread string through the arms and handles. (Place the monkey upside down to simplify threading the string.)

Frog Beanbag

Here's a happy substitute for that time in life when children long to collect frogs. It will appeal especially to mothers who wish all their son's or daughter's frogs were made of felt. Actually, this smiling frog has a dual personality — it can be used as a plaything, or it can serve as a paperweight on an adult's desk.

Materials:
Green felt; gold felt; scraps of pink, orange, and white felt; ½ pound dry beans or split peas; black ball fringe; and fabric glue.

Directions:
Cut head shapes from two 6x6½-inch pieces of green felt. Cut the legs from two 4½x5-inch pieces of gold felt.

Topstitch the two leg pieces together, leaving top open. Fill legs ¾ full with dry beans or split peas. Cut a slit in one head piece to accommodate top of legs. Insert leg section in slit and stitch across on wrong side.

Topstitch the two head pieces together, leaving a 2-inch opening on the bottom. Fill head with beans or peas and stitch opening closed.

Cut the facial features from felt and attach them with fabric glue. (Cut two pompons from ball fringe and hand-sew them securely to the eyes before gluing eyes on.)

Katy the Cat

Children are always eager to explore the world of crafts. So, why not get yours started out the easy way with applique, a craft that involves simple, graphic forms. The stitching of Katy the Cat is simplified still further because it is constructed of felt. Upon its completion, it will repose languorously on your child's bed and be a steadfast companion during the nighttime hours. The finished size is 12½x13½ inches (at the longest dimension).

Materials:
Two 16x16-inch turquoise (A) felt squares, 9x12-inch rectangles or scraps of felt in green (B), blue (C), navy (D), and chartreuse (E), small amount of white yarn for mouth, and polyester stuffing. (If you are purchasing felt, buy one square of each color.)

Directions:
Enlarge the pattern on paper, using the drawing as a guide. The full-size pattern should measure 13x14 inches. Press all of the felt pieces with a steam iron. Tape the pattern to the turquoise felt, allowing ½ inch all around the edges for a seam allowance. Trace outline of cat. Make marks for the placement of the eyes, nose, and circles.

Place carbon paper underneath the traced cat so that the carbon side is up and touching the wrong side of the felt. With a tracing wheel, press hard over the outline of the cat. You will now have the cat outline on both sides of the felt.

Tape the pieces of felt in the appropriate colors to the back of the pattern and trace the shapes onto the felt. The repeated flowers and circles need to be traced only once (use these pieces as models from which to cut the rest). Cut out all of the felt pieces. Lay out the design on the cat and pin all of the pieces into place before stitching.

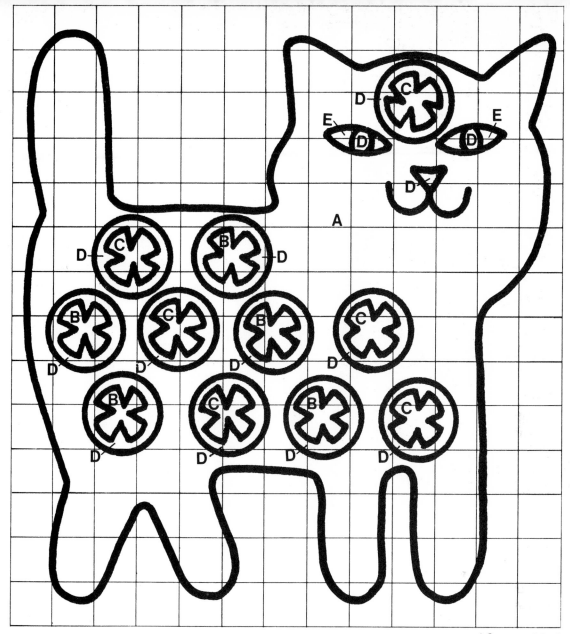

1 Square = 1 Inch

Sew around the circles, nose, and eyes, using a medium-width zigzag stitch on your sewing machine (10 stitches to the inch). Stitch across through the middle of the flowers, bisecting the petals.

Set the zigzag stitch for 8 stitches to the inch, and couch a piece of the white yarn onto the mouth line of the cat, as shown in drawing.

Carefully steam press the sections. Place the appliqued cat (face down) on the other piece of turquoise felt and pin them together. Stitch the two pieces together along the traced outline on the wrong side. Leave a large enough opening below the tail so you can insert your hand while you stuff the cat.

Trim around the cat, ⅜ inch away from the sewn edge. Clip the corners and curves, and trim the ear points close to the seam. Turn the cat right side out. Push out the ears, legs, and tail with the eraser of a pencil or other blunt-pointed object. Insert the stuffing, starting with the legs, ears, body, and ending with the tail. Hand-stitch the back seam opening closed, stuffing as you sew.

Peggy the Pig

Here's a pal for Katy the Cat on the previous page. These two animals, with their stylized designs, make quite a team and look as though they belong together. Children will enjoy making this pink felt, flower-adorned pillow. And Peggy will be right at home in a youngster's room. The completed size is 12½x14 inches at the largest dimension — just the right size to stand guard over a juvenile bed.

Materials:

Two 15x17-inch pieces of cerise felt (F); 9x12-inch rectangles or scraps of felt in hot pink (G), orange (H), golden yellow (I), lemon yellow (J), green (K), and olive (L); small amounts of green yarn; polyester stuffing; and one pipe cleaner. (If you purchase felt, buy one square of each color.)

Directions:

Enlarge the pattern on paper so the pig design measures 15x17 inches. Press the felt pieces with a steam iron. Tape the pattern to the cerise felt, allowing ½ inch of felt all around the edges for seams. Trace the outline of the pig. Make marks for the placement of the flowers, leaves, eye, and cheek. Untape the pattern.

Place carbon paper underneath the traced pig, with the carbon side up, touching the wrong side of the felt. With a tracing wheel, press hard over the outline of the pig. (You will now have the outline of the pig on both sides of felt.)

Tape the felt pieces to the back of the pattern and trace the other shapes in the appropriate colors. Cut out all of the pieces. (If you have pinking shears, use them for cutting

1 Square = 1 Inch

out the flower centers.) Lay out the design on the pig, and pin all pieces in place.

Sew around the flowers, leaves, eye, cheek, and hooves, using a medium-width zigzag stitch (10 stitches to the inch). Stitch across the flower centers with a straight stitch.

Using the sewing machine, couch the yarn to the stem line, as shown in the illustration on page 187. Carefully steam press.

Place the pig face down on the other piece of cerise felt, and pin the two together. Sew the pieces together along the traced outline of the wrong side. Leave a large enough opening along the top so you can insert your hand while you are stuffing the pig.

Trim around the pig ⅜ inch from the sewn edge. Clip all the corners and curves. Trim the hoof and snout points close to the seam. Turn the pig right side out. Use blunt-pointed tool, such as the eraser of a pencil, to push out the snout and the hooves.

Beginning with the hooves and snout and ending with the body, insert stuffing. Stitch up the seam opening by hand, stuffing as you sew.

Cut two ear pieces from orange felt. Sew the two pieces together around the edge, using zigzag stitch. Follow the dotted line on the pattern for placement. Crease the ear down the middle, and sew the blunt end to this spot. Tack down the underside of ear and underlayer of topside with a stitch.

Curl the pipe cleaner around a pencil or dowel for the tail, and turn back the tips to prevent scratching a child. Sew one end to the appropriate place on the back of the pig.

Heloise the Hippo

Children of all ages love to play with cuddly, stuffed animals, so it's only natural that they will want to learn to make them, too. As soon as they are old enough to learn to stitch a simple seam on the sewing machine, it's time for them to undertake a stuffed toy project such as this. Heloise is more than just a tuck-under-the-arm toy, she's actually large enough for a small child to sit on.

Making Heloise the Hippo, who measures about 30 inches in length and stands about 16 inches high, will require the guidance of an adult seamstress for some of the procedures, but it will be fun as well as a learning experience for youngsters to take part in its construction.

Materials:
One yard 45-inch cotton print fabric, several colors of felt scraps, 2 yards gift-tie yarn for tail, ribbon for neck bow, polyester stuffing, and fabric glue.

Directions:

Enlarge the pattern pieces, using the illustrations as a guide. Cut out the body, underbody, back gusset, and head gusset pieces from the printed fabric. Cut two mouth pieces, two nostrils, two eyes, two eyelashes, four ears, and four feet from felt scraps. The pattern allows for a ⅜-inch seam allowance.

Stitch the head gusset to the main body pieces, matching points A and B under the chin and over the head. Stitch the back gusset to the body pieces from points A to C (do not join the gussets to each other). Stitch the underbody piece to the body at the sides of the legs and tummy. Stitch the underbody center seams B and C to each other, leaving an opening in the center.

Stuff the nose and the legs firmly with polyester stuffing first, then stuff the rest of the body a little less firmly. Hand-stitch the openings closed at the gussets and tummy. Run a gathering stitch by hand around the bottom of the feet; pull the stitches up tight and whipstitch them to the felt foot soles.

For the curly tail, cut three 20-inch lengths of gift-tie yarn; fold them in half, hold two strands together, and braid the six strands as you would three strands. Sew the tail to the hippo and tie a ribbon bow at the end of the tail to embellish it. Stitch the ears and the contrasting lining together, right sides together, around the curved part, in a ⅛-inch seam. Turn the ears to the right side and press. Take a small tuck in the ear lining fabric, and hand-sew it to the head with the lining ½ inch in front of the outer ear.

Hand-sew a gathering stitch around the edges of the eyes and pull up the stitches slightly. Put a little stuffing in the eyes to give them a three-dimensional effect, and sew them to the head over slightly larger half-circles of felt that have been glued in place. Glue the felt eyelashes in place. Glue on the mouth and nostrils, and tie a ribbon bow around the neck.

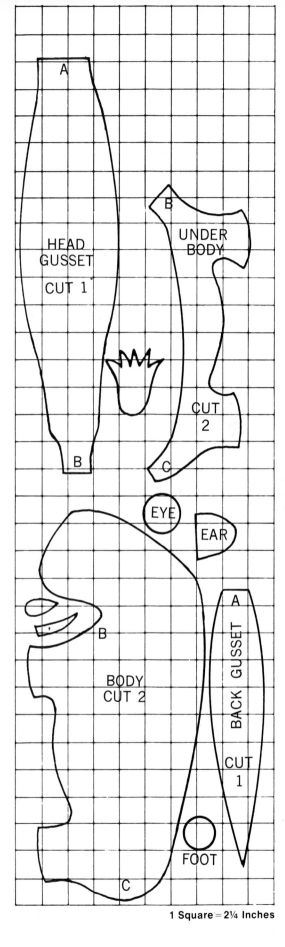

HEAD GUSSET CUT 1

UNDER BODY CUT 2

EYE

EAR

BODY CUT 2

BACK GUSSET CUT 1

FOOT

1 Square = 2¼ Inches

191

Frolicking Caterpillar

This fanciful felt caterpillar will add a lively note to a child's room, and it's fun to play with, too. Actually, it's more than just a plaything — snapping and unsnapping the various sections of the caterpillar teaches small children how to manage the snaps on their own clothing when they are learning to dress themselves.

This project has a fair amount of hand sewing, but it is one a child will enjoy. It provides an opportunity to display inventiveness — the color combinations for the caterpillar can be as lifelike or as imaginative as the child wants — and it can be made in any length.

Materials:

Two ¼-yard pieces of felt in contrasting colors; small scraps of black, red, white, and gold felt; 10 large-size snaps, old nylon stockings or pantyhose, one pipe cleaner, several pieces of shirt cardboard, fabric glue, and a compass.

Directions:

Using a compass, draw circles on the shirt cardboard in the following diameters: 1 inch, 1¼ inches, 1½ inches, 1¾ inches, 2 inches, 2¼ inches, 3 inches, 3½ inches, and 4 inches. Cut out these circle patterns and use them to cut out the felt circles; cut two of each size, one from each of the contrasting colors.

Cut the felt pieces for the facial features, following the illustration below. For the eyes, cut two gold circles, two white triangles, and two black pupils. Cut the nose and mouth from red felt. Sew or glue the facial features to one of the two largest circles — whichever color you want to "face forward."

On all of the circles that will face backward (except for the very smallest one), center and sew the socket side of the snap. On all forward-facing circles (except for the largest one), center and sew the ball side of the snap. Be sure to sew the snaps securely.

Match the contrasting colored circles according to size and so that one color faces forward and the other is on the back. Place each set of circles together with the snaps to the outside. Sew the edges of each set of circles in an overcast stitch, leaving an opening measuring about ¾ of the way around. Fill each circle with cut-up nylon hosiery until it has a plump look, then finish overcasting the circle. Snap the finished circles together.

Bend a pipe cleaner to resemble antennae. Sew it in place in the center of the head right between the eyes.

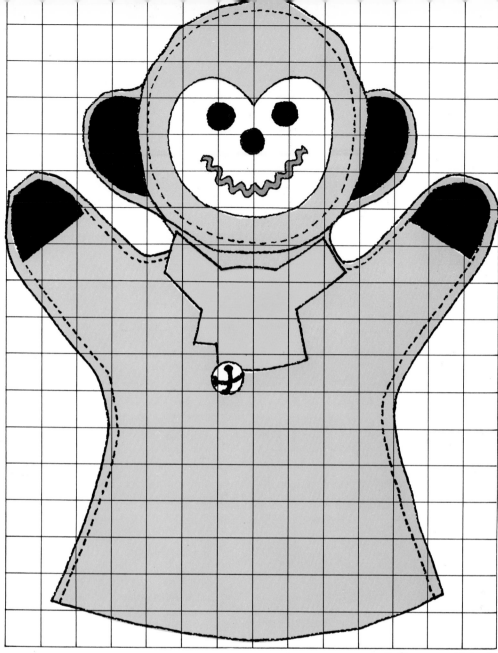

1 Square = ½ Inch

Teddy Bear Puppet

Puppets come in many forms and designs, and this smiling felt hand puppet is one of the easiest to make and to operate. Children love to use their imaginations and play "let's pretend," and with the aid of a puppet they can channel their creativity by manipulating the puppet. Who knows, the hand puppeteer of today may be a part of the theater tomorrow.

Materials:
10x15-inch piece of yellow felt; scraps of black, white, green, and red felt; polyester stuffing; and fabric glue.

Directions:
Enlarge and cut two body pieces, following outline of bear. Machine-stitch sides together, leaving bottom open. Next, cut two circles for head. In one piece, cut a heart-shaped opening; from wrong side, cover this opening with white felt. Glue it in place. Sew the head circles together, leaving a small opening. Stuff head with filling, and finish stitching around it. Glue nose, eyes, ears, hands, and scarf in place; zigzag-stitch green mouth to bear's white face.

Oven-Baked Jewelry

Your children will need only a little assistance from you to make this assortment of jewelry. Once the forms are baked, children can paint and assemble to their heart's content. And when they're through, no one will ever suspect that these artistic creations were born in the kitchen.

Materials:
Plastic modeling clay, gesso, acrylics, dye, glue, yarn, earring bases, and jewelry clasps.

Directions:
First, roll small lumps of plastic modeling clay in your hands until they become soft and malleable, then shape into the desired forms.

For the beads, roll small bits of clay between your palms to make the pellets. Press and squeeze them into simple shapes. To make holes in the beads, pierce them with a round toothpick, knitting needle, or skewer.

To make the flat pieces of jewelry, roll out the clay on a flat surface and cut the pendant shapes with a knife.

Arrange the pieces of jewelry on a foil-lined cookie sheet and bake them in a 300° oven for 18 to 20 minutes. When the plastic clay is properly cured it will be firm, but a little resilient to the touch.

After curing, enlarge the holes in beads and pendants. To do this, hand-twist a drill bit through each piece. Use a lipstick case like a cookie cutter to make large holes in the pendants. Cut through the flattened modeling clay wherever you want a hole. On the larger pieces, notch the edges with a sharp knife so the yarn will rest in the notches as you wrap the jewelry.

Color the jewelry after it's cooled; sand lightly, if necessary. Use a coat of gesso as a primer, then finish with acrylics. When you're painting the beads, spear them on toothpicks and stick them into a block of plastic foam while the paint dries.

You can also color jewelry by dyeing it. Mix 2 or 3 teaspoons of liquid dye or ½ to 1 teaspoon powdered dye with 1 cup water and ½ teaspoon salt in a saucepan. Bring the mixture to a boil. Stir until the dye dissolves, then drop in the plastic pieces; simmer about 15 minutes. Stir frequently. Let the dye go darker than the final tint you desire, because the jewelry becomes lighter after several weeks of exposure to sunlight. Rinse thoroughly; roll the pieces on paper towels to dry.

Make the cords by twisting together 8 strands of fine yarn, using knots as spacers. Suspend the small yarn-covered beads from strands of yarn to create cluster pendant, or attach a small yarn tassel to the white flower-petal pendant to make it even more effective.

King-Sized Key Rings

You won't lose your keys easily, once you attach them to a large key ring such as those shown here. Made of wood and decorated with vivid colors of enamel, these key rings almost resemble mini wall hangings when they are suspended by their chains from hooks.

Children can make these key rings easily. And once they master these simple woodworking techniques, they can advance to more complex carpentry projects.

Materials:
¼x3-inch strips of balsa wood, strips of wood molding in different shapes, several sizes of dowels, key chains, small jars of assorted colors of acrylics, white glue, gesso, and sandpaper.

Directions:
Cut the shapes from balsa wood with a saw. Sand the edges with fine sandpaper. Cut ¼-inch-thick sections crossways from moldings and dowels. Sand these pieces. Arrange the molding and dowel pieces in desired patterns and glue them to the balsa wood base. Allow to dry.

Coat the entire surface of the key ring with gesso, using a small brush. Let dry. Paint the entire surface with one color of acrylics. When this is dry, paint the molding sections with contrasting colors. Drill a hole for the key chain and attach it.

Ticktacktoe

This is a game that never goes out of fashion, and that people of all ages enjoy playing. It's a game for two players, who alternately put crosses and ciphers in squares formed by two horizontal lines crossing two vertical lines. Each player tries to get three crosses or ciphers in a row before his opponent does.

This wooden version of a ticktacktoe board and markers will last for many years. It is a simple woodworking project—and an excellent joint venture for a parent and a child.

Materials:
Small piece of ¾x6-inch pine board, 1-inch wooden dowel, stain, and clear varnish.

Directions:
Cut a 6-inch-square base from the ¾x6-inch pine board. Mark the position for the 9 holes and drill the holes ½ inch deep with a 1-inch spade bit. Cut ten 1-inch lengths from the dowel. Use a ¼-inch drill to mark the five 0s and a saw to cut the Xs in the other five markers. Sand the markers to fit the recesses. Stain the base only. Coat all the pieces with a coat of clear varnish.

Rope Craft

In today's assembly-line world, it is important for children to rediscover the thrill of making handcrafted toys. In this case, it's a craft technique that fascinates children. Boys, especially, seem to have a special talent for making something unusual from a piece of rope or twine. And when the project involves an adult and a youngster, there's a special kind of comradeship that evolves.

Once you have mastered the simple techniques for making this woolly lion, use this talent to concoct a collection of jungle beasts.

Materials:
12 inches of 1½-inch rope, 24 inches of ½-inch rope, 10 inches of ⅜-inch rope, 2 yards of sisal twine, scraps of red and green felt, and 6 pieces of 18-inch-long florist wire.

Directions:
To make the body, begin by cutting the 24-inch piece of ½-inch rope in half. Unwind one strand, and insert two pieces of florist wire cut same length as the rope. Replace the strand over the wire, then tie ends with small lengths of florist wire. Lay the two leg pieces flat.

Add the 12-inch piece of 1½-inch rope and 10-inch piece of ⅜-inch rope; wind all pieces together for about one inch. Continue wrapping for approximately three more inches, then fasten them together with a knot. You'll have eight inches left for neck and head. Unwind three strands and follow sketches to make lion's head. Comb out ends of rope for mane and tail. Cut out eyes and tongue from scraps of red and green felt and attach with glue.

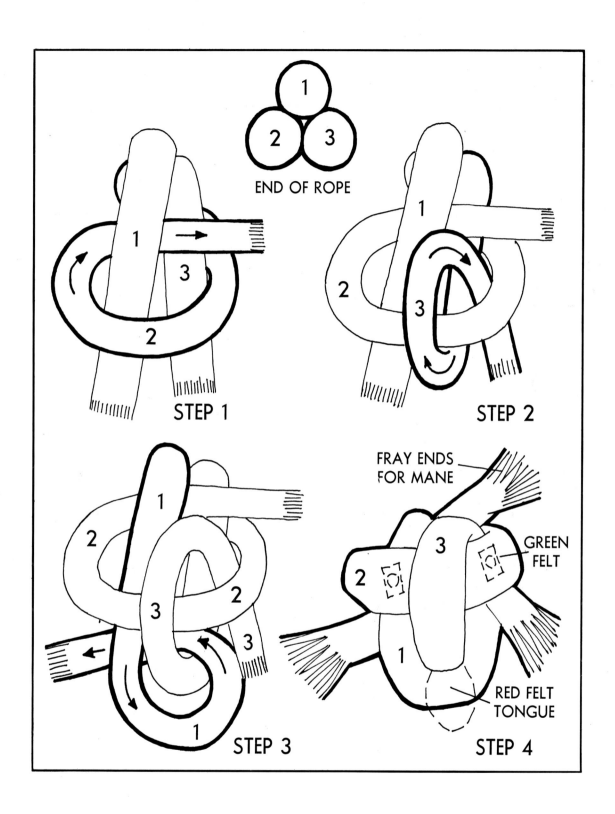

1

2

3

END OF ROPE

STEP 1

STEP 2

STEP 3

FRAY ENDS
FOR MANE

GREEN
FELT

RED FELT
TONGUE

STEP 4

Potholder Pets

Children will enjoy making decorative pot-holders for gift-giving occasions. It's mostly a cut-and-paste project, with a little stitching.

Materials:
Owl—2 12-inch squares of dark brown felt, scraps of tan and yellow felt, and fabric glue.
Pussycat—2 12-inch squares of dark brown felt, 1 12-inch square of tan felt, scraps of white and yellow felt, brown floss, and fabric glue.

Directions:
Owl: Cut two 7x8-inch pieces of dark brown felt for the owl background, using the photo as a guide. Cut circles for eyes from brown and yellow felt. Cut the wings and beak section from tan felt. Glue brown eye circles on top of yellow circles, then glue eyes to tan felt. Top-stitch the tan piece to one layer of the brown felt. Add a felt hanger at the top, and top-stitch the two brown pieces together.

Pussycat: Cut two 7x8-inches pieces of dark brown felt for the pussycat background, using the photo as a guide. Cut out inner tan sections of felt, embroider on the features with dark brown embroidery floss. Glue on the felt eyes. Add a felt hanger at the top, and top-stitch the two felt pieces together.

Cardboard Cache Pots

Once children find out how easy and inexpensive these sculptured-effect plant containers are to make, they'll want to create a variety of sizes and distinctive designs. They are perfect for both flowering and foliage plants—all you have to do is slip the decorative plant containers over regular flowerpots.

Materials:
Cardboard paint cartons, cotton clothesline, white glue, gesso, and flat white paint.

Directions:
Mark the design of your choice on the cardboard paint container with a pencil. Saturate the clothesline with a half-and-half mixture of white glue and water. Attach the wet clothesline to the container, as shown in the picture.

Let the project dry for several days. Cover all the spaces that are not covered with cord with gesso. When the gesso is dry, cover the entire container with a coat of flat white paint.

Novelty Napkin Rings

You'll be amazed at the ease with which you can make these fragile-appearing, lacy napkin rings. And would you believe, they are made of plaster surgical bandages. Make them in sets of four, eight, or twelve, and give them to your favorite people on special occasions.

Materials:
4-inch-wide surgical plaster bandage; white paint; an assortment of white laces, colored rickracks and ribbons; and glue.

Directions:
Use a 2-inch-diameter glass jar to shape the napkin rings. Fold the 4-inch-wide plaster bandage in half (down through the middle of the strip) and wrap it twice around the glass jar. Remove it from the jar, dip the bandage in water, and rewind around the jar.

Smooth the bandage surface with your fingers and let it set for a few minutes. Then, slide the ring off the jar gently and let it dry thoroughly. Cover the hardened bandage with a coat of white paint and decorate the ring by gluing on lace, ribbon, and rickrack.

Patriotic Wastebasket

With the red, white, and blue patriotic color scheme so popular these days, it's only natural that the same theme should make its mark on room accessories. Here's a handsome and functional wastebasket that's easy to make and requires very few purchased materials.

Materials:
Two-gallon ice cream container (you can get this from an ice cream shop); red, white, and blue shiny patent paper; and vinyl adhesive.

Directions:
Cut 2x9-inch strips of red and white patent paper (the number will depend on the dimensions of the container). Using vinyl adhesive, glue the strips to the midsection of the carton. Glue on a 2-inch-wide strip of blue patent paper around both the top and bottom edges, lapping it over the ends of the red and white stripes. From the white patent paper, cut star shapes that measure 1¾ inches across and paste them onto the blue borders.

Rainy-Day Blanket Game

The world of make believe can wend its way down the winding streets of this rainy-day blanket game. Your youngster will spend hours pushing his toy cars and trucks on imaginary trips. There are no rules, no scoring, and no time limit for this captivating pastime.

Materials:
An inexpensive neutral-color or earth-tone blanket, patterned edging, fabric glue, and felt in assorted colors.

Directions:
Cut the blanket in half and edge it with the patterned border. Cut out colorful pieces of felt in shapes representing areas of the town your youngster knows best — the shopping center, school, library, airport, Grandma's house, and church. Add some colorful fun places he enjoys — the lake with a fleet of sailboats, the county fair with midway rides, campgrounds with small tents, and parks with playground equipment.

Make felt driveways and highways wide enough for toy cars and trucks to make their "necessary" trips. Let your youngster join in the project by drawing his favorite places and then translating the drawings into felt pieces.

Lay the pieces out on the blanket in a pleasing design. Use various shades of green felt for the landscaping in order to give the game some dimension. Use fabric glue to attach groupings of buildings to the blanket background. For added strength, sew the tiny street markers and flowers instead of gluing them.

Wide-Eyed Beanbags

These fringed and faced velveteen beanbags will be fun for children to toss back and forth when they are playing games. They also are ideal as paperweights. Beanbags have been favorite toys of childhood for many generations, and they are just as popular today as they were in years past.

These lighthearted versions are so much fun to make, and children can give vent to their creative impulses and make the faces as original as they desire. They can give variety and character to the faces of these fringed beanbags by changing the shapes and sizes of the eyes and moustaches. And, even though the lion and cat faces seem to lend themselves well to this project, experiment with other faces to see how effective they can be.

Materials:
Velveteen scraps, felt scraps, small amounts of fringe, yarn or string for whiskers and moustaches, kidney beans, and fabric glue.

Directions:
First, cut out 5-inch diameter circles of velveteen in various colors (two for each beanbag). Then, sew or glue to the fronts, the facial features cut from felt scraps, adding yarn or string for the whiskers or moustaches and for the embroidered mouths.

Next, measure a ¼-inch border within each circle, and sew fringe around the edge of the front face piece within the ¼-inch border, being careful to maintain the circular shape.

Place a front and back piece together, right sides facing, and stitch a ¼-inch seam around the circle, leaving a 2½-inch opening. Turn the beanbag right side out and fill it about ⅔ full with kidney beans.

Hand-sew the 2½-inch opening closed, using a blind hem stitch and turning the raw edges underneath to match the rest of the seam.

Bundles of Toys

These toy totes are great projects for the budding seamstress — there're only a couple of seams to stitch on the sewing machine, and the rest is just cutting designs and gluing them on.

These make wonderful gifts for young children who need an incentive to pick up their playthings. In addition to their practicality, these burlap toy totes add color and individuality to the sleep/playroom.

Materials:

Clown toy bag — ½ yard of burlap or sturdy cotton fabric, scraps of colored felt, three green and three red ball fringe segments, double-fold bias tape, fabric glue, and pinking shears.
Large T-O-Y bag — one yard of burlap, felt scraps of various colors, fabric glue, and cord or elastic for drawstring.

Directions:

Clown toy bag: Fold the fabric in half, selvage to selvage, and machine-stitch a ½-inch seam down the side and across the bottom. Bind the side seam with bias tape to within 1½ inches of the top to keep it from fraying. Leave the top open. Turn the bag to the right side. Turn under a 1-inch hem across the top to form a casing, and machine-stitch.

Next, stitch two strips of bias tape lengthwise to form the ties. Thread the strips through the casing in opposite directions and tie the ends together on each side.

With pinking shears, cut out the clown applique from pieces of felt. Glue the figure in place with fabric glue. Then, attach ball fringe for the buttons and the hair.

Large T-O-Y bag: Fold the fabric in half, selvage to selvage, and machine-stitch ½-inch seams along the side and across the bottom. Make a 2-inch hem around the top to form a casing for a draw cord.

Make the giraffe, flower, and letters out of bright-colored felt scraps. Glue the designs to the tote in a random fashion.

Quacking Good Bank

This humorous duck bank will encourage young-sters to start saving at an early age. Not only will the young coin collectors enjoy watching coins disappear into the duck, they also will be learning a lesson in thrift.

This is a combination sewing-craft project that can be shared by a child and an adult.

Materials:

4-inch foam ball, black grosgrain ribbon, white and yellow felt, white glue, 16-inch mailing tube, stuffing, ½ yard of printed fabric, and cardboard for feet and beak.

Directions:

Enlarge the pattern, following the diagram, and make a paper pattern. Cut out the body parts from the print fabric. Seam the tail, and turn to the right side. Sew one side of the tail to the body. Seam the body, leaving the tail, neck, and bottom open. Stitch in the bottom circle. Turn the bird right side out.

Cut a cardboard circle for the bottom. Place it inside the bird and pin it from the bottom to hold it in place. To cover the mailing tube, glue on fabric.

Stuff the bird chest, slide in the mailing tube (neck). Stuff the bird from the tail. When the bird is stuffed, slip-stitch the tail closed and glue the neck seam allowance to the neck.

Sew on the wings and remove the pins from the bottom. Cover the cardboard feet with yellow felt and glue them onto the bird.

For the head and beak, cut a section 1½x1½ inches from the foam ball. Push the ball onto the neck top, centering the beak hole. Remove the ball and deepen the neck hole.

Cut four head pattern pieces and stitch them together, covering the ball one side at a time, pulling and pinning the fabric to fit. Hold the fabric in position with pushpins while you glue it to the inside beak edges and the inside neck hole.

From yellow felt, cut one whole beak and two halves. Glue slightly smaller cardboard halves to the whole felt beak, leaving ⅜ inch free at the center. Cut the money hole. Glue the felt-covered side to the ball, centering in the hole, and pin it to hold. Glue the felt halves to the beak on the open side.

Add the collar and tie. Push on the head and cut the money hole through the ball to the neck. Glue on the eyes. Leave the head loose so the bank can be emptied.

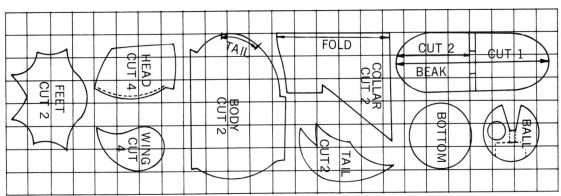

1 Square = 1½ Inches

203

Coffee Can Characters

◀ Just think how much fun it would be for your children to create the collection of fabulous faces pictured at the left. Besides being a craft project that will stir their inventiveness, it is one that requires no expensive materials and tools. The bases for these amusing characters are nothing but discarded coffee cans in one-, two-, and three-pound sizes. Don't stop when you've completed this assortment — dream up some ideas of your own and create your own collection.

These decorated containers will hold many small items: candies, pretzels, cookies, pencils, crayons, string, and various paraphernalia. Or, you can even use one as a bank if you just make a slit in the top for inserting coins.

Materials:
1-, 2-, and 3-pound coffee cans; craft paper, adhesive-backed paper, or felt to cover cans; fringe, rickrack, and braid in assorted colors, and metallic trim; pipe cleaners; and glue.

Directions:
Start by covering both the outside and inside of the cans with craft paper or felt, glued on, or adhesive-backed paper.

Make the faces by using numerous trims creatively. For example, use brush fringe for the hair, ball fringe for the eyes and nose, rickrack for the mouth, and decorative braids for the neckline or headband. Make the cone-shaped hats from craft paper or use a party souvenir hat; glue on decorative trim — metallic braid or rickrack, and pompons.

Cut the witch's pointed nose out of a divider from an egg carton and glue it in place. Make the flower out of shirred rickrack with a ball fringe center, and glue it onto a pipe cleaner stem. The dog ears are made out of fake fur fabric, with one pleat at the top; glue them to the sides of the can.

Dough Dolls

The playful people shown above are sculptured from baker's clay — that never-fail craft material that you bake in the oven just as you would a batch of cookies. Use these baker's clay figures as wall plaques or even as ornaments on your Christmas tree.

Materials:
4 cups flour, 1 cup salt, wire, strawflowers, water colors or felt-tip pens, and foil.

Directions:
To make the dough, mix together 4 cups unsifted flour and 1 cup salt. Add 1½ cups of water gradually. (Do not halve or double the recipe; make a separate batch for each project.) Knead the mixture for about five minutes.

Set the dough on a large piece of aluminum foil, and mold into figures as you would modeling clay. Make the balloon string of wire for the one doll. Insert a small curved piece of wire at the top of each figure for hanging.

Place the figures on a cookie sheet and bake in the oven, preheated to 325°, until the dough-clay is hard, about 1 hour. Remove from oven and allow the clay to cool. Use either water colors or felt-tip marking pens to color the facial features and balloon. Place a sheaf of strawflowers in the hand of the one doll. (Glue it in position.) As a final loving touch, give each figure a coating of clear varnish.

Index

A-B

C-D-E

F-G-H

Acknowledgments

We are happy to acknowledge our indebtedness and to express our sincere thanks to the following who have been helpful to us in producing this book:
  American Mart Corporation
  Arno Adhesive Tapes, Inc.
  Bernhard Ulmann
  Coats & Clark
  Jan DeBard
  Fieldcrest
  Kathy Keating
  Window Shade Manufacturers Association
  Wm. E. Wright Co.